New
MARITIMES
Seasonal
COOKING

New MARITIMES *Seasonal* COOKING

DONNA YOUNG & MARG ROUTLEDGE

**OVER 200 DELICIOUS RECIPES
FOR LIGHT AND HEALTHY MEALS,
YEAR ROUND**

FIREFLY BOOKS

A FIREFLY BOOK

Published by Firefly Books Ltd. 1999

First published by Numbus Publishing Limited

Second Printing

Library of Congress Cataloguing-in-Publication Data available.

Canadian Cataloguing in Publication Data
Young, Donna
    New Maritimes seasonal cooking : delicious recipes for light and healthy meals year round

Includes index.
ISBN 1-55209-390-5

1. Cookery, Canadian – Maritime style. 2. Low-fat diet – Recipes. 3. Cookery – Maritime Provinces. I. Routledge, Marg. II. Title.

TX715.6.Y68 1999   641.5'638   C98-932687-X

Published in Canada in 1999 by
Firefly Books Ltd.
3680 Victoria Park Avenue
Willowdale, Ontario M2H 3K1

Published in the United States in 1999 by
Firefly Books (U.S.) Inc.
PO Box 1338, Ellicott Station
Buffalo, New York 14205

Design: Arthur B. Carter, Halifax NS
Food Photography: Hawk Communications Inc., Sackville NB
Stoneware Pottery: Flo Grieg, Elizabeth Lord, Rachel Morouney, Joan Shaw
Cover photo: summer menu
Printed and bound in Canada

The Publisher acknowledges the financial support of the Government of Canada through the Book Publishing Industry Development Program for our publishing activities.

CONTENTS

PREFACE

Food with a maritime flavour, made with local, readily available ingredients, and typical of the cultures that make up Atlantic Canada is what this book is about. It's rooted in traditional, tasty dishes we all want to eat. Today, many of us can't have them, and the rest of us shouldn't eat them. Therefore, we analyzed the recipes, adjusting, substituting, testing, and yes, putting some of them in the wastebasket. We arranged what was left, into seasonal menus. There's lots of cultural variation in the book; there's nothing trendy. It's designed for people who love seasonal food and want to prepare that food at home, quickly. Because cooking must keep pace with lifestyle change, we made this book fit the new North American food guidelines: meals with less than 30 per cent of calories from fat, high in fibre content, and reduced in salt. We have also paid close attention to minimum sugar content.

Marg and I are practical working women, graduate home economists. Marg came from Central Canada, I from the US. We both married New Brunswickers and stayed, juxtaposing career, homemaking, child-rearing, and community service. We both have worked as rural extension workers, teachers, good food promoters, and business women. Marg's business as a food marketing consultant led her to recipe development and food styling. My business as a food market analyst led me to food journalism. We understand nutrition and food chemistry; we love to cook; and while we are devout breakfast eaters, at least one of us is not above replacing routine cereal with fresh fruit pie in August. In our homes, the entertainment is meal-centred.

That's why this book is meal-centred, divided by seasons, and arranged by menus rather than categories. In consideration of working couples, main dishes serve two or four and offer ideas for leftovers (plan-overs); baked recipes are in quantities that will feed you today and your freezer for tomorrow. This is a cookbook that brings the everyday—potatoes, wild blueberries, molasses, fish, and scones—alongside the distinctive fare—roschti, pavlova, satay, and ratatouille. It includes recipes from our grandmothers and for our grandchildren and yours. Affordable recipes that will take your family into the twenty-first century. A few special occasion recipes from each of our families are in the last chapter because they didn't fit the guidelines for the others. However, they were "too good to leave out."

ACKNOWLEDGEMENTS

This book exists because we poured into it a couple of years of energy and decades of recipe development. While we didn't ask our families' permission, we quickly obtained their approval of our decision. Some members of each family tasted and tested, others gave professional advice from their own fields, and all supported and cajoled us. They include Cheryl, Jane, Kirsten, Margot, Nancy, Peter, Ross, Scott, and Sherman. Don Young humoured us, taste-tested everything (some things, many times), and suffered with our setbacks. Mary Breau provided nutrition consultation; Anita Landry supplied fisheries information; Muriel Gorman contributed recipe monitoring and Pat Beaney cooking finesse. Darrell Munro, art director, and David Corkum, photographer, gave stalwart service for the photographs.

Our sincere thanks to each one.

INTRODUCTION

Food appeals to us when it tastes good. Only in recent years have we begun to show as much concern about the nutritional value of food as we have about its taste. That concern is changing what we eat. It is a significant change because the way we live has also changed. Today we sit—in vehicles, behind desks, and in front of computers and televisions. We used to walk, carry, chop, knead, scrub, dig, and push.

Urban dwellers are adjusting their lifestyle and eating habits more quickly than rural residents. Maritimers continue with traditional eating patterns, while those in other parts of Canada are changing theirs. One reason for the difference may be our enjoyment of a delicious, home style cuisine.

We know that dieting is not the way to change our eating style. We know that waiting until the boom is lowered by a doctor because we have cancer, heart disease, or diabetes is not the solution. We also know that eating what appeals to us is what we want to do, but not always what we should do.

That's why we wrote this book. To provide an improved, daily eating regime for the early decades of life so that we won't be denied the foods we love later on, when food becomes a leading pleasure of life. We structured it by seasons to capture the most natural, fresh taste from seasonal foods. We prepared menus, combining foods that taste good together, for meals that balance nutrients and high-and low-fat foods.

WHAT IS MEANT BY LOW-FAT EATING

The new rule is: Choose less than 30 per cent of the day's calories from fat. This does not mean every food eaten must have less than 30 per cent of its calories from fat. If it did, we'd have to say goodbye to whole milk, ground beef, many fat-rich snack foods, and most salad dressings. It does mean a day's food should not have more than 30 per cent of its calories from fat. So, you may sneak in a high-fat food if you balance it with low-fat foods. It's also possible to remove much of the fat from some foods by altering ingredients.

There are only a couple of things to remember about fat. First of all, the per cent of fat in a food, by weight, is entirely different from the per cent of calories from fat in that food. Every gram of fat contains nine calories; every gram of carbohydrate or protein (the other two major components of food) contains four calories. Thus, a gram of fat has more than twice as many calories as a gram of carbohydrate or protein.

Another thing to know about fat is how much is appropriate to eat each day. This is related to body size. Healthy body weight (in pounds) divided by two, gives the approximate number of grams of fat that should be eaten each day. For example, if healthy body weight is 130 pounds, daily fat intake should be about 65 grams.

Food stores have many "light" foods. Label reading is one way to determine whether a light food actually has fewer calories from fat or whether it has low salt, or is merely light in colour. Even though the food has fewer calories from fat, it may still contain too much fat to be used regularly. It is often better to substitute an ingredient that contains much less fat, for example, quark or yogurt cheese in place of light cream cheese or light sour cream.

Fat composition is an important consideration for people with a family history of atherosclerosis (hardening of the arteries and heart disease). Composition of fat is much less important to others. The bar graph, in the Appendix, shows the composition of each of the common fats we use.

Fat in food is a mixture of three types of fat: saturated, monounsaturated and polyunsaturated. Fats containing a high percentage of polyunsaturates and/or monounsaturates are healthier ones to use on a regular basis. This makes canola oil, along with many other liquid oils, better fats to choose for regular cooking and baking. Fats high in saturates—all animal fats and coconut oil—should be restricted if the family has a history of atherosclerosis. Since the disease is the number one killer of adults, fat composition is of concern to many families. Manufacturers use that concern to promote the strengths of their products. Research is producing a constant stream of information on preferred fats. Technology will make more healthful solid fats, probably improved soft margarines.

In a broader context, high-fat diets result in a great number of health problems in addition to atherosclerosis, which is why most people need to reduce fat intake. A person may switch to 1 per cent milk; give up butter and margarine on toast, sandwiches and rolls; give up salad dressings and/or doughnuts, croissants and high-fat cheeses; or do all of these things. For each of us everyday, the bottom line is quite simply: eat less until total calories from fat is below 30 per cent of daily calorie intake.

It is difficult to know when the magic plateau is reached, when enough fat has been removed. Once that point is reached, dieticians and food scientists say there will be a cleaner taste and an absence of coating in the mouth. There will be less consciousness of body after dinner. A person may simply get on with life. It will not happen in a day or a week. Initially, there will be a lack of taste. Herbs and spices may help during this period. Gradually, a cleaner taste and a greater appreciation of food texture will come. Later on, the preference for fat-rich foods will disappear.

WHAT IS IN THE NEW NORTH AMERICAN FOOD GUIDES

Canada's food guide is represented by a rainbow; the United States chose a pyramid (see Appendix). In both cases the message is the same: Eat more fruits, vegetables, and grains and less animal products. The outside bands of the rainbow and the base of the pyramid display dozens of grains, vegetables, and fruits to combine in interesting meals. The inside bands of the rainbow and the pointed top of the pyramid crowd the smaller quantities of dairy and meat products that are needed. The visual impact of the rainbow or the pyramid is striking. It emphasizes the necessity of and the safety in eating five to twelve servings of grains (cereals, breads, pastas, and rice) and five to ten servings of vegetables and fruits each day. It's the reason we've put breads into family meals; filled plates, bowls, and lunch bags with vegetables; and made desserts with fruits.

It's also the reason we use 1 per cent milk, low-fat dairy products, and limit meat, fish, and poultry servings to 4 ounces (115 grams). Nutritionists suggest visualizing a deck of cards on the dinner plate; the deck being the recommended size for a serving of meat, fish, or poultry. Another way to change what's on the plate is to adopt the five to one rule. It puts five parts vegetable, potato, legume and/or grain on the plate for each part of meat, fish, or poultry. In that ratio, protein foods become flavour and texture enhancers.

The food guides recommend that salt, alcohol, caffeine, and foods that are mostly sugar be consumed in moderation. The taste for salt and sugar is acquired. The easy way to adjust taste buds is to cut back gradually. When prepared and processed foods taste too salty, a healthier level of consumption has been reached. When plain dry cereals taste sweet enough and commercial desserts too sweet, a person is on the right track. Caffeine dependence is induced. Canada's Food Guide recommends a maximum of four cups of coffee per day. Tea, cola, and instant coffee have about half as much caffeine as dripped or perked coffee. Chocolate also contains a form of caffeine. Alcohol in moderation means one alcoholic drink per day or not more than seven drinks per week. A drink is a bottle of beer, a glass of wine, or a spirit drink. Abstinence is strongly recommended for pregnant women. Food guides do not speak of dessert. However, dessert is part of our heritage and must be addressed. Fruit-based dishes are excellent choices when dessert seems essential.

A food guide is a visual presentation of recommended foods based on availability, knowledge, culture, and lifestyle. It is constantly evolving. Understanding the structure of a food guide and transposing it into meals on the plate is one key to improved eating.

How We Developed Low-Fat Recipes

We began by shuffling through cookie and square recipes. None of them seemed to have potential. We almost despaired. We shifted our attention to breads and muffins and were able to get our bearings. We had been substituting whole wheat flour for half the all-purpose flour in baked goods and had been fiddling with the kinds and amount of fat used. We had two muffin recipes that made a dozen good muffins with one-quarter cup of oil. We set that as a guideline and developed two more. We discovered sweet fruit breads were low in fat. We adjusted and tested those. We don't butter them—a habit of the past.

We went on to an easy category—breads. We changed yeast bread recipes from solid fat to oil; we reduced salt and sugar; and we increased whole grain content. We met resistance from family and friends who said the products didn't taste quite the way they remembered. They were experiencing the taste adjustment we mentioned earlier. The adjusted recipes are decidedly better in texture and nutrition. We were offered favourite bread recipes, most of which contained two or three times as much salt and sugar as required, and only all-purpose flour.

Quick breads were painful. We wanted to include them for cooks who haven't the patience or time to make yeast breads. We wanted quick, simple recipes with short ingredient lists. But they too had to taste good. We argued and made dozens of scones and biscuits before we threw out soda bread and achieved good buttermilk scones, blueberry tea bread, and potato bannock.

We went back to cookies, squares, and cakes. The Maritimes are famous for delicious, rich morsels that we call squares; other geographic areas call them bars or fingers. A couple of those were so good we decided to preserve them in a special section at the end.

We discarded layered pastries, croissants, and doughnuts. We kept sponge cakes, fruit cakes, and crumble-topped cakes. While we expected to eliminate cheesecake, we were overjoyed with the quality product we got when quark was substituted for cream cheese. Imagine, cheesecake without calorie-overload.

Cookies were next. We set a guideline of four parts whole grain flour and/or cereal to one part soft margarine. With a lot of finicking, we got six cookie recipes that passed the "kid test."

Puddings and pies are heritage foods along the Atlantic seaboard. We had fun with the puddings, updating them, cutting back the sugar and salt, reducing and changing fats, adding whole grains and more fruit.

Finally we faced pies. We each had a dozen favourites. Our pies have one crust; we believe in thin, flaky crusts. We also believe in thick fillings and either meringue or no topping. Our children say they had to go to university to learn there was such a thing as a two-crust pie with ice cream on the side.

You may want to convert favourite recipes as well as trying ours. Following are two examples of our original and the revised recipe ingredients.

BANANA MUFFINS (ORIGINAL)

½ cup	butter
1 cup	granulated sugar
1	egg
½ tsp	vanilla
½ tsp	nutmeg
1½ cups	all-purpose flour
2 tsp	baking powder
2	bananas, mashed
¼ cup	hot water
1 tsp	baking soda

BANANA MUFFINS (REVISED)

¼ cup	oil	50 mL
½ cup	granulated sugar	125 mL
1	egg	1
½ tsp	vanilla	2 mL
½ tsp	nutmeg	2 mL
1½ cups	whole wheat flour	375 mL
1 tsp	baking powder	5 mL
1	large banana	1
¼ cup	hot water	50 mL
1 tsp	baking soda	5 mL
2 tbsp	poppy seeds	25 mL

The sugar and salt have been cut in half; the butter has been replaced with half as much oil, and the all-purpose flour has been replaced with whole wheat flour. The poppy seeds are added for nourishment and crunch. The original recipe used a cake mixing method: whip, cream, and fold. The resulting muffins were miniature cakes. We simplified the method to obtain bread texture.

CRANBERRY COBBLER (ORIGINAL)

1 cup	cranberries
1 cup	water
¾ cup	granulated sugar
2 tsp	cornstarch
1 tbsp	butter
1¼ cups	all-purpose flour
2 tsp	baking powder
½ cup	granulated sugar
¼ cup	shortening
½ cup	milk
½ cup	raisins
½ cup	dates
½ cup	walnuts
1 tbsp	sugar

CRANBERRY COBBLER (REVISED)

1 pkg	cranberries (12 oz)	340 g
1½ cups	water	375 mL
¾ cup	granulated sugar	175 mL
1 tsp	soft margarine	5 mL
½ cup	all-purpose flour	125 mL
½ cup	whole wheat flour	125 mL
2 tsp	baking powder	10 mL
¼ cup	granulated sugar	50 mL
2 tbsp	soft margarine	25 mL
½ cup	raisins	125 mL
½ cup	1% milk	125 mL

The quantity of cranberries has been doubled while that of biscuit topping remains almost the same. The biscuits have half as much sugar and fat and some whole wheat flour.

We were not always successful. Recipes containing peanuts, peanut butter, and quick cooking oats are difficult to change. They tend to be dry and have poor texture when fat is removed. Corn syrup moistens a baked product and is an excellent substitute for half the fat. Sugar content needs to be reduced accordingly. Good luck as you experiment to bring family favourites to a modern standard.

STOCKING THE KITCHEN FOR THIS BOOK

Changes will be required in the shopping list to use this book. Our categories correspond to food store departments. In each department, we identify foods the recipes use frequently.

In the grains category, you will need whole wheat flour. It's in most baked goods. Quick cooking oats, cornmeal, rye flour, brown and white rice, bulgur, and baking beans are used. For convenience, we use canned kidney beans and chick peas. Dried ones are cheaper.

The fats we use constantly are canola oil and olive oil; canola is the only one required in quantity. We appreciate the unique taste of butter and use it discerningly. Soft margarine is used for creaming in baked goods and lard for flakiness in pastry. We do not use shortening.

In the staple vegetable department, we use lots of potatoes, as well as onions, carrots, celery, rutabaga, sweet peppers, and romaine.

The herb and spice list is topped by fresh garlic and black pepper. Dried herbs are used in winter, including a maritime favourite, summer savoury. We use fresh basil, thyme, tarragon, rosemary, parsley, and mint when available and list the quantity of dried alternative when practical. During summer, fresh dill and chives are used. Maritime recipes require ground cinnamon, nutmeg, and ginger. We also use ground cloves and allspice, fresh ginger, whole cloves, and stick cinnamon.

In condiments, molasses is used regularly; corn syrup, maple syrup, and honey, are used less frequently. Light soya, oyster, and Hoisin sauces are used. Light mayonnaise is essential. We use many vinegars and recommend you purchase white, balsamic, rice, and one more of choice (tarragon or wine). Hot pepper sauce may be Tabasco, the universal brand, or any other one.

Fresh fruits used often include apples, lemons, and cranberries. Seasonal fruits are featured in their fresh and frozen forms, particularly wild blueberries and rhubarb. Canned plum tomatoes and tomato paste are used frequently. They are the least expensive of the canned tomato products. Seedless raisins are the one dried fruit used often, dried apricots less often, other dried fruits are used infrequently.

Dairy counter shopping for this book is different. Buttermilk is used. It is thick and creamy, a quarter the price of yogurt, yet it contains almost no fat. Vanilla skimmed milk yogurt and plain skimmed milk yogurt are used regularly in a variety of ways. Quark cheese and yogurt cheese replace high-fat dairy products. Quark is a soft, unripened cheese available in the dairy case at an increasing number of stores; it is usually cheaper at farm markets. It is of German origin, and is dense and mild-flavoured compared to yogurt. Read labels to get low-fat quark. Yogurt cheese, not really a cheese, is made by straining plain, skimmed milk yogurt. All four have extended refrigerator shelf life. All may be frozen. We tested our recipes with 1 per cent fresh milk. Creamed cottage cheese is in the book three times; watch its salt content. Hard cheeses play a reduced role in our recipes compared to the usual Canadian diet. Regular hard cheeses contain 25 per cent to 35 per cent fat (by weight).

In protein foods, we have selected widely, including pork, beef, and lamb, as well as poultry, fish, and seafood. We chose the leanest cuts of meat and used low-fat cooking procedures. Because the popular press offers so many chicken breast recipes, we neglected them. Because there is a dearth of modern roasted meat recipes, we included a lean one from each animal. We have not avoided eggs; rather, we have used them sparingly. Egg yolk adds tenderness to a product. Substituting two whites for a whole egg gives baked products a rubbery texture. Egg yolk does contain fat. We like to say it's one of the few high-fat ingredients that keeps good nutritional company. Our recipes were tested with large eggs.

There is nothing exotic on our shopping list. For the most part, we tried to use foods that can be grown in a northern climate and purchased at regular food stores.

Nutritional analysis of our recipes is based on the Nutrient Analysis Program, using 1991 Canadian Nutrient File, by Elizabeth Warwick, of Cornwall, Prince Edward Island. Where the yield gives two values, the nutrient analysis is based on the first figure. Ingredients listed as optional are not included in the analysis. The nutritional value for chicken broth in our recipes is based on our chicken broth recipe rather than canned chicken broth as listed in the nutrient file. Our recipe consists of vegetables simmered with meaty chicken bones but is free of chicken skin and fat.

We found analyzing the nutrient content of our recipes an enlightening experience. While most of them did not have more fat than we had anticipated, many recipes had too much protein. Traditionally we have eaten large servings of protein foods (meats, fish, poultry, eggs, and dairy products). We reduced the portion size of these foods in order to reduce protein content of our meals. We added whole grains and legumes to get a healthier, fibre-rich diet. Because these foods also contain protein, our meals are still high in protein. We were amazed at how little oil it took to push a salad to more than 50 per cent of calories from fat, simply because there are so few calories in salad ingredients other than the dressing. We were so surprised by the fat content of poultry skin, we have given the nutrient analysis for both roasted chicken and turkey, with and without skin, so you can see the difference.

Fats, carbohydrates, and protein are the major components of food; their interrelationships are important in meal planning. Selecting a wide variety of foods from each of these categories, with emphasis on carbohy-drate foods, as we have done, eliminates concern about intake of individual vitamins and minerals. We included grams of fibre and fat and total calories in the nutrient analysis for people on restricted diets who want that infor-mation. We have not included grams of sodium (salt). However, we have selected foods that are low in salt; we have used few processed foods; and we have eliminated or greatly reduced the salt in most baked goods. The calorie breakdown portion of the nutrient analysis on our recipes gives the percent-age of calories in the food that comes from each major food component: protein, fat, and carbohydrate. The total adds up to 100 per cent. We hope you will find the nutrient analysis as informative as we did.

Welcome to *New Maritimes Seasonal Cooking*.

WELCOME TO SPRING

There comes a day when the breeze is as gentle as the caress of pussy willow against the cheek; when the grinding of ice floes is a joyful reminder of hand-churned maple ice cream; when the setting sun trails the sky with irridescent rose, the same colour as the nectar of stewed rhubarb. There's one word for it. Spring.

The fitting colour for the season is spring green. The green of emerging asparagus shoots and fiddlehead fronds from the dank, sandy loam of tended garden and rough river bank. The tender green of leaf and bib lettuce, of watercress and dandelion. Because we want to celebrate the renewal of life in the kitchen, as well as in the barn and the meadow, we search our books for innovative ways to serve eggs, lamb, and veal. We put away the stews, pot pies, and chowders and bring out recipes for biscuits and maple cakes, fruited breads and rolls.

While spring is the season of renewal, joy, and hope, the food store in a northern climate cannot keep pace, cannot satisfy our yearning. So, it is the laborious season for the seasonal cook. It requires that you not only go to markets and farms as well as stores but that you plan for this season well in advance. You need to know where to find rhubarb and fiddleheads, you must plant parsnips a year in advance and shepherd early spinach and lettuces in a sheltered garden. You do become ingenious with dried fruits, stored potatoes, and the ubiquitous lemon. Finally, you watch the weather to catch every gentle, sunny hour for that memorable picnic or barbecue. It may not be easy; however, it's the essence of spring green.

BREAKFAST (4)*
Pink Grapefruit Juice
Apricot Sauce with Green Grapes
    and Yogurt 62
Hot Cross Buns 50-51

BRUNCH (6)
Swiss Cheese Spread, Crackers 7
Asparagus on Toast 19
Citrus Compote
Rhubarb Surprise Cake 40

BOX LUNCH (2)
Oatmeal Carrot Muffins 52
Yogurt Slaw 9

LUNCH (2)
Fiddlehead Soup 8
Multi-grain Bread 53
Apple Waldorf Salad 10
Marshland Crisps 55

LUNCH (4)
Fiddlehead Stir-fry 20
Potato Bannock 56
Apricot Bread 57

FAMILY SUPPER (4)
Swiss Carrot Salad 11
Microwaved Pork Steak 21
Whipped Potatoes
Beet Greens
Rhubarb Meringue Pie 41

SUNDAY DINNER (4)
Sardine Cucumber Cups 4
Roasted Leg of Lamb with
    Rosemary Jelly 34-35
Baked Parsnips 38
Steamed Green Beans
Lemon Potato Wedges 39
Strawberry Parfait 49

QUICK SUPPER (4)
Basil Hamburger 24
Cucumber Salsa 25
Ovened French Fries 26
Strawberry Smoothie 63

OUTDOOR SUPPER (6)
Barbecued Chicken 27
Molded Spinach Salad 12
Marinated Potato Salad 13
Granary Rolls 58-59
Jumbo Raisin Cookies 60

CANDLELIGHT DINNER (2)
Wilted Spinach and Bean Salad 16
Veal Scaloppini 28
Noodles
Three Coloured Pepper Stir-fry
Raspberry Ice 45

SUNDAY DINNER (4)
Jane's Scallop Seviche 5
Pork Medallions with
    Green Peppercorns 29
Baked Brown and Wild Rice 30
Peas and Onions 31
Lemon Sponge Pudding 48

PARTY DINNER (6 TO 8)
Stuffed Mushrooms 6
Baked Whole Salmon 32-33
Parsley Potatoes
Fiddleheads
The Working Cook's Rolls 61
New Brunswick Spring Delight 46

VEGETARIAN SUPPER (4)
Roschti 22
Red Cabbage with Apple 23
Pineapple Upside Down Cake 44

PLAN-OVER DINNER (4)
Salmon Fishcakes 36
Marinated Asparagus Salad 17
Granary Rolls 58-59
Marshland Crisps 55

PLAN-OVER DINNER (3)
Romaine and Watercress Salad 18
Curried Lamb 37
Rhubarb Chutney 64
Basmati Brown Rice
Fresh Pineapple Spears

*indicates number served

STARTERS
Jane's Scallop Seviche
Sardine Cucumber Cups
Stuffed Mushrooms
Swiss Cheese Spread

SOUPS & SALADS
Apple Waldorf Salad
Cheryl's Salad Dressing
Fiddlehead Soup
French Dressing
Marinated Asparagus Salad
Marinated Potato Salad
Molded Spinach Salad
Romaine and Watercress Salad
Swiss Carrot Salad
Wilted Spinach and Bean Salad
Yogurt Slaw

MAIN COURSE FOODS
Asparagus on Toast
Baked Brown and Wild Rice
Baked Parsnips
Baked Whole Salmon
Barbecued Chicken
Basil Hamburger, Cucumber Salsa
Curried Lamb
Fiddlehead Stir-fry
Lemon Potato Wedges
Microwaved Pork Steak
Ovened French Fries
Peas and Onions
Pork Medallions with Green
   Peppercorns
Red Cabbage with Apple
Roasted Leg of Lamb,
   Rosemary Jelly
Roschti
Salmon Fish Cakes
Veal Scaloppini

DESSERTS
Lemon Sponge Pudding
Maple Seven-Minute Frosting
New Brunswick Spring Delight
Pie Pastry
Pineapple Upside Down Cake
Raspberry Ice
Rhubarb Meringue Pie
Rhubarb Surprise Cake
Strawberry Parfait

BAKED GOODS
Apricot Bread
Granary Rolls
Hot Cross Buns
Jumbo Raisin Cookies
Marshland Crisps (cookie)
Multi-grain Bread
Oatmeal Carrot Muffins
Potato Bannock
The Working Cook's Rolls

MISCELLANEOUS
Apricot Sauce with Green Grapes
   and Yogurt
Rhubarb Chutney
Strawberry Smoothie

Sardine Cucumber Cups

When the Youngs were building their house, they noticed the carpenters ate the same lunch everyday: a can of sardines with bread. When they lived in Guyana, the Routledges found empty Connors' sardine tins in the South American rainforest. Maritimers continue to eat sardines and ship them around the world.

Sardines are rather high in fat, but they contain omega-3 fat, which is one of the better types of fat to eat. Sardines also contain protein and a wide array of minerals and vitamins. Those packed in tomato or mustard sauce have less fat. However, our choice for this recipe is tabasco sardines.

1	English cucumber	1

Filling:

1 (3.7 oz)	can tabasco sardines in oil	106 g
1 tbsp	freshly squeezed lemon juice	15 mL
1 tsp	Dijon mustard	5 mL
1 tbsp	low-fat mayonnaise	15 mL

Wash cucumber and cut into 1-inch (2.5 cm) slices. With teaspoon or melon-baller, scoop out top centre of each slice.

Drain sardines on paper towel to remove oil. In small bowl, using a fork, mash sardines with lemon juice, mustard, and mayonnaise. Scoop onto cucumber cups, filling cavity and mounding. Chill until serving time.

Yield: about 15 filled cups

Variation:
Filling may be served on crackers or used in a sandwich with thinly sliced cucumber.

per filled cup	**calorie breakdown**
calories 18.3	% protein 35
g fat 1.0	% fat 50
g fibre 0.1	% carbohydrate 15

JANE'S SCALLOP SEVICHE

Peruvians use a lime juice marinade in place of cooking to develop an unusual flavour in fish and seafoods. We hesitate to eat uncooked fish. For a relatively safe seviche, find out from your fishmonger when the fresh fish comes in and buy it that day. Freeze for 48 hours. Thaw in microwave and make seviche. Keep refrigerated until serving time. Dispose of leftovers. Alternatively, cook scallops by poaching in the lime juice only until opaque and marinate in refrigerator for several hours.

½ lb	fresh scallops	250 g
½ cup	lime juice	125 mL
2 tbsp	bottled, sliced jalapeño peppers *or* 1 fresh, sliced	25 mL
1	medium tomato, peeled, seeded, and chopped	1
½	red onion, sliced thinly, separated into rings	½
1 tbsp	chopped, fresh coriander	15 mL

If scallops are large, cut in half or quarters. Place scallops and lime juice in shallow glass dish. Cover and marinate in refrigerator 4 to 6 hours, stirring several times. Scallops should be opaque and appear cooked. Add peppers, tomato, onion, and coriander; refrigerate at least 4 hours. To serve, remove scallops with slotted spoon.

Yield: 4 servings as appetizer

Variation:
Make with white fish fillets, cut into bite-size pieces.

per serving	calorie breakdown
calories 70	% protein 56
g fat 0.6	% fat 8
g fibre 0.7	% carbohydrates 36

Stuffed Mushrooms

If you've dribbled appetizer mushrooms down your front, you'll appreciate the consistency, as well as the uniqueness, of these stuffed mushrooms.

1	medium sweet potato	1
18	medium mushrooms	18
1 tbsp	oil	15 mL
1	small onion, finely chopped	1
1	clove garlic, minced	1
1 tsp	grated fresh ginger	5 mL
½ tsp	dried summer savoury	2 mL
¼ tsp	salt	1 mL
pinch	cayenne	
2 tbsp	brandy (optional)	25 mL

Scrub sweet potato, pierce, and microwave on high until cooked, 4 to 5 minutes. Wash mushrooms, drain well, remove stems and chop finely. Rub outside of caps with some of the oil. Place on baking sheet. Heat remaining oil in small skillet, sauté onion and garlic 1 minute. Add chopped stems, ginger, savoury, salt, and cayenne; stir-fry 1 minute. Peel sweet potato, mash, and blend with skillet mixture and brandy. Spoon into mushroom caps, rounding tops. Bake in 400°F (200°C) oven 10 minutes. Serve hot.

Yield: 6 servings

per serving	**calorie breakdown**
calories 59	% protein 7
g fat 2.5	% fat 39
g fibre 1.3	% carbohydrate 55

SWISS CHEESE SPREAD

The nuttiness of Swiss cheese makes this a good starter with coffee.

4 oz	Swiss cheese, coarsely grated	115 g
3 tbsp	low-fat salad dressing	45 mL
2	cloves garlic, minced	2
pinch	black pepper	
	rye bread, thinly sliced	
	sliced olives for garnish	

Blend Swiss cheese, salad dressing, garlic, and black pepper. Spread on thin slices of rye bread; top with black or green olive slices. Spreads best at room temperature.

Store in refrigerator for up to one week.

Yield: 1 cup (250 mL)

per tablespoon	**calorie breakdown**
calories 34	% protein 27
g fat 2.4	% fat 64
g fibre 0	% carbohydrate 9

SWEET POTATOES AND YAMS

Native to tropical areas of the Americas, sweet potatoes are available in many varieties. Two are widely grown commercially: the pale sweet potato and the darker-skinned variety that is erroneously called "yam" by many people. The pale sweet potato has a thin, light yellow skin and pale yellow flesh. It is not sweet to taste and after being cooked is dry and crumbly, similar to a white baking potato. The darker variety has a thicker, dark orange skin and sweet, vivid orange flesh. It is the one usually sold in our food stores.

Fresh sweet potatoes are readily available most of the year (except summer). Choose ones that are smooth and unbruised. Store in a dry, dark, cool location and use within one week of purchase. Do not refrigerate.

Dark-skinned sweet potatoes are readily microwaved. Wash, pierce, and microwave on high, about 4 minutes per potato.

Fiddlehead Soup

Potato is an excellent thickener for soup. Both taste and texture are better than when the same soup is thickened with wheat, corn, or tapioca flour.

1 tbsp	oil	15 mL
¾ cup	sliced leeks*	175 mL
1 cup	diced potatoes	250 mL
3 cups	fiddleheads, fresh or frozen	750 mL
2 cups	chicken broth	500 mL
1 tsp	salt (less if broth already salted)	5 mL
¼ tsp	pepper	1 mL
1 tbsp	chopped, fresh coriander or parsley	15 mL
2 cups	1% milk	500 mL
3 tbsp	plain yogurt for garnish	45 mL

*Onions may be substituted for leeks.

In large, heavy saucepan, heat oil. Add leeks; sauté 2 minutes. Add potatoes and fiddleheads; cover pan, reduce heat, and steam vegetables 5 minutes. Remove six large fiddleheads for garnish. Stir in chicken broth and simmer until vegetables are tender, 10 to 15 minutes. Add salt, pepper, and herb. Purée mixture in blender or food processor.* Return to heat, stir in milk. Heat thoroughly, but do not boil. Taste and adjust seasonings. Serve garnished with yogurt and reserved fiddleheads.

*This soup may be made in quantity and frozen for winter. Freeze puréed mixture; add milk before serving.

Variations:
Replace fiddleheads with broccoli, spinach, or carrots.

Yield: 6 servings

per serving	**calorie breakdown**
calories 229	% protein 21
g fat 5.1	% fat 19
g fibre 0.8	% carbohydrate 59

YOGURT SLAW

Cabbage is readily available all year. It is an inexpensive and nutritious vegetable that used to be a staple in Canadian kitchens. We would like to bring cabbage back in appropriate, modern ways.

1 cup	thinly sliced cabbage	250 mL
1	small red-skinned apple, quartered, cored, and chopped	1
½ cup	pineapple chunks, fresh or canned	125 mL
½ cup	vanilla skimmed milk yogurt	125 mL

Combine cabbage, apple, pineapple, and yogurt. Toss with fork and pack in sealed container. Will store in cool place for 24 hours.

Yield: 2 servings

per serving	calorie breakdown
calories 117	% protein 13
g fat 0.5	% fat 3
g fibre 2.6	% carbohydrate 84

Apple Waldorf Salad

A cross between salad and dessert, this is a perfect finish to a soup lunch.
Make it with any red-skinned apple. Our preference would be Cortland
because it's slow to brown once it is cut.

½ cup	diced celery	125 mL
½ cup	grated cabbage	125 mL
¼ cup	chopped dates	50 mL
1	large red apple	1

Dressing:

2 tbsp	low-fat salad dressing	25 mL
2 tsp	lemon juice	10 mL
1 tsp	honey	5 mL

Place celery, cabbage, and dates in small bowl. Leaving skin intact, quarter,
core, and chop apple. Add to other ingredients. Whisk salad dressing,
lemon juice, and honey. Pour over salad ingredients and toss. Refrigerate.
Serve cold.

Yield: 2 servings

per serving	**calorie breakdown**
calories 181	% protein 2
g fat 4.4	% fat 20
g fibre 4.5	% carbohydrate 78

Swiss Carrot Salad

Donna's father immigrated from Switzerland as a child. Years later, she recalls, his eyes would light up when there was carrot salad for supper.

1 lb	(4 medium) carrots, peeled and sliced	450 g
1	small red onion, halved and thinly sliced	1
1	sweet green pepper, cut into 1-inch (2 cm) strips	1
¼ cup	granulated sugar	50 mL
½ tsp	salt	2 mL
¼ tsp	pepper	1 mL
½ cup	vinegar (preferably balsamic)	125 mL
½ cup	tomato juice	125 mL
2 tsp	olive oil	10 mL
1 tsp	Dijon mustard	5 mL
2 tsp	Worcestershire sauce	10 ml
	lettuce cups	

Steam carrots 4 to 5 minutes until tender crisp. Plunge into ice water to stop cooking process; drain. Place carrots, onion, and green pepper into container with lid. In shaker, combine sugar, salt, pepper, vinegar, tomato juice, oil, mustard, and Worcestershire sauce. Shake and pour over vegetables. Cover and refrigerate at least 6 hours. Serve on lettuce cups.

Keeps well in refrigerator for 2 weeks.

Yield: 6 servings

per serving	calorie breakdown
calories 91.9	% protein 6
g fat 1.8	% fat 16
g fibre 2.5	% carbohydrate 78

Molded Spinach Salad

This is one of the first recipes we shared during our thirty-five-year friendship. In Marg's recipe box, it was identified as "Donna's Green Salad Mold." Excellent for entertaining, it is enjoyed by people who are surprised by its tang and the lack of sweetness generally associated with jellied salads.

1 (6 oz) pkg	lime flavoured gelatin	170 g
1½ cups	boiling water	375 mL
1½ cups	cold water	375 mL
¼ cup	red wine vinegar	50 mL
2 tbsp	lemon juice	25 mL
2 tbsp	granulated sugar	25 mL
½ tsp	salt	2 mL
¼ tsp	pepper	1 mL
few drops	hot pepper sauce	
2 cups	chopped fresh spinach	500 mL
½ cup	sliced green onions	125 mL
1 cup	diced celery	250 mL
½ cup	grated carrot	125 mL
	spinach leaves, salad dressing, and carrot curls for garnish	

Dissolve gelatin in boiling water. Stir in cold water, vinegar, lemon juice, sugar, salt, pepper, and hot pepper sauce. Chill in refrigerator until partially set (egg white consistency). Fold vegetables into gelatin mixture. Pour into 6 cup (1.5 L) oiled mold. Refrigerate until set. At serving time, unmold on spinach leaves. Garnish with salad dressing and carrot curls.

Yield: 10 to 12 servings

per serving
calories 51
g fat 0.1
g fibre 0.8

calorie breakdown
% protein 10
% fat 1
% carbohydrate 88

Marinated Potato Salad

Donna's mother made great potato salad. The things she did differently from most people were to undercook, dry off, and marinate the potatoes. It meant you needed little salad dressing to make a tasty salad. Last fall's stored potatoes are best for this spring salad.

6	medium potatoes	6
¼ cup	French dressing (recipe follows)	50 mL
2	hard cooked eggs	2
1 cup	diced celery	250 mL
4	green onions, sliced *or* ¼ cup (50 mL) diced onion	4
¼ tsp	salt	1 mL
⅛ tsp	pepper	0.5 mL
¼ cup	Cheryl's Salad Dressing (recipe follows)	50 mL

Peel potatoes, cut in half lengthwise and cook in ½ cup (125 mL) boiling water in a covered saucepan until barely tender, about 10 minutes. Drain, dry off by holding saucepan over warm burner 1 minute. Drizzle French dressing over potatoes, turning to coat all sides. Refrigerate to cool. To assemble salad, cube potatoes, chop eggs, and combine with celery, onions, salt, and pepper. Carefully stir in Cheryl's cooked salad dressing (see page 15), adding only enough to hold the salad together. Refrigerate until serving time.

Yield: 6 servings

per serving   **calorie breakdown**
calories 188   % protein 10
g fat 5.0   % fat 23
g fibre 2.3   % carbohydrate 66

French Dressing

¼ cup	oil	50 mL
½ cup	white or tarragon vinegar	125 mL
¼ tsp	salt	1 mL
pinch	pepper	
1 tsp	granulated sugar	5 mL
1	clove garlic, cut in half	1

Combine all ingredients in glass jar, cover, and shake vigorously. Store in refrigerator.

Yield: ¾ cup (175 mL)

CHERYL'S SALAD DRESSING

A true mayonnaise is made with egg yolks, vinegar or lemon juice, and lots of oil—far too high in fat for today's salads and sandwiches. Cheryl, Marg's daughter, makes this cooked, low-fat salad dressing in a double boiler. We have adapted it for the microwave. The quantity is small because the dressing will not keep as long as sterilized commercial products.

½ cup	sugar	125 mL
2 tbsp	all-purpose flour	25 mL
1 tsp	dry mustard	5 mL
¼ tsp	salt	1 mL
dash	cayenne	
⅔ cup	1% milk	150 mL
½ cup	white vinegar	125 mL
1	egg, beaten	1
1 tbsp	butter *or* olive oil	15 mL

In 2 cup (500 mL) microwave-safe measure, mix sugar, flour, dry mustard, salt, and cayenne. Stir in milk and microwave on high for 2½ minutes or until thick, stirring twice. Add vinegar; microwave on high 1 minute, stirring once. Whisk some of the hot mixture into beaten egg, then stir egg mixture into hot mixture. Microwave on medium for about 40 seconds, until thick.

Stir in butter or oil. Store in jar in refrigerator for up to 2 weeks.

Yield: 1½ cups (375 mL)

Variation:
To dress tossed salads, thin with equal amounts of lemon juice and sugar.

per 2 tablespoons (30 mL)	**calorie breakdown**
calories 62	% protein 8
g fat 1.7	% fat 24
g fibre 0	% carbohydrate 68

WILTED SPINACH AND BEAN SALAD

Make this spring salad when tender, fresh spinach comes on the market. You might even have it growing in a sheltered garden. The recipe comes from Marg's gourmet group.

1 cup	diagonally sliced green beans	250 mL
4 oz	fresh spinach leaves	125 g
½ cup	thinly sliced mushrooms	125 mL
1 tbsp	olive oil	15 mL
2	green onions, sliced	2
2 tbsp	balsamic or red wine vinegar	25 mL
2 tsp	brown sugar	10 mL
¼ tsp	curry powder	1 mL
⅛ tsp	freshly ground pepper	0.5 mL
2	cherry tomatoes, halved, for garnish	2

Steam green beans until tender crisp; drain and plunge into ice water to stop cooking. Drain well, pat dry. Wash spinach, spin or pat dry, remove heavy stems, and break into large pieces. Place spinach, beans, and mushrooms in salad bowl. In small skillet, heat oil; stir in onions, vinegar, sugar, curry powder, and pepper. Bring to boil, stirring constantly. Remove from heat, pour over salad and toss gently. Serve immediately on individual plates, garnished with tomato halves.

Yield: 2 servings

Variation:
For a luncheon salad entrée, garnish with wedges of hard-cooked egg.

per serving	**calorie breakdown**
calories 193	% protein 14
g fat 7.8	% fat 34
g fibre 2.5	% carbohydrate 51

MARINATED ASPARAGUS SALAD

It takes years and appropriate conditions to establish an asparagus bed. No wonder we cherish this delicate, unparalleled vegetable. Like corn, asparagus tastes better if cooked immediately after harvesting. If you must store it, wrap in a damp cloth and refrigerate.

1 lb	fresh asparagus	450 g
⅓ cup	apple juice	75 mL
2 tbsp	lemon juice	25 mL
1 tbsp	powdered fruit pectin*	15 mL
1 tsp	Dijon mustard	5 mL
1	clove garlic, minced	1
pinch	pepper	
4	romaine leaves	4
	chopped fresh chives for garnish	

*Pectin is a thickening agent that dissolves readily when combined with liquids. Commonly used for setting jams and jellies, it may be substituted for oil in salad dressings or marinades as we have done here.

Trim or snap woody ends from asparagus. Wash, tips up, under stream of cool water. Turn tips down and drain thoroughly. Combine apple and lemon juices, pectin, mustard, garlic, and pepper in non-aluminum saucepan. Bring to boil; add asparagus. Reduce heat, cover and simmer for 4 minutes, until asparagus is tender crisp. Chill in marinade. Drain and serve on romaine. Garnish with chives.

Yield: 4 servings

Tip:
To snap woody ends from asparagus, hold ends of stalk (tip end just below head) between thumb and forefinger of each hand and bend stalk until it breaks just above the tough part.

per serving	calorie breakdown
calories 44	% protein 26
g fat 0.5	% fat 8
g fibre 2.2	% carbohydrate 66

Romaine and Watercress Salad

Add a spring green, such as watercress, to a winter green like romaine, dress it, and you will have a surprisingly crunchy salad.

½ head	romaine	½
½ bunch	watercress	½
2	oranges, peeled and sectioned	2

Sesame Dressing:

1 tbsp	sesame seeds	15 mL
1 tbsp	olive oil	15 mL
2 tbsp	lemon juice	25 mL
2 tsp	honey	10 mL
	pepper to taste	

Wash and dry romaine and watercress; break into bite-size pieces, removing coarse stalks. Place in salad bowl. Cut orange sections in half and add to greens.

In small skillet, toast sesame seeds, about 2 minutes. In a shaker, combine oil, lemon juice, honey, pepper, and toasted sesame seeds. Cover and shake well; immediately pour over greens. Toss and serve.

Yield: 3 to 4 servings

per serving	calorie breakdown
calories 123	% protein 7
g fat 6.2	% fat 43
g fibre 2.9	% carbohydrate 50

ASPARAGUS ON TOAST

Your grandmother may have served this as a supper dish, with no knowledge of the nutrient balance it provided. We serve it for brunch, but it's equally good as an entrée for lunch or as a light supper.

1½ lb	fresh asparagus	675 g
1 tbsp	butter	15 mL
2 tbsp	all-purpose flour	25 mL
¾ cup	1% milk	175 mL
½ cup	cooking water from asparagus	125 mL
¼ tsp	salt	1 mL
⅛ tsp	pepper	0.5 mL
1 tsp	fresh thyme or tarragon *or* ¼ tsp (1 mL) dried	5 mL
8	slices whole grain bread, toasted	8
2	hard-cooked eggs, sliced	2

Trim or snap woody ends from asparagus. Wash, tips up, under stream of cool water. Steam until tender crisp, about 4 minutes. Meanwhile, in small skillet, over medium heat, melt butter, work in flour with a fork. Gradually whisk in milk, and cook, stirring constantly until sauce begins to thicken. Add sufficient cooking water from asparagus to make a smooth, medium sauce. Add seasonings. Cut 4 slices of toast into diagonal quarters. To serve, arrange one full slice of toast and four points on each hot plate. Top full slice with asparagus, sliced egg, and hot sauce. Serve immediately.

Yield: 4 servings

Variations:
As the first spinach, snowpeas, and green beans mature, make the same dish with each one instead of asparagus.

per serving	**calorie breakdown**
calories 272	% protein 22
g fat 7.9	% fat 24
g fibre 6.5	% carbohydrate 54

Fiddlehead Stir-Fry

When you've had several meals of fiddleheads and you want a new way to enjoy this delicate spring green, try this recipe for lunch or supper.

4 cups	fresh fiddleheads	1 L
1 tbsp	butter	15 mL
2	medium carrots, cut julienne*	2
3	green onions, sliced	3
1 cup	sliced, fresh mushrooms	250 mL
½	lemon, grated rind and juice	½
¼ tsp	pepper	1 mL
2 tbsp	grated Romano cheese (optional)	25 mL

*matchstick strips

Simmer fiddleheads in small amount of boiling water in covered saucepan for about 4 minutes, until they brighten in colour and are tender crisp. Turn into colander, rinse with cold water to stop cooking process, set aside to drain. Add butter to hot wok or heavy skillet. Stir-fry carrot strips for 1 minute. Add onions and mushrooms; stir-fry 1 minute. Carefully fold in fiddleheads, keeping them intact. Sprinkle with lemon rind and juice and pepper. Cover just long enough to heat through. Serve on hot plates. If desired, top with cheese.

Yield: 4 servings

per serving	**calorie breakdown**
calories 74	% protein 17
g fat 3.4	% fat 36
g fibre 1.6	% carbohydrate 47

MICROWAVED PORK STEAK

Cutlets, or steaks as they are called today, make attractive servings that look large on the plate. Microwaving this dish eliminates the need to add fat.

1 lb	boneless loin *or* leg pork steaks	450 g
1 tbsp	all-purpose flour	15 mL
½ tsp	dried sage	2 mL
¼ tsp	salt	1 mL
pinch	cayenne	
3 tbsp	red wine *or* apple juice	45 mL
4	mushrooms, sliced	4

Trim all fat from pork, score edges to prevent rolling, and cut into 4 serving-size pieces. On a plate, combine flour, sage, salt, and cayenne. Dredge pork steaks on both sides. Pour wine or apple juice into shallow, microwave dish. Add pork, arrange mushroom slices on top. Cover with vented plastic wrap and microwave on medium (50%) for 10 to 12 minutes. Drain drippings into liquid measure; microwave on high to reduce to sauce consistency. Serve with meat on hot plates.

Yield: 4 servings

per serving	**calorie breakdown**
calories 200	% protein 39
g fat 4.7	% fat 22
g fibre 1.7	% carbohydrate 39

COVERING FOOD IN THE MICROWAVE

Paper towels or napkins allow steam to escape, making them excellent covers for bread and cured meats such as bacon and weiners. Select unrecycled and unprinted paper products.

Vented plastic wrap holds moisture in, making it a good cover for vegetables, meats, and seafoods. Plastic wrap should not come in contact with the food.

Waxed paper distributes heat evenly, making it a good cover for fruits and chicken. It absorbs spatters, which makes it a good cover for sauces and fatty foods.

Heat-proof glass and ceramic ovenware are inert products, making them the safest to use for covers. They can be difficult to vent.

ROSCHTI

This Swiss recipe is an adaptation from "Donna's Kitchen," a CBC Radio program. Roschti means "crisp and golden."

4	medium potatoes	4
½ tsp	salt	2 mL
¼ tsp	pepper	1 mL
2 tbsp	butter	25 mL
1 tbsp	oil	15 mL
½ cup	diced onion	125 mL
1 cup	grated Swiss cheese	250 mL

Peel and halve potatoes. Simmer, covered, in a minimum amount of boiling water until underdone (the point of a knife can be inserted one quarter the way into a potato before meeting resistance). Drain and cool. When ready to make the roschti, coarsely grate potatoes and toss with salt and pepper. In heavy 10-inch (25 cm) skillet, heat 1 tablespoon (15 mL) butter and oil; add onions and sauté until translucent. Over medium heat, spread onions evenly in skillet. Spread potatoes over onions and flatten with spatula. Cook, uncovered, for 5 to 6 minutes, using a wide spatula to check underside for colour. When brown, carefully turn potato cake. Place a plate upside down over the skillet, grasp plate and skillet firmly together and invert them quickly. Add remaining tablespoon (15 mL) butter and carefully slide potato cake, browned side up, back into skillet. Sprinkle with cheese, continue to cook for 5 to 6 minutes until cheese melts and underside is browned. Serve immediately.

Yield: 4 servings

per serving
calories 315
g fat 14.8
g fibre 3.1

calorie breakdown
% protein 13
% fat 41
% carbohydrate 45

RED CABBAGE WITH APPLE

The authentic German version, "Rotkohl mit apfeln," which Marg included in her gourmet cooking classes, called for bacon and bacon fat. In the '90s, we eliminate bacon and substitute olive oil for bacon fat. We find the flavour of seasoned red cabbage and apple is just as exciting. This is a large recipe that keeps well for another dinner or box lunch.

1 (2 lb)	head red cabbage	1 kg
2	large apples	2
1 tbsp	olive oil	15 mL
¼ cup	water	50 mL
1	bay leaf, crushed	1
2 tbsp	granulated sugar	25 mL
½ tsp	salt	2 mL
¼ tsp	pepper	1 mL
¼ cup	rice *or* red wine vinegar	50 mL

Wash cabbage, remove and discard outer leaves. Cut into quarters and slice thinly. Peel, core, and cube apples. Add oil, water, bay leaf, cabbage, and apples to heavy saucepan. Bring to a boil, reduce heat, cover tightly, and steam gently for about 20 minutes, until cabbage is tender but crisp. Stir occasionally to prevent burning, adding 1 tbsp water, if necessary. Add sugar, salt, pepper, and vinegar; mix well. Serve hot. Refrigerate leftover.

Yield: 8 servings

per serving	**calorie breakdown**
calories 87	% protein 7
g fat 2.2	% fat 20
g fibre 3.4	% carbohydrate 72

Basil Hamburger

Ground beef needs to be frozen immediately if not to be cooked within 48 hours of purchase. To prevent moisture loss, rewrap the meat in proper freezer paper or seal in a heavy plastic bag with air removed. Label with date and use within 3 months. It is safest to thaw ground beef in the refrigerator (12 hours per pound/450 g) or in the microwave just before cooking. If necessary to refreeze, cook the meat first.

To destroy all harmful bacteria, cook ground beef to an internal temperature of 160°F (75°C) or until no pink colour remains. Always place cooked meat on a clean surface, never on the container that held the raw meat. (See lean ground beef information, page 25.)

1 lb	lean ground beef	450 g
1	small onion, diced	1
2 tbsp	chopped fresh basil	25 mL
¼ tsp	salt	1 mL
¼ tsp	pepper	1 mL
few drops	hot pepper sauce	
4	hamburger buns	4
	cucumber salsa (recipe follows)	
4	lettuce leaves	4

In medium bowl, combine beef, onion, basil, salt, pepper, and hot pepper sauce; using hands, mix well. Form 4 patties about ¾-inch (2 cm) thick. Broil under or barbecue over medium heat, 5 to 7 minutes on each side. Fully cook beef (no pink in centre), without drying it out. Meanwhile split hamburger buns and toast inside. Place a patty on bottom half of each bun, top with cucumber salsa and lettuce; replace top and serve.

Yield: 4 servings

per serving with salsa	**calorie breakdown**
calories 300	% protein 30
g fat 11.2	% fat 35
g fibre 1.3	% carbohydrate 35

CUCUMBER SALSA

We used to serve salted fresh cucumber in lemon-clotted cream. This salsa is more piquante, better for us, and a refreshing replacement for ketchup on hamburgers.

1	medium cucumber	1
½ tsp	salt	2 mL
½ cup	quark or yogurt cheese*	125 mL
½	lime, juice of	½
1	clove garlic, minced	1
1 tbsp	chopped fresh coriander *or* ½ tsp (2 mL) dried	15 mL

*see page 49

Peel cucumber, cut into quarters, remove seeds, and coarsely grate. Place in non-metal colander on a tray, sprinkle with salt, and refrigerate for several hours. Rinse cucumber under cold, running water, allow to drain and pat dry. Blend with quark or yogurt cheese, lime juice, garlic, and coriander. Will keep 3 days in the refrigerator.

Yield: 1¼ cups (300 mL)

Variation: In the fall, make with two large, firm, chopped green tomatoes.

per 2 tablespoons	calorie breakdown
calories 23	% protein 60
g fat 0.1	% fat 4
g fibre 0.2	% carbohydrate 36

LEAN GROUND BEEF

In Canada, regular ground beef contains up to 30 per cent fat; medium ground beef 23 per cent fat; and lean ground beef 17 per cent fat. The percentage figures are deceiving because this is a per cent of fat by weight —quite different from a per cent of calories from fat. There are 9 calories in each gram of fat and 4 calories in each gram of protein. An 88 g broiled patty has 254 calories if made from regular ground beef and 209 calories if made from lean ground beef. The caloric difference is because of the greater number of calories in the extra fat in regular ground beef. Regular ground beef, broiled to well done, has 63 per cent of calories from fat; lean ground beef 54 per cent of calories from fat. For leaner ground beef, ask a meat cutter to grind 5 lbs (2 kg) of round steak for you. Divide it into meal-size portions and/or patties; package, seal, and freeze. Be prepared for a chewy, dry, flavourful product.

Ovened French Fries

Marg first found this recipe in the Time-Life Books Healthy Home Cooking series. It has since appeared in several cookbooks, but we feel it is worth repeating.

4	large baking potatoes	4
1 tsp	chili powder	5 mL
1 tbsp	oil	15 mL
½ tsp	salt	2 mL

Place large baking sheet in oven and preheat to 450°F (230°C). Scrub potatoes (for fibre leave skins on). Cut lengthwise into slices about ½-inch (1 cm) thick. Cut each slice lengthwise into ½-inch (1 cm) thick strips and place in large bowl. Toss with chili powder to coat evenly. Sprinkle with oil and toss again. Arrange in single layer on hot baking sheet. Bake 15 minutes, turn and continue baking until crisp and browned, about 15 minutes more. Sprinkle with salt and serve hot.

Yield: 4 servings

per serving
calories 210
g fat 3.8
g fibre 3.5

calorie breakdown
% protein 9
% fat 16
% carbohydrate 75

French Fry Comparison

While we want to believe in home-made, oven-baked French fries, you can't beat the commercial product for texture and convenience. Now processors have made one that is also relatively low in fat. Our home-made fries have 16 per cent of calories from fat. The best industry fries, cooked according to package directions, have 28.6 per cent of calories from fat. If you want the healthiest industry fries, you must know what to buy. The rule of thumb is: the bigger the cut, the lower the fat content. So, large pieces of potato—straight cut as opposed to crinkle cut—and fries free of batter coating contain the least fat. To prepare, oven roast following package directions. Eat them with salsa, chili sauce, or ketchup. Avoid adding gravy or cheese. McCain Foods, a New Brunswick based company, has made a nutrition claim on their Superfry package indicating they are under the 30 per cent of calories from fat guideline. Other companies may have a similar product; the nutrition claim is the consumer's guide.

BARBECUED CHICKEN

With the popularity of the outdoor grill, barbecued chicken became a family favourite. The challenge was to cook the meat well without burning the skin. Now that we remove the skin, the challenge is to cook the chicken without drying the meat.

2 (3lb/1.5 kg)	chickens	2

Barbecue Sauce:

1	small onion, chopped	1
1 tsp	oil	5 mL
¾ cup	tomato juice	175 mL
1 tbsp	cider vinegar	15 mL
2 tbsp	molasses	25 mL
1 tbsp	Worcestershire sauce	15 mL
1 tbsp	prepared mustard	15 mL
1 tsp	salt	5 mL
⅛ tsp	pepper	0.5 mL
	hot pepper sauce to taste (optional)	

Remove and discard chicken skin. Cut into serving-size pieces. Save wing tips and backs for stock. Divide chicken pieces into two lots, based on size, and refrigerate.

To make sauce, combine all ingredients in small saucepan. Gently bubble-boil, uncovered, for 10 minutes. Blend or process sauce until smooth; set aside. Place larger chicken pieces on microwave rack with meatier portions to outside. Cover loosely and microwave on high for 6 minutes. Rearrange pieces and continue cooking, removing pieces as they turn white and appear cooked. Cook smaller pieces. Brush chicken with barbecue sauce and place on heated grill. Place dark meat on hottest space and white meat on less hot section. Cook about 10 minutes, turning once and basting often. Serve hot from clean tray. Boil leftover sauce and use for dipping. Boiling is required because brush was in contact with uncooked chicken.

Yield: 8 servings

per serving	calorie breakdown
calories 221	% protein 67
g fat 5.8	% fat 24
g fibre 0.3	% carbohydrate 9

Veal Scaloppini

Veal is a luxury meat, unknown in many homes and absent from most restaurant menus. Veal served with spring vegetables and flat noodles affords a quality dining experience.

½ lb	boneless veal cutlet	225 g
2 tbsp	whole wheat flour	25 g
⅛ tsp	salt	0.5 mL
¼ tsp	pepper	1 mL
1 tbsp	finely chopped fresh parsley	15 mL
2 tsp	olive oil	10 mL
½ cup	dry red wine	125 mL
	watercress or spinach for garnish	

Divide veal into two slices and dry thoroughly. On a plate, blend flour, salt, pepper, and parsley. Dredge veal slices on each side. Heat oil in heavy skillet. Fry cutlets 3 to 5 minutes on each side (depending on thickness). Remove to hot platter. Pour wine into skillet; heat and stir to deglaze pan and reduce sauce. Pour around hot cutlets. Garnish generously with fresh watercress or spinach and serve immediately.

Yield: 2 servings

per serving	**calorie breakdown**
calories 244	% protein 53
g fat 7.8	% fat 35
g fibre 0.9	% carbohydrate 12

PORK MEDALLIONS WITH GREEN PEPPERCORNS

This dish can be made as quick as a flash; have the rest of the meal ready to serve before starting to cook the meat.

1 lb	pork tenderloin	450 g
pinch	cayenne	
2 tbsp	all-purpose flour	25 mL
1 tbsp	olive oil	15 mL
¼ cup	white wine *or* chicken broth	50 mL
1 tbsp	chopped fresh thyme (optional)	15 mL
2 tbsp	green peppercorns	25 mL
1 tbsp	skimmed milk yogurt	15 mL

Slice pork tenderloin into ½-inch (1 cm) medallions. Between sheets of waxed paper, roll to ¼-in (0.5 cm) thickness. Blend cayenne and flour; dredge pork pieces on both sides. Heat oil in skillet and quickly brown medallions on both sides (don't overcook). Remove to hot plate. Add wine, thyme, and half the peppercorns to skillet. Crush peppercorns with wooden spoon while reducing liquid to sauce consistency. Stir in remaining whole peppercorns and yogurt. Pour sauce onto hot serving plate. Arrange medallions on top and serve immediately.

Yield: 4 servings

per serving	calorie breakdown
calories 192	% protein 58
g fat 7.4	% fat 37
g fibre 0.1	% carbohydrate 5

GETTING YOUR THIAMINE

Pork has high thiamine content. It's quite difficult to get enough thiamine unless you eat one serving of pork each week. Dried beans, wheat bran, and wheat germ are other reasonably good sources of thiamine. When we select more of our calories from carbohydrates, rather than protein and fat, we require more thiamine.

Baked Brown and Wild Rice

We add whole wheat flour to baked products to increase the fibre content of our diet. Another way to increase fibre is to put brown and wild rice, barley, and whole wheat pasta on the dinner plate.

2 cups	chicken broth	500 mL
¾ cup	brown rice	175 mL
¼ cup	wild rice	50 mL
1	clove garlic, minced (optional)	1
1 tsp	salt (if broth unsalted)	5 mL
1 tsp	celery seed	5 mL
	pepper to taste	
2 tbsp	chopped fresh parsley	25 mL

In 2 quart (2 L) covered casserole, blend chicken broth, both rices, garlic, salt, celery seed, and pepper. Cover and bake in 350°F (180°C) oven 1 hour until liquid is absorbed and rice is tender. Fluff with a fork and sprinkle with parsley before serving.

Yield: 4 servings

Variations:
May be cooked in microwave on medium for 25 to 30 minutes. Let stand 15 minutes. If serving with beef, use beef broth in place of chicken.

per serving	**calorie breakdown**
calories 396	% protein 18
g fat 4.4	% fat 10
g fibre 1.8	% carbohydrate 72

PEAS AND ONIONS

Because peas are the seed of a vegetable, they concentrate nourishment. As well, the tough coating on the seeds provides fibre.

1 tsp	butter	5 mL
1	medium onion, diced	1
2 cups	frozen green peas	500 mL
⅛ tsp	pepper	0.5 mL
⅛ tsp	granulated sugar	0.5 mL
1 tsp	water	5 mL

In microwave dish, melt butter; add onion and microwave on high for 2 minutes. Add peas, pepper, sugar, and water. Stir to blend, cover and microwave on high for 6 minutes. Let stand 5 minutes. Serve hot.

Yield: 4 servings

per serving	calorie breakdown
calories 74	% protein 22
g fat 1.3	% fat 15
g fibre 3.7	% carbohydrate 63

SAFE MICROWAVE COOKING CONTAINERS

Vessels that convert little or none of the microwave energy to heat are the safest ones to use. Heatproof glass, such as Pyrex, Fire King, Glasbake, and Corelle are examples. Ceramic ovenware that stays cool while the food in it heats up is also a good microwave cooking container. Plastic and paper disposable food containers that we recycle in the kitchen should not be used for microwave cooking unless labelled "microwave-safe."

Baked Whole Salmon

Farm fresh Atlantic salmon is available year-round, but it is an especially good companion for fiddleheads. The bright colours and distinctive flavours blend to create a meal to remember. We recommend fresh or dried tarragon as the herb but dill, thyme, or parsley work equally well.

1 (3 to 4 lb)	salmon	1.5 kg
¼ tsp	pepper	1 mL
2 tsp	soft butter *or* olive oil	10 mL
2	lemons	2
8	sprigs of fresh tarragon *or* 1 tbsp (15 mL) dried	8

For easy serving ask your fishmonger to butterfly the salmon (remove the bones). You may have the choice of keeping the head on or having it removed; it is easier to handle with the tail and skin intact. To prepare for cooking, scrape off scales, feel for small bones and remove with tweezers. Rinse fish and sprinkle cavity with pepper. With butter or oil, grease shiny side of heavy foil sheet large enough to wrap fish. Thinly slice one lemon and lay half the slices along centre of foil, top with 3 sprigs fresh or half dried tarragon. Place salmon on top and arrange another row of lemon and 3 sprigs fresh or remaining dried tarragon. Fold foil securely to prevent leakage. Bake in 400°F (200°C) oven for 25 to 30 minutes. Remove, open foil at one end and drain juices into a glass measure. Open foil completely, and insert a fork into thickest part; fish is cooked if flesh flakes easily and is opaque. If undercooked, reseal and bake 5 minutes longer. Remove skin from top side, place platter over fish and invert. Remove remaining foil and skin. Keep warm while preparing sauce. To serve, cut remaining lemon into six wedges and arrange on platter with remaining tarragon.

Sauce for Salmon:

1 tbsp	butter	15 mL
1½ tbsp	all-purpose flour	22 mL
1 cup	drained fish broth plus white wine	250 mL
1 tsp	sugar	5 mL
¼ cup	skimmed milk yogurt	50 mL

In a small saucepan, heat the butter, work in flour to make a roux. Add broth and wine and cook over medium heat, stirring constantly, until it thickens. Stir sugar into yogurt and add to sauce mixture, heat through but do not boil. Pour sauce into a warm pitcher and serve with baked salmon.

Yield: 10 servings

On the Barbecue:
Prepare salmon as for baking and place on the grill over high heat. Cook for 30 minutes, carefully turning at halfway point.

per serving	calorie breakdown
calories 116	% protein 53
g fat 5.5	% fat 44
g fibre 0	% carbohydrate 3

ROASTED LEG OF LAMB

Fresh lamb is available from local producers and is regularly air-freighted from New Zealand. Frozen New Zealand lamb is available in most supermarkets. Modern lamb is uniform in age and tenderness, though not necessarily uniform in trimming. Let your eye be the judge of leanness since almost all fat on the leg is on the surface.

1 (4 to 6 lb)	leg of lamb	1 (2 to 3 kg)
2	cloves garlic, minced	2
2 tsp	dried rosemary	10 mL
2 tsp	dried thyme	10 mL
½ tsp	pepper	2 mL

Sauce:

2 tbsp	all-purpose flour	25 mL
½ cup	vegetable cooking water	125 mL
¼ tsp	salt	1 mL
pinch	pepper	
½ cup	red wine	125 mL
	or ½ cup (125 mL) grape juice	

Wipe roast with wet cloth, pat dry. Make a paste of garlic, rosemary, thyme, and pepper using a mortar and pestle or back of a spoon in a bowl. Make several small slits on both sides of leg and spoon some paste into each slit. Place on rack in shallow roasting pan. Insert meat thermometer into thickest part of muscle, avoiding fat and bone. Roast, uncovered, in a 325⁰F (160⁰C) oven until internal temperature reaches 150⁰F (65⁰C) for medium, or 160⁰F (70⁰C) for well done. If you like a crisp crust, sear the roast for 10 minutes in 425⁰F (220⁰C) oven and then reduce temperature to 325⁰F (160⁰C). Remove roast to hot platter and cover with cloth to keep hot. Skim fat from roasting pan, leaving brown drippings (at least 2 tbsp or 25 ml). Place pan over direct heat and work in flour, making a paste. Add vegetable water while stirring and scraping to deglaze pan. Taste, add salt, pepper, and wine or grape juice. Pour into hot gravy boat.
To serve lamb, keep platter, gravy boat, and plates very hot.

Yield: 8 servings

per serving	calorie breakdown
calories 236	% protein 69
g fat 6.8	% fat 28
g fibre 0.1	% carbohydrate 3

Rosemary Jelly for Lamb (Refrigerate overnight)

While the traditional complement to lamb is mint jelly or mint sauce, we have opted for rosemary jelly. We prefer rosemary quince jelly; however, it must be made in the late fall or be purchased from a specialty shop.
A quick and satisfactory alternative may be made from crabapple jelly. In a saucepan, over low heat, warm jelly to liquify and add a 4-to 5-inch (10 to 13 cm) sprig of fresh rosemary. Return to jar and refrigerate overnight.

ROASTING MEAT

This is the first of six lean roasts included in this book. The stuffed pork roast is from the loin of the animal; the most tender cuts are from the loin. Ham, eye of round, and leg of lamb are from the hip of animals. Hip cuts tend to be the leanest ones. In lamb and pork, all cuts (except for hocks) are tender enough to dry roast. In beef, only cuts from the loin and rib are tender enough to dry roast without concern. Medium tender cuts of beef (round, sirloin tip, cross rib, and blade) may be dry roasted if marinated and cooked slowly only to medium rare doneness. Roasting (or dry heat roasting) means placing a tender roast on an open pan, fat side up, and cooking, uncovered, in 325°F (160°C) oven until a meat thermometer indicates appropriate doneness.

Braising is better for cooking medium tender cuts of beef. To braise, place the roast in a covered pan with ½-inch (1 cm) of liquid and cook in the oven or on top of stove until desired doneness is achieved. Braising time will be similar to dry roasting time. Temperature should be 300°F (150°C) in the oven and simmer on top of the stove. For tender, moist meat, braise only to medium rare.

Less tender cuts of beef (chuck, brisket, stew meat) and shank of all animals require long, slow cooking in liquid, until meat is fork-tender rather than done.

It is important to monitor meat while cooking because overcooking results in a dry, tough product.

Salmon Fish Cakes

Fish cakes, made by forming patties from a mixture of mashed potato, flaked salt fish, and onion, were a staple of the Maritime diet. Fishmongers still sell prepared fish cakes. To get fish cakes suited to the new century, we have adapted a recipe that was introduced at an Atlantic seafood exhibit. Use it with other leftover cooked fish.

¾ lb	Atlantic salmon, cooked and flaked	350 g
2 cups	cooked, coarsely chopped potato	500 mL
1	medium onion, finely chopped	1
1	large dill pickle, finely chopped (optional)	1
¼ cup	low-fat salad dressing	50 mL
1 tsp	Dijon mustard	5 mL
2 tsp	chopped fresh parsley *or* ½ tsp (2 mL) dried	10 mL
½ tsp	salt	2 mL
pinch	pepper	
2 tbsp	all-purpose flour	25 mL
¼ cup	fine bread crumbs	50 mL
1 tbsp	olive oil*	15 mL

*Oil not necessary if using non-stick baking sheet.

Mix salmon, potato, onion, pickle, salad dressing, mustard, parsley, salt, and pepper together. Form into 3-inch (8 cm) patties. Combine flour and bread crumbs; dredge patties in this mixture. Lightly oil baking sheet if not non-stick and place fish cakes on it. Broil on high until cakes are golden, flip over and repeat (3 to 4 minutes total).

Yield: 8 fish cakes; 4 servings

per serving	**calorie breakdown**
calories 235	% protein 6
g fat 7.8	% fat 29
g fibre 2.8	% carbohydrate 64

CURRIED LAMB

When there's a little meat left on the lamb leg and some drippings in a container, you can have one more delightful, easy dinner of lamb.

2 tsp	olive oil	10 mL
1	medium onion, chopped	1
1	clove garlic, minced	1
1 tsp	curry powder	5 mL
¼ tsp	pepper	1 mL
¼ tsp	nutmeg	1 mL
¾ lb	leftover roasted lamb, coarsely chopped	350 g
1 cup	dripping	250 mL
1	large banana, mashed	1
½ cup	raisins	125 mL

Heat oil in heavy skillet. Sauté onion and garlic for one minute. Stir in curry, pepper, and nutmeg; add lamb, dripping, banana, and raisins. Cover and simmer for 5 minutes to blend flavours, stirring frequently. Check and adjust seasonings. Serve with rice.

Yield: 3 servings

Variation:
If short on meat, add sliced vegetables such as celery, carrots, and/or zucchini.

per serving	calorie breakdown
calories 306	% protein 30
g fat 9.3	% fat 26
g fibre 3.1	% carbohydrate 44

Baked Parsnips

We don't know why people don't eat parsnips as often as beans or carrots. They grow readily; they are available from early fall until late spring; they cook quickly; and they taste wonderful.

4	medium parsnips	4
2 tsp	butter	10 mL
⅛ tsp	pepper	0.5 mL
pinch	brown sugar	

Peel parsnips, cut into 4-inch (10 cm) sticks. Simmer, covered in ½ cup (125 mL) boiling water until tender crisp, about 6 minutes. Drain and transfer to baking dish. Dot with butter, sprinkle with pepper and brown sugar. Bake in 350°F (180°C) oven for 10 to 15 minutes. Serve at once.

Yield: 4 servings

Variation:
Sliced on diagonal, parsnips may be combined with green beans, peas, or sliced carrots.

per serving	calorie breakdown
calories 74	% protein 4
g fat 2.1	% fat 25
g fibre 0	% carbohydrate 71

LEMON POTATO WEDGES

Potatoes cooked with garlic and lemon complement lamb. This adapted recipe comes from Greece.

3	baking potatoes	3
2 tbsp	lemon juice	25 mL
1	clove garlic, minced	1
1 tbsp	olive oil	15 mL
½ tsp	salt	2 mL
¼ tsp	pepper	1 mL
1 tsp	dried oregano	5 mL

Scrub potatoes well. Leaving skin on, cut in half lengthwise and then cut each half into 4 wedges. Bring 1 cup (250 mL) of water, lemon juice, and garlic to boil in saucepan. Add potato wedges, reduce heat and simmer, covered, for 12 minutes or until undercooked; drain. Combine oil, salt, pepper, and oregano in 9-inch (23 cm) square baking dish. Add potato wedges, turning each piece to coat. Arrange wedges, skin side down and bake in 400°F (200°C) oven 15 to 20 minutes, until brown and crisp. Serve immediately.

Yield: 4 servings

per serving	**calorie breakdown**
calories 134	% protein 13
g fat 3.6	% fat 23
g fibre 5.8	% carbohydrate 64

Rhubarb Surprise Cake

The most colourful harbinger of spring must be rhubarb. Its stalks are a blend of yellow green and pink rose; a combination of the two colours are what we associate with the season. This simple cake is made exceptional with the addition of maple syrup.

½ cup	maple syrup	125 mL
4 cups	sliced (1-inch/2 cm) fresh rhubarb	1 L
¼ cup	butter or soft margarine	50 mL
1 cup	granulated sugar	250 mL
2	eggs	2
1 tsp	vanilla	5 mL
1½ cups	all-purpose flour	375 mL
2 tsp	baking powder	10 mL
½ cup	1% milk	125 mL

Pour maple syrup into 8-inch (2 L) square cake pan. Arrange rhubarb in rows over syrup to cover bottom of pan. In medium bowl, cream butter and sugar. Add eggs one at a time, beating after each addition. Add vanilla. In separate bowl, blend flour and baking powder. Add half the flour to creamed mixture; stir to combine. Mix in milk, then remaining flour. Spoon cake batter over rhubarb and spread evenly. Bake in 350°F (180°C) oven 45 minutes or until cake is golden brown on top and centre springs back when touched. Loosen edges of cake from sides of pan; invert onto wire rack and carefully remove pan. Serve warm or cold.

Yield: 12 servings

per serving
calories 234
g fat 4.5
g fibre 1.5

calorie breakdown
% protein 7
% fat 17
% carbohydrate 76

RHUBARB MERINGUE PIE

In spring, both our families keep a close eye on the rhubarb patch, looking for enough stalks to make a rhubarb pie.

1	unbaked pastry crust (9-inch 23 cm)	1
5 cups	chopped rhubarb	1.25 L
	boiling water	
1½ cups	granulated sugar	375 mL
¼ cup	all-purpose flour	50 mL
2 tbsp	tapioca	25 mL
2	egg whites	2
pinch	cream of tartar	
¼ cup	granulated sugar	50 mL

Line pie plate with pastry and refrigerate while preparing rhubarb. Pour boiling water over rhubarb and let stand 2 minutes. Drain well. Blend sugar and flour; stir into rhubarb. Sprinkle tapioca over pastry; cover with rhubarb mixture. Bake in 350°F (160°C) oven for 30 minutes. Near end of cooking time, prepare meringue. Beat egg whites and cream of tartar until foamy. Gradually add sugar, beating constantly until meringue forms stiff peaks. Remove pie from oven; spread with meringue. Reduce heat to 325° (160°C) and bake 20 minutes longer, until meringue is set and lightly browned. Cool on wire rack.

Yield: 8 servings

per serving	**calorie breakdown**
calories 330	% protein 5
g fat 6.2	% fat 17
g fibre 2.1	% carbohydrate 78

PIE PASTRY

Most of our pies have pastry crusts, in keeping with the maritime tradition, but all of them are single, bottom crusts made with lard pastry. We make no apologies. When the family gathers or the guests have been invited, it's time to have a genuine pie with tasty, flaky pastry. It can be made with fats that are better for those with atherosclerosis. However, for most of us, on those special occasions, a pie cannot be made better than with lard pastry. We offer two versions. The first makes six or seven pastry crusts which may be stored in the freezer. The second makes two pastry crusts; one for today, and a second to be refrigerated or frozen as a ball of pastry for future use.

Pie Crust Mix

6 cups	all-purpose flour	1.5 L
2 tsp	salt	10 mL
1 lb	cold lard	454 g
1	egg	1
1 tbsp	white vinegar	15 mL
	water to fill 1 cup (250 mL) measure	

In large bowl, combine flour and salt. Cut lard into about 24 squares; add to flour mixture and cut in, using pastry blender or two knives, until lard is the size of small peas. Break egg into a liquid measure, beat lightly. Add vinegar and enough water to egg to make 1 cup (250 mL); stir to blend. Drizzle liquid over flour mixture while tossing with a fork. Add only enough liquid to make dough cling together. Overmixing makes tough pastry. Press into ball by kneading 2 or 3 times. Cut into 6 or 7 slices, depending on size of pie plates. Dough will roll easier if refrigerated for an hour. Form slice into 1-inch (2.5 cm) thick circle and place on floured surface. Sprinkle with flour and roll from centre to edges until smooth, flat, and thin. Do not turn over. Loosen from surface with long, thin spatula, fold in half, and fit into pie plate easing rather than stretching pastry. Trim edges. Make pastry medallions from leftover bits for topping fruit pies. Flute edges if making pie but not if freezing pastry shell.

To store: Stack pastry shells, separated with waxed paper and sealed in plastic. Store in refrigerator for 1 week; in freezer for 3 months.

Yield: 6 or 7 pastry crusts

Pastry for Two Crusts

2 cups	all-purpose flour	500 mL
1 tsp	salt	5 mL
¾ cup	lard	175 mL
5-6 tbsp	cold water	75-90 mL

In medium bowl, combine flour and salt. Cut lard into small squares; using pastry blender or two knives, cut into flour mixture, until the size of small peas. Drizzle water over flour mixture while tossing with a fork, adding only enough liquid to make dough cling together. Press into ball by kneading 2 or 3 times. Divide in half and roll, following method described on previous page.

Yield: 2 pastry crusts

Folacin

Folacin (sometimes called folic acid) comes from the same root as foliage. The best food sources of folacin are leafy greens (chard, spinach, bok choy, romaine, etc.) and broccoli. Whole grains such as whole wheat, rye, oats, barley, and brown rice along with dried beans contain folacin. Breakfast cereals (dry, ready-to-eat) have small amounts of folacin added.

Folacin plays an important role in preventing some birth defects and is believed to reduce the risk of certain cancers. Historically, many women in Canada had low levels of folacin in their bodies. The increased consumption of whole grain flours and of broccoli should change that.

PINEAPPLE UPSIDE DOWN CAKE

When Donna asked her husband, Don, a born and bred Maritimer, what favourite traditional recipes should be in the book, he recommended fish chowder and pineapple upside down cake. Here's the cake, albeit with less butter than he remembered.

1 tbsp	melted butter	15 mL
¼ cup	brown sugar	50 mL
6 or 7	pineapple rings, canned or fresh	6 or 7
6 or 7	dried apricots	6 or 7
1 cup	all-purpose flour	250 mL
1 tsp	baking powder	5 mL
3	eggs, at room temperature	3
1 cup	granulated sugar	250 mL
1 tbsp	lemon juice	15 mL
6 tbsp	hot 1% milk	90 mL

In a 9-inch (1.5 L) round, deep, pie plate or cake pan, blend melted butter with brown sugar and spread evenly. Arrange pineapple rings around perimeter of pan and one in centre. Place an apricot in each ring. Blend flour and baking powder; set aside. In medium bowl, beat eggs until thick and lemon-coloured. Gradually add sugar, while beating. Fold in half flour mixture. Fold in lemon juice, then remaining flour. Do not overmix. Add hot milk, all at once, and blend. Spoon batter over pineapple rings. Bake in 375⁰F (190⁰C) oven 30 to 35 minutes, until centre springs back when touched. Cool on wire rack for 10 minutes. Loosen edges, invert on cake plate. Serve warm or cold.

Yield: 8 servings

per serving	**calorie breakdown**
calories 268	% protein 7
g fat 3.7	% fat 12
g fibre 1.1	% carbohydrate 81

RASPBERRY ICE

The new, insulated ice-cream makers produce a quality product. Churning during freezing keeps the crystals small and the texture smooth. Home-made "ices" have shorter freezer life than commercial products.

2 cups	raspberries, fresh or frozen	500 mL
¾ cup	granulated sugar	175 mL
2 tbsp	lemon juice or Kirsch	25 mL
2 cups	plain, skimmed milk yogurt	500 mL
2	egg whites	2

Purée raspberries in blender or food processor. Press half the purée through a sieve to remove some seeds. In medium bowl, combine raspberries, sugar, lemon juice or Kirsch, and yogurt. Mix well and refrigerate until chilled. When ready to make ice, beat egg whites until stiff but not dry and fold into raspberry mixture. Freeze in ice-cream maker following manufacturer's instructions.

Yield: 6 servings

per serving	**calorie breakdown**
calories 124	% protein 14
g fat 0.2	% fat 2
g fibre 1.6	% carbohydrate 84

EGGS IN UNCOOKED PRODUCTS

Salmonella bacteria may be found in raw eggs. There are no reported cases in Canada. However, to date, there have been a number of confirmed cases in the United States of *Salmonella Enteritidis*, which compel us to discontinue using egg yolks in uncooked foods. However, it is acceptable to use egg whites when the food is prepared, immediately frozen, and eaten while still frozen. The above recipe is an example of a safe raw egg white recipe.

New Brunswick Spring Delight

The Algonquin word for maple sap is "sinzibukwud," meaning to draw from wood. Natives used two methods to make maple syrup. They condensed sap by plunging hot stones into it. They made a lighter syrup by freezing the sap, discarding the ice, and repeating the procedure for several days until a thick syrup remained.

1 cup	(7 or 8) egg whites	250 mL
1 tsp	cream of tartar	5 mL
1¼ cups	granulated sugar	300 mL
1¼ cups	sifted cake and pastry flour	300 mL
4	egg yolks	4
¼ cup	maple syrup	50 mL
1 tsp	maple extract (optional)	5 mL

When beating egg whites, beaters and bowl must be clean, dry, and free of grease. To increase volume, warm bowl in which egg whites are to be beaten. Using stand mixer, beat egg whites with cream of tartar until soft peaks form. Gradually beat in 1 cup (250 mL) sugar, a tablespoon at a time, until stiff peaks form. Mix flour with remaining ¼ cup (50 mL) sugar and carefully fold into whites, one half at a time. In separate bowl, beat egg yolks, maple syrup and extract, if using, until thick and light coloured. Fold into egg white mixture. Carefully spoon into ungreased 9-inch (3 L) tube pan. Bake in 375°F (190°C) oven 25 to 30 minutes, until cake springs back when touched. Invert in pan until cake cools. Loosen around edges and remove from pan. Frost with Maple Seven-Minute Frosting.

Opposite *(clockwise from centre bottom): Baked Brown and Wild Rice (page 30), Peas and Onions (page 31) and Pork Medallions with Green Peppercorns (page 29); Jane's Scallop Seviche (page 5); Lemon Sponge Pudding (page 48).*

MAPLE SEVEN-MINUTE FROSTING

2	egg whites	2
½ cup	granulated sugar	125 mL
½ cup	maple syrup	125 mL
⅛ tsp	salt	0.5 mL

Combine all ingredients in top of double boiler. Beat with hand mixer until frothy. Place over boiling water and beat until stiff peaks form, 3 to 4 minutes. Remove from heat, beat 1 minute longer. Spread over top and sides of New Brunswick Spring Delight maple sponge cake.

Yield: 16 servings

per serving	**calorie breakdown**
calories 177	% protein 7
g fat 1.4	% fat 7
g fibre 0	% carbohydrate 86

Opposite *(clockwise from centre bottom): Wild Blueberry Muffins (page 108); Cornbread with Jalapeño Pepper (page 117); Granary Rolls (pages 58-59); Hot Cross Buns (page 50); Multi-grain Bread (page 53); Flatbread with Olives (page 111); Maritime Brown Bread (page 251); Genuine Bran Muffins (page 109); Potato Bannock (page 56).*

Lemon Sponge Pudding

Marg's children used to call this "magic pudding" because the batter separates during baking to produce a tart lemon sauce and a delicate cake.

1 cup	1% milk	250 mL
1 tbsp	butter or soft margarine	15 mL
2	eggs, separated	2
¾ cup	granulated sugar	175 mL
⅓ cup	all-purpose flour	75 mL
1	lemon, grated rind and juice	1

In liquid measure, in microwave, heat milk and butter. In small bowl, beat egg yolks until frothy. Gradually whisk milk into yolks. Combine sugar and flour; stir into yolk mixture. Add lemon juice and rind. In clean bowl, beat egg whites until stiff but not dry; fold into yolk mixture. Pour into 1½ quart (1.5 L) round baking dish; set dish in pan of hot water and bake in 350°F (180°C) oven 45 minutes, until centre springs back when touched. Serve warm.

Yield: 5 servings

per serving	calorie breakdown
calories 218	% protein 9
g fat 5	% fat 20
g fibre 0.3	% carbohydrate 71

Why We Use 1 Per Cent Milk

The amount of fat consumed with the milk you drink is up to you. Skimmed milk contains less than 0.1 per cent milk fat. Whole milk, commonly labelled and called homogenized milk, contains approximately 3.3 per cent milk fat (by volume). While that doesn't sound like a large difference, it is a marked difference in terms of per cent of calories from fat. A cup of whole milk contains 9 g of fat; multiplied by 9 (the total number of calories in each gram of fat) equals 81 calories from fat. The total number of calories in a cup of whole milk is 159. So, 50 per cent of the calories are from fat.

By contrast, a cup of 1 per cent milk contains 2.5 g of milk fat; multiplied by 9 equals 22.4 calories. A cup of 1 per cent milk contains 110 calories. In other words, about 24 per cent of the calories are from fat. Switching from whole milk to 1 per cent milk, cuts in half the per cent of calories from fat.

Nutritionists advise that children under two years should only be given whole milk because of their high energy requirement.

STRAWBERRY PARFAIT

Attractive, delicious, and good for you, this is a perfect parfait, paticularly when compared with some that are served at banquets as an excuse for dessert.

2 tbsp	granulated sugar	25 mL
2 cups	sliced, fresh strawberries	500 mL
1½ cups	skimmed milk yogurt cheese	375 mL
½ tsp	almond extract	2 mL
2 tbsp	icing sugar	25 mL
¼ cup	sliced almonds, toasted*	50 mL

Sprinkle sugar over berries and toss. In separate bowl, combine yogurt cheese, almond extract, and icing sugar. Carefully spoon strawberries and yogurt cheese into parfait glasses, making layers ¾-inch (2 cm) thick. End with yogurt cheese and top with almonds. Serve cold.

*To toast almonds: Stir-fry in small, heavy skillet over medium heat about 2 minutes, until lightly browned.

Yield: 4 servings

per serving	**calorie breakdown**
calories 205	% protein 22
g fat 3.5	% fat 15
g fibre 2.8	% carbohydrate 63

TO MAKE YOGURT CHEESE

You will need twice as much yogurt as the quantity of cheese in the recipe. Pour plain skimmed milk yogurt into a sieve lined with a coffee filter or into a screened funnel. Cover and refrigerate 4 hours or overnight. Yogurt cheese will keep in covered container in refrigerator for up to 1 week. Whey (the drained liquid) may be used to replace milk or water in bread or sauce recipes.

HOT CROSS BUNS

Some people believe you should not have hot cross buns until Easter weekend, but in Marg's house Ash Wednesday brings the first of many batches of this Easter bread. Several years ago, she tried to replace the icing crosses with cut crosses; she was quickly told that was not acceptable.

½ cup	lukewarm water	125 mL
1 tsp	granulated sugar	5 mL
1 tbsp	active dry yeast	15 mL
1½ cups	hot water	375 mL
½ cup	granulated sugar	125 mL
¼ cup	oil	50 mL
4½ to 5 cups	all-purpose flour	1250 mL
1	egg, lightly beaten	1
2 tsp	cinnamon	10 mL
½ tsp	nutmeg	2 mL
1 tsp	salt	5 mL
½ cup	currants	125 mL
2 tbsp	corn syrup	25 mL
1 tbsp	water	15 mL

Icing:

1 tbsp	butter	15 mL
1 tbsp	milk	25 mL
1 cup	icing sugar	250 mL

In liquid measure, dissolve 1 tsp (5 mL) sugar in ½ cup (125 mL) water; sprinkle in yeast and let stand 10 minutes, until frothy. In large bowl, combine 1½ cups (375 mL) hot water, sugar, and oil. Add 2½ cups (625 mL) flour and egg; beat 2 minutes to develop gluten. Add yeast mixture, cinnamon, nutmeg, salt, currants, and enough of remaining flour to make soft dough. Turn on floured surface and knead until smooth and elastic, about 5 minutes. Form into ball, return to bowl, cover and let rise in warm place until double in bulk, about 1 hour. Punch down, let rest 10 minutes and cut into 30 pieces. Shape round, smooth balls; place 2 inches (5 cm) apart on lightly oiled baking sheet and flatten with palm of hand. Cover and let rise in warm place until doubled in size, about 1 hour. Bake in 375°F (190°C) oven 18 to 20 minutes, until browned. In microwave, heat corn syrup and water; brush over hot buns. Remove from pan and cool on wire rack.

Beat butter, milk, and enough icing sugar to form stiff icing. Pipe crosses on cooled buns. If freezing, ice at serving time.

Yield: 30 buns

Variation:
Use half whole wheat flour.

per bun	**calorie breakdown**
calories 141	% protein 7
g fat 2.1	% fat 14
g fibre 0.9	% carbohydrate 79

CHOOSING MUFFIN RECIPES

All our recipes for muffins contain oil, the preferred fat. When searching for new recipes, select ones that call for oil or *melted* shortening. Then oil may be substituted for the shortening. Corn syrup is a good muffin ingredient because it moistens the product and usually replaces some of the fat. It also increases shelf life of the muffin.

Oatmeal Carrot Muffins

Because rolled oats is such a nutritious food, it forms the basis of many North American baked goods. We made dozens of oatmeal muffins from a variety of recipes before finally getting the taste we wanted.

1 cup	quick cooking oats*	250 mL
1½ cups	whole wheat flour	375 mL
¾ cup	firmly packed brown sugar	175 mL
2 tsp	baking powder	10 mL
1 tsp	baking soda	5 mL
2 tsp	cinnamon	10 mL
¼ cup	oil	50 mL
¾ cup	buttermilk**	175 mL
¼ cup	corn syrup	50 mL
1	egg	1
1 cup	grated carrot (1 large)	250 mL

*For better taste, spread oats in large, heavy frying pan and toast over medium heat, stirring constantly for 5 to 8 minutes.
**May substitute equal parts plain skimmed milk yogurt and 1% milk.

In a medium bowl, blend oats, flour, brown sugar, baking powder, baking soda, and cinnamon. In liquid measure, whisk oil, buttermilk, corn syrup, and egg. Add liquid ingredients to dry ones, stirring only to moisten. Fold in carrot. Spoon batter into lightly oiled or lined muffin tins. Bake in 400°F (200°C) oven 20 to 25 minutes, until centre springs back when touched. Remove from pans and cool on wire rack. These freeze well.

Yield: 12 medium muffins

per muffin	**calorie breakdown**
calories 199	% protein 9
g fat 5.1	% fat 22
g fibre 2.9	% carbohydrate 69

MULTI-GRAIN BREAD

If you like to take a small loaf of bread to a shut-in, this is an excellent choice. Divide the dough in half to make two small gift loaves.

1 cup	multi-grain cereal*	250 mL
1 cup	boiling water	250 mL
¼ cup	molasses	50 mL
1 tbsp	oil	15 mL
1 tsp	salt	5 mL
½ cup	warm water	125 mL
1 tsp	granulated sugar	5 mL
1 tbsp (1 pkg)	active dry yeast	15 mL
2 cups	all-purpose flour	500 mL
1 cup	whole wheat flour	250 mL

*Made with 7 or 8 different grains; available in bulk food stores.

In large bowl, combine cereal and boiling water; stir in molasses, oil, and salt. Dissolve sugar in warm water; add yeast and let stand 10 minutes until frothy. Add 1 cup (250 mL) all-purpose flour to cereal mixture and beat until elastic. Stir in yeast mixture; add whole wheat flour and enough of remaining all-purpose flour to make a soft dough. Turn onto floured surface and knead for 5 minutes, adding only enough flour to keep dough from sticking. Return to bowl, cover and let rise in warm place until double in bulk, about 1 hour. Punch down, let rest 10 minutes. Shape into round loaf, place on lightly oiled baking sheet. Cover with tea towel and let rise until double in size, about 1 hour. Bake in 375⁰F (190⁰C) oven 35 to 40 minutes or until crust is golden brown and bread sounds hollow when rapped with knuckles. Remove from baking sheet and cool on wire rack. Store in air tight container.

Yield: 1 round loaf (25 slices)

per slice	calorie breakdown
calories 94	% protein 12
g fat 1.2	% fat 11
g fibre 1.8	% carbohydrate 77

FUNCTION OF BREAD INGREDIENTS

Unlike other baked goods, there is considerable flexibility in ingredients used in bread. Salt and sugar may be reduced; liquids may be varied; seasonings may be added and flours altered. Understanding the function of each of the ingredients helps to make reliable ingredient changes.

Yeast is a living plant that leavens bread. Correct temperature is vital so that yeast creates gas bubbles and makes the bread rise; if the liquid is too hot, it will kill the yeast.

Flour usually means all-purpose flour made from wheat. It has the greatest gluten producing potential and thus is the easiest flour to use when learning to make bread. Gluten in the flour stretches to make an elastic framework, which holds the gas bubbles produced by the yeast. Stirring and kneading develop the elasticity of the gluten. More stirring and kneading are required to develop gluten with whole wheat and other whole grain flours. Adding too much flour is a common error. Dough should be soft, just past the sticky stage.

Liquids commonly used are milk, water, and dripping from potatoes. Milk gives bread a soft crust and creamy crumb. Water makes bread more chewy and crusty. Potato water keeps bread moist. Whey, from the making of yogurt cheese, may be less commonly used but is a nutritious liquid for bread.

Sugar is the food required by yeast to form gas bubbles that make the dough rise. It also adds flavour and helps brown the crust.

Salt brings out flavour and controls the action of the yeast. Too much salt slows the rate of gas formation.

Fat makes bread tender, keeps it soft, and gives a silky crust.

Eggs add food value, colour, flavour, and help make the crumb fine.

MARSHLAND CRISPS

Marshland's Inn in Sackville, New Brunswick, serves cookies and hot cocoa at 9 P.M. For decades this was one of their cookies, a recipe ahead of its time.

1 cup	soft margarine	250 mL
2 cups	loosely packed brown sugar	500 mL
1	egg	1
¼ cup	frozen orange juice concentrate (undiluted)	50 mL
3 cups	whole wheat flour	750 mL
2 tsp	baking powder	10 mL
1½ cups	Kellogg's All-Bran cereal	375 mL

Beat margarine, sugar, egg, and orange juice concentrate until smooth and fluffy. Add flour, baking powder, and All-Bran and stir with wooden spoon until well mixed. Drop by teaspoonsful onto lightly oiled cookie sheets and flatten with a fork dipped in flour. Cookies should be less than ¼-inch (0.5 cm) thick when flattened. Bake in 350⁰F (180⁰C) oven 8 to 10 minutes, until brown and crisp on edges. Transfer to wire rack immediately. When cool, store in sealed container. Freeze well. Serve with coffee or milk.

Yield: 4½ dozen

per cookie	**calorie breakdown**
calories 96	% protein 6
g fat 3.7	% fat 33
g fibre 1.6	% carbohydrate 61

Potato Bannock

A quick bread that is kneaded and baked as a flattened round is a bannock. If you cut the flattened round into wedges, it becomes scones. This is probably the only potato bannock containing finely chopped raw potato rather than mashed potato.

2¼ cups	all-purpose flour	550 mL
½ tsp	salt	2 mL
2 tbsp	baking powder	25 mL
3 tbsp	granulated sugar	45 mL
⅔ cup	1% milk	150 mL
3 tbsp	oil	45 mL
1 cup	peeled diced potato*	250 mL

*A yellow-fleshed potato gives bannock golden flecks.

In medium bowl, blend flour, salt, baking powder, and sugar. In blender or food processor, combine milk and oil. Add potato and pulse to finely chop but not purée it. Pour milk mixture into dry ingredients, stirring only to moisten. Turn onto floured surface; knead 10 times. Form into 1-inch (30 cm) thick round. Place on lightly oiled or non-stick baking sheet. Bake in 375⁰F (190⁰C) oven 30 minutes, until toothpick comes out clean. Remove from pan and cool on wire rack. Serve warm or cold.

Yield: 10 servings

Variation:
Form dough into two round disks—one for dinner and one for the freezer. Cooking time will be reduced about 5 minutes.

per serving	calorie breakdown
calories 197	% protein 9
g fat 4.7	% fat 21
g fibre 1.4	% carbohydrate 70

APRICOT BREAD

Before home freezers, dried fruits were common winter fare. It is no wonder fruit breads were popular. The colour of this one brought spring to the tea table. Today we can keep it in the freezer for unexpected company.

1 cup	chopped dried apricots	250 mL
2 cups	all-purpose flour	500 mL
1 tsp	baking soda	5 mL
½ cup	granulated sugar	125 mL
1 cup	orange juice	250 mL
2 tbsp	oil	25 mL
1	egg	1

If apricots are hard, soak in warm water 15 minutes; drain and discard liquid. In medium bowl, combine flour, baking soda, and sugar. In liquid measure, whisk orange juice, oil, and egg. Pour into flour mixture and stir until combined. Fold in apricots. Turn into an oiled 8 x 4 x 2½ inch (1.5 L) loaf pan. (A long, 12-inch/30 cm, narrow loaf pan also works well.) Let rest on counter 15 minutes. Invert another loaf pan over top and bake in 325°F (160°C) oven for 30 minutes. Remove inverted pan and bake another 25 to 30 minutes, or until toothpick inserted in centre comes out clean. Cool in pan for 10 minutes, remove and cool completely on wire rack. Freezes well.

Yield: 16 slices

per slice	**calorie breakdown**
calories 145	% protein 8
g fat 2.1	% fat 13
g fibre 0.5	% carbohydrate 79

SWEET BREAD BAKING

The top of a sweet bread tends to crack as it bakes because the bread rises too quickly and the crust forms too soon. Allowing the bread to rest on the counter permits rising to begin slowly, before baking starts. Covering with an inverted pan during the first half of baking delays crust formation. Removal of the inverted pan during the last 30 minutes of baking results in formation and browning of a crust.

GRANARY ROLLS

As the serving size of meat or fish is reduced to 4 ounces (112 g), vegetables and rolls must be added to satisfy our appetite.

1 tsp	granulated sugar	5 mL
½ cup	lukewarm water	125 mL
1 tbsp (1 pkg)	active dry yeast	15 mL
3½ cups	hot water	875 mL
½ cup	brown sugar	125 mL
1 tbsp	salt	15 mL
½ cup	oil	125 mL
4 cups	all-purpose flour	1 L
2½ cups	rye flour	625 mL
2 cups	natural bran	500 mL
3 cups	whole wheat flour	750 mL

Topping: (optional)

1	egg yolk	1
2 tbsp	water	25 mL
	natural bran	

In liquid measure, dissolve sugar in ½ cup (125 mL) lukewarm water; sprinkle in yeast and let stand 10 minutes, until frothy. In large bowl, combine hot water, brown sugar, salt, oil, 2 cups (500 mL) of the all-purpose flour, and all the rye flour; beat for 2 minutes to develop gluten. Stir in yeast mixture, natural bran, whole wheat flour, and enough remaining all-purpose flour to make a soft dough. Turn onto floured surface and knead 6 minutes, until smooth and elastic. Place dough in large bowl, cover and let rise in warm place until double in bulk, about 1½ hours. Punch down and let rest 10 minutes. Cut and shape dough into 36 round, smooth balls and place 2 inches (5 cm) apart on baking sheets. For hamburger buns, flatten with palm of hand. Cover and let rise in warm place until double in size, about 1 hour.

For topping, whisk egg yolk and water; brush on rolls and sprinkle with natural bran.

Bake in 375°F (190°C) oven 20 to 25 minutes, until brown. Remove from pans, cool on wire racks. Freeze well.

Yield: 36 large rolls

per roll	calorie breakdown
calories 153	% protein 10
g fat 3.8	% fat 21
g fibre 4.0	% carbohydrate 69

VITAMIN E

Few nutrients have generated as much public interest as has Vitamin E. If all the claims made for its curative and health-promoting effects were true, it would be a wonder ingredient. The claims gained public attention because early research showed that Vitamin E components were essential for fertility in rats. While it is possible to feed laboratory animals controlled diets and thus produce Vitamin E deficiencies, such is not the case in humans. Vitamin E is widely available in a normal diet; it is stored throughout the body and its release is so gradual that depletion of body stores would take months. No symptoms of deficiency have been identified.

The best source of Vitamin E is vegetable oil, including all the common oils we use for cooking. This offers another reason for cooking and baking with vegetable oil. Other excellent food sources include wheat germ and corn meal. The processing of flours and cereals removes most of the Vitamin E, so whole wheat flour and whole grain cereals are moderate sources of Vitamin E while refined flours contain only traces. Most of our bread recipes would be good sources of Vitamin E because they use vegetable oil and some whole grains and whole wheat flour.

Jumbo Raisin Cookies

This is a genuine, Maritime, school lunch cookie. We were surprised to find one that our children had loved also met the guidelines for this book. We did add whole wheat flour to the recipe.

2 cups	seeded raisins*	500 mL
1 cup	water	250 mL
1 cup	soft margarine	250 mL
2 cups	granulated sugar	500 mL
3	eggs	3
2 cups	all-purpose flour	500 mL
2 cups	whole wheat flour	500 mL
1 tsp	baking soda	5 mL
1 tsp	baking powder	5 mL
½ tsp	salt	2 mL
1 tsp	cinnamon	5 mL
¼ tsp	allspice	1 mL
1 cup	chopped walnuts (optional)	250 mL

*may substitute Thompson seedless

In saucepan, combine raisins and water; simmer 5 minutes and set aside. Cream margarine and sugar; beat in eggs, one at a time. Stir in raisin mixture. Blend flours, baking soda, baking powder, salt, cinnamon, and allspice. Add to batter along with walnuts, if using, and stir to blend. Drop by spoonfuls onto lightly oiled or non-stick cookie sheets, 2 inches (5 cm) apart, and bake in 400°F (200°C) oven 12 to 15 minutes, until browned and centre springs back when touched. Store in sealed container between layers of waxed paper. These freeze well.

Yield: 6 dozen

per cookie	**calorie breakdown**
calories 88	% protein 6
g fat 2.9	% fat 29
g fibre 0.9	% carbohydrate 66

THE WORKING COOK'S ROLLS

Marg's mom found this recipe many years ago, when she rejoined the work force and still wanted to make home-made rolls. The dough may be mixed while supper is cooking, the rolls put into pans before going to bed and baked while eating breakfast. It may be made into rolls, cinnamon buns, or tea rings.

1 tsp	granulated sugar	5 mL
½ cup	lukewarm water	125 mL
1 tbsp (1 pkg)	active dry yeast	15 mL
3½ cups	hot water	875 mL
½ cup	oil	125 mL
1 tbsp	salt	15 mL
¾ cup	granulated sugar	175 mL
1	egg, beaten	1
6 cups	all-purpose flour	1500 mL
5 cups	whole wheat flour	1250 mL

In liquid measure, dissolve 1 tsp (5 mL) sugar in ½ cup (125 mL) luke-warm water; sprinkle in yeast and let stand 10 minutes, until frothy. In large bowl (6 quart/6 L), combine hot water, oil, salt, and sugar. Add 5 cups (1250 mL) all-purpose flour; beat until smooth and elastic. Add yeast mixture, egg, whole wheat flour, and enough of the remaining all-purpose flour to make a soft dough. Turn onto floured surface; knead 6 minutes, until smooth and elastic. Dough should remain soft. Place dough in bowl, cover and let rise on counter until double in bulk, 3 to 4 hours. Punch down, cut into four parts and cover with tea towel. Work with one part at a time. Cut and shape rolls; place in lightly oiled pans. Cover with tea towels and let rise in cool (16⁰ to 18⁰C) place overnight. In the morning, bake rolls in 350⁰F (180⁰C) oven until golden brown and hollow sounding when rapped with knuckles. Time depends on whether rolls are separate or joined, at least 20 minutes. Remove from pans; cool on wire racks; store in sealed container or wrap and freeze.

Yield: about 7 dozen medium rolls

per roll	calorie breakdown
calories 80	% protein 10
g fat 1.7	% fat 18
g fibre 1.3	% carbohydrate 71

APRICOT SAUCE WITH GREEN GRAPES AND YOGURT

A thoroughly modern dish that combines two purchased ingredients with a microwaved sauce. Donna used to make it with sour cream.

| 1 lb | green grapes, stemmed | 450 g |
| ¾ cup | plain skimmed milk yogurt | 175 mL |

Sauce:

½ cup	chopped, dried apricots	125 mL
1 tbsp	lemon juice	15 mL
2 tbsp	corn syrup *or* honey	25 mL
¾ cup	apple cider *or* juice	175 mL

Place green grapes in glass dishes. Top each with 3 tablespoons yogurt. In glass liquid measure, combine apricots, lemon juice, and corn syrup or honey. Microwave on high for 2 minutes. Pour apple cider or juice into blender or food processor; add apricot mixture and process until smooth. Spoon over grapes and yogurt.

Yield: 4 servings

per serving	calorie breakdown
calories 210	% protein 7
g fat 0.9	% fat 4
g fibre 1.6	% carbohydrate 89

STRAWBERRY SMOOTHIE

In June we are apt to pick more strawberries than we will eat during winter.
Spring cleaning of the freezer reminds us that June is coming again, making
it time to use up those frozen berries from last year.

1 cup	plain skimmed milk yogurt	250 ml
1 cup	1% milk	250 mL
½ cup	frozen lemonade concentrate	125 mL
2 cups	sweetened, frozen strawberries, thawed	500 mL

In blender or food processor, process ingredients until smooth. Serve
immediately.

Yield: 4 servings

per serving
calories 235
g fat 1.0
g fibre 2.6

calorie breakdown
% protein 10
% fat 4
% carbohydrate 86

MILK STORAGE

Refrigerate milk as soon as possible after purchase, in the coldest part of
the refrigerator. Keep milk in closed containers to prevent absorption of
flavours from other foods. Return unused portions to the refrigerator as
soon as possible; a temperature of 7°C or higher reduces the shelf life of
milk. Sealed containers keep longer than opened ones. Milk may be frozen
and kept for two months. Unopened containers retain better flavour in the
freezer; milk with some fat content retains better texture than skimmed
milk.

RHUBARB CHUTNEY

Made as a replacement for mango chutney, this spicy condiment is delicious with lamb, pork, or fish. Try it as a spread on bread. With frozen rhubarb, it can be made any time of the year.

3 cups	sliced rhubarb, fresh or frozen	750 mL
2	large onions, diced	2
2 cups	lightly packed brown sugar	500 mL
½ cup	cider vinegar	125 mL
½ tsp	cinnamon	2 mL
¼ tsp	ground cloves	1 mL
⅛ tsp	cayenne	0.5 mL

Into large, heavy saucepan, measure all ingredients. Bring to boil, stirring frequently. Reduce heat and boil gently for 1 hour, until mixture is the consistency of marmalade. Store in refrigerator 1 month; in freezer 1 year.

Yield: 2 cups (20 servings)

per serving	**calorie breakdown**
calories 87	% protein 1
g fat 0	% fat 1
g fibre 0.6	% carbohydrate 98

WELCOME TO SUMMER

Summer is a colourwashed meadow carpeted with daisies and dandelions, Queen Anne's lace, devil's paintbrushes, purple vetch, thistles, and clover. Hundreds of plants (some say weeds) that bring a spring-green pasture into full bloom. Swaying in the soft, southeasterly breeze, a meadow hides wild strawberries and blueberries. Its fragrance calls forth insects by day; its blanket of dew brings out spiders by night.

We will need to sneak away from the crowd at the barbecue or around the picnic table to study cloud formations, listen to and smell the meadow, and share the night sky with the stars. Summer is so short in the Maritimes; it would be a shame to be slaving at the computer or baking bread when it peaks.

We have created relaxed summer menus to be served outdoors—cold food and barbecued meals. We have quick, simple desserts, punctuated with a few special ones that take advantage of fresh summer fruits.

We remembered our Maritime heritage. Into summer we put one genuine lobster party, including the seaweed and salt water. You may eat it on the beach, on the deck, or in a meadow. If it rains, the kitchen table covered with newspapers will do nicely.

Whether your summer focus is golf, tennis, sailing, swimming, or gardening, the food should be appropriate to the activity and complement what is fresh and available in this season of new potatoes, ripe tomatoes, and tender peas—a veritable meadow of colours and flavours.

BREAKFAST
Rhubarb Juice 121
Vanilla Yogurt and Cantaloupe
Wild Blueberry Muffins 108

BRUNCH (6)*
Easy Brunch Squares 82
Dilled Snow Peas and Carrots 75
Genuine Bran Muffins 109
Cinnamon Coffee Cake 110
Sparkling Berry Punch 122

LUNCH (4)
Gazpacho 73
Flatbread with Olives 111
French Vanilla Ice Cream 99
Doohickies 113

BOX LUNCH
Tabbouleh Pita Bread Wedges 76
Fresh Fruit

SPECIAL LUNCH (4)
Leaf Lettuces with Vinaigrette 77
Brie, Basil, and Tomato Pasta 83
Bread Sticks
Chocolate Crunchies 114

SUPPER (6)
Mediterranean Salad 78
Italian Crusty Bread 115
Strawberry Glazed Pie 100

VEGETARIAN SUPPER (4)
Hodge Podge 84
Jiffy Rolls 116
Blue and Green Crisp 101

BARBECUED DINNER (4)
Tomato Bruschetta 68
Grilled Fish 85
Vegetable Pouch 86
Minted Red Potato Salad 79
Grilled Peaches and Blueberries 102

*indicates number served

FAMILY DINNER (4)
Pork Kebobs 87
Breaded Zucchini Parmesan 88
Potato Fans 90
Fire and Ice Tomatoes 80
Peach Yogurt Pops 103

PARTY DINNER (6)
Mackerel Mousse 69
Mike's Sirloin Steak 91
Seasoned Potatoes in Foil 89
Broiled Tomatoes 92
Italian Crusty Bread 115
Pavlova with Lemon Filling 104-05

OUTDOOR SUPPER (3)
Mary's Delicious Dip with
   Crudities 70
Flank Steak Teriyaki 93
Barbecued Corn on the Cob 94
Potato Kebobs 90
Peach Custard Pie 106

OUTDOOR LATE DINNER (4)
Pickled Mackerel 71
Ross's Cowboy Beans 95
Sliced Tomatoes
Cornbread 117
Wild Blueberry Cake 107

PICNIC (4)
Chicken Satay 96
Marinated Summer Vegetables 81
Casserole Rye Bread 118
Prune Brownies 119

BEACH PARTY (6)
Steamed Clams 72
Boiled Lobsters 97
Jiffy Rolls 116
Marinated Potato Salad 13
Almond Biscotti 120

PLAN-OVER SUPPER (6)
Cold Potato Soup 74
Lobster Rolls 98
Plums & Peaches

STARTERS
Mackerel Mousse
Mary's Delicious Dip
Pickled Mackerel
Steamed Clams
Tomato Bruschetta

SOUPS AND SALADS
Cold Potato Soup
Dilled Snow Peas and Carrots
Fire and Ice Tomatoes
Gazpacho
Marinated Summer Vegetables
Mediterranean Salad
Minted Red Potato Salad
Tabbouleh
Vinaigrette

MAIN COURSE FOODS
Barbecued Corn on the Cob
Boiled Lobsters
Breaded Zucchini Parmesan
Brie, Basil, and Tomato Pasta
Broiled Tomatoes
Chicken Satay
Easy Brunch Squares
Flank Steak Teriyaki
Grilled Fish
Hodge Podge
Lobster Rolls
Mike's Sirloin Steak
Potato Fans
Potato Kebobs
Pork Kebobs
Ross's Cowboy Beans
Seasoned Potatoes in Foil
Vegetable Pouch

DESSERTS
Blue and Green Crisp
French Vanilla Ice Cream
Grilled Peaches and Blueberries
Pavlova with Lemon Filling
Peach Custard Pie
Peach Yogurt Pops
Strawberry Glazed Pie
Wild Blueberry Cake

BAKED GOODS
Almond Biscotti (cookie)
Casserole Rye Bread
Cinnamon Coffee Cake
Chocolate Crunchies (cookie)
Cornbread
Doohickies (cookie)
Flatbread with Olives
Genuine Bran Muffins
Italian Crusty Bread
Jiffy Rolls
Prune Brownies
Wild Blueberry Muffins

MISCELLANEOUS
Rhubarb Juice, Rhubarb Punch
Sparkling Berry Punch

Tomato Bruschetta

A true Italian bruschetta is made by roasting bread over the coals, rubbing the slices with garlic and drizzling with olive oil. This version adds fresh tomatoes and basil to create a fast and easy summer appetizer or lunch.

2	tomatoes, peeled, seeded, and chopped	2
2 tbsp	chopped fresh basil	25 mL
⅛ tsp	pepper	0.5 mL
8	diagonally cut slices Italian or French bread	8
1	clove garlic, cut in half	1
1 tbsp	olive oil	15 mL
1 tbsp	grated Romano or Parmesan cheese	15 mL

In small bowl, combine tomatoes, basil, and pepper; set aside. Place bread slices on baking sheet and broil on each side until lightly toasted. Rub top side with cut edge of garlic clove. Lightly brush with oil. Spoon on tomato mixture; sprinkle with cheese. Return to broiler for 1 minute to warm tomatoes. Serve immediately.

Yield: 4 servings

per serving	calorie breakdown
calories 225	% protein 12
g fat 4.7	% fat 19
g fibre 2.2	% carbohydrate 69

To Peel and Seed a Tomato

Immerse ripe tomato in boiling water for 30 seconds, then plunge into cold water. When cool, cut out stem end and peel off skin. If tomato is not fully ripe, it will need 1 minute in boiling water.

To remove seeds, slice tomato in half. Squeeze each half, forcing out seeds and juicy pulp. Use fingers to dislodge any stubborn seeds. Removing seeds takes a minute, but it eliminates the bitter taste.

MACKEREL MOUSSE

This sharp tasting starter is made with 1 cup (250 mL) of our Pickled Mackerel on page 71. If you haven't made the mackerel, substitute marinated herring, purchased at the fish counter. This mousse is attractive when made in a fish-shaped mold.

1 tbsp	unflavoured gelatin	15 mL
¼ cup	yogurt whey* *or* water	50 mL
1 cup	pickled mackerel (including onions, juice)	250 mL
1 tbsp	seafood or chili sauce	15 mL
1 cup	yogurt cheese**	250 mL
¼ cup	sweet red pepper strips	50 mL
¼ cup	sliced green onion *or* 2 tbsp (25 mL) sliced chives	50 mL
½ cup	low-fat salad dressing	125 mL

*liquid that drains off when making yogurt cheese
**see page 49

Sprinkle gelatin over whey or water in microwave dish; let stand 1 minute. Microwave on high for 40 seconds until gelatin is dissolved; set aside. In food processor or blender, purée pickled mackerel, seafood sauce, and yogurt cheese. Add red pepper and green onion or chives; pulse to coarsely chop. Pour into bowl and fold in gelatin mixture and salad dressing. Pour into 1-quart (1 L) oiled mold. Refrigerate until firm. Unmold on lettuce, serve with light crackers.

Yield: 12 to 15 servings

per serving
calories 102
g fat 1.1
g fibre 0.2

calorie breakdown
% protein 27
% fat 33
% carbohydrate 40

MARY'S DELICIOUS DIP

Mary Pomeroy gave Marg this recipe in the '60s. Make it when you need a dip in a hurry; the ingredients are always on hand.

1 cup	low-fat salad dressing	250 mL
1 tsp	garlic powder	5 mL
1 tsp	curry powder	5 mL
1 tsp	vinegar	5 mL
1 tsp	horseradish	5 mL

Mix all ingredients together. Let sit 1 hour before serving. Serve with raw vegetables such as broccoli, cauliflower, carrots, green onions, cucumber, zucchini, green pepper, and rutabaga. Store in refrigerator.

Yield: 1 cup (250 mL) (12 servings)

per serving	**calorie breakdown**
calories 35	% protein 10
g fat 2.1	% fat 52
g fibre 0	% carbohydrate 57

Pickled Mackerel

Donna loves mackerel. For years she ate it with guilt because of high fat content. We are learning more about the benefit of omega-3 fatty acids, so the guilt is gone, and she can share her favourite mackerel recipe. Incidentally, she is also a mackerel fisher, mostly because she can catch them with a bare hook.

2 (about 1 lb)	mackerel fillets	454 g
3 tbsp	lemon juice	45 mL
¼ tsp	salt	1 mL
1 cup	water	250 mL
¾ cup	brown sugar	175 mL
1 cup	vinegar	250 mL
5	whole cloves	5
⅛ tsp	pepper	0.5 mL
2	small onions, thinly sliced	2

Lay mackerel fillets in heavy skillet. Drizzle with lemon juice; sprinkle with salt. Add water and slowly bring to boil. Reduce heat, cover, and poach until fillets are cooked, about 10 minutes. Cool, drain, and discard liquid. Refrigerate fish until cold and firm. Meanwhile, in a saucepan combine brown sugar, vinegar, cloves, and pepper. Bring to a boil and simmer 3 minutes. Set aside. Scrape skin and surface fat from fillets. Break into bite-size chunks; drop into glass jar, alternating with onion rings. Pour marinade over fish. Cover and refrigerate at least 24 hours. Keeps in refrigerator 4 weeks. Serve as a starter with crackers or as a salad lunch on lettuce.

Yield: 3 cups (12 servings)

per serving	calorie breakdown
calories 137	% protein 21
g fat 5.4	% fat 35
g fibre 0.3	% carbohydrate 44

Steamed Clams

To cook on open fire:
Scrub clams with bristle brush, particularly along seams. Discard any that are not closed or do not close when touched. After cooking, discard any that do not open.

Indirect grilling is recommended. Divide hot, ashy-white coals into two banks, the width of the grill apart. Set grill between the banks and place clams on top. They will cook by both heat and hot smoke. Natural juices will be preserved. As soon as they open, remove from grill.

To keep hot on the grill and prevent drying out, place seaweed, damp leaves, or foil over coals to deflect heat.

To cook on barbecue:
The method is similar to above but grill should be 6 inches (15 cm) above the coals.

Variation:
This method also works for mussels, oysters, quahogs, or scallops in the shell.

per clam	calorie breakdown
calories 24	% protein 73
g fat 0.3	% fat 13
g fibre 0	% carbohydrate 15

GAZPACHO

Hailing from the Andalusian region of Spain, this cold, refreshing summer soup is a low-fat salad in a bowl.

2 cups	tomato juice	500 mL
1 tbsp	olive oil	15 mL
1 tbsp	vinegar (wine or herbed)	15 mL
½	lemon, juice of	½
1	clove garlic	1
2	slices bread, quartered	2
½ tsp	salt	2 mL
¼ tsp	pepper	1 mL
few drops	hot pepper sauce (optional)	
1	large tomato, peeled, seeded, and diced	1
1	small stalk celery, diced	1
½	cucumber, diced	½
½	red pepper, diced	½
½	medium onion, diced	½
4	parsley sprigs for garnish	4

In blender or food processor, purée tomato juice, oil, vinegar, lemon juice, garlic, bread, salt, pepper, and pepper sauce. Refrigerate until well chilled. When ready to serve, stir in the vegetables and garnish each bowl with parsley.

Yield: 4 servings

per serving	calorie breakdown
calories 123	% protein 11
g fat 4.2	% fat 28
g fibre 3.4	% carbohydrate 62

Cold Potato Soup

The classic French "vichyssoise" sounds exotic but is only a puréed, cold leek and potato soup. Serve cold in summer, piping hot in winter.

1 tsp	olive oil	5 mL
1	large leek (white and light green parts), sliced	1
¼ cup	diced celery	50 mL
1½ cups	chicken broth	375 mL
1½ cups	sliced potatoes	375 mL
¼ tsp	salt (less if broth is salted)	1 mL
⅛ tsp	white pepper	0.5 mL
⅓ cup	homogenized milk	75 mL
	sliced fresh chives for garnish	

Heat oil in heavy saucepan, add leek and celery. Reduce heat, sauté for 3 minutes. Add chicken broth, bring to a boil, cover and simmer 10 minutes. Add potatoes, continue cooking until potatoes are very soft (about 10 minutes). Pulse in blender or food processor until mixture is a coarse rather than smooth purée. Add salt and pepper. Refrigerate until thoroughly chilled. Before serving, add milk, using more or less to adjust thickness; taste and adjust seasoning (a cold soup requires more than a hot). Serve in chilled bowls, garnished with chives.

Yield: 4 servings

per serving	calorie breakdown
calories 244	% protein 18
g fat 4.5	% fat 16
g fibre 1.6	% carbohydrate 66

DILLED SNOW PEAS AND CARROTS

Thinning carrots is a tedious job. Its one reward is a jar of dilled carrots.

2 cups	snow peas (½ lb/225 g)	500 mL
2 cups	baby carrots (¾ lb/345 g)	500 mL
2	sprigs fresh dill	2
2	cloves garlic	2
1 cup	vinegar	250 mL
2 tbsp	granulated sugar	25 mL
2 tsp	salt	10 mL
1 tsp	horseradish	5 mL

Scrub carrots; remove tips from snow peas. Place sprig of dill and clove of garlic in bottom of 2 preserving jars (1 pint/0.5 L each). Pack each jar with carrots and snowpeas. In liquid measure, combine vinegar, sugar, salt, and horseradish. Microwave on high 2 minutes, until sugar is dissolved. Pour half into each jar and fill with boiling water. Cover, cool, and refrigerate at least 24 hours before serving.

Yield: 8 servings

per serving
calories 46
g fat 0.1
g fibre 1.8

calorie breakdown
% protein 10
% fat 2
% carbohydrate 87

Tabbouleh (Parsley with Bulgur)

Basic dishes originating from the eastern Mediterranean, like tabbouleh and hummus, have become nutritious delights in our diet. While they are available at delicatessens and market stalls, you can easily make them at home.

⅓ cup	bulgur	75 mL
⅔ cup	boiling water	150 mL
2 cups	fresh parsley (1 bunch)	500 mL
3	large green onions, thinly sliced	3
⅓ cup	fresh lemon juice (1 lemon)	75 mL
2 tbsp	olive oil	25 mL
2	cloves garlic, minced	2
1 tsp	salt	5 mL
pinch	black pepper	
3 tbsp	chopped fresh, mint leaves (optional)	45 mL
2	small tomatoes, peeled, seeded, and diced (optional)	2

Pour boiling water over bulgur and let soak for 20 minutes. Drain well through a sieve, pressing to remove as much moisture as possible. Wash and drain parsley; remove tough stems, and in blender or food processor, pulse to chop *or* chop finely with knife. Combine parsley with onions and bulgur. In small bowl, whisk lemon juice, oil, garlic, salt, and pepper. Drizzle over bulgur mixture and stir to blend. Refrigerate at least 2 hours before serving. May add chopped mint and/or tomatoes before serving.

Stores in refrigerator for several days, longer if tomatoes are not added.

Yield: 6 servings

per serving	**calorie breakdown**
calories 84	% protein 9
g fat 4.1	% fat 41
g fibre 3.2	% carbohydrate 50

VINAIGRETTE

This is a basic dressing to serve on lettuces. You may vary the seasonings depending on the rest of the meal.

3 tbsp	lemon juice	45 mL
3 tbsp	rice vinegar	45 mL
¼ cup	olive oil	50 mL
⅛ tsp	pepper	0.5 mL
1	clove garlic, split (optional)	1
¼ tsp	dry mustard (optional)	1 mL

Measure ingredients into a glass jar. Seal and shake. Store on cupboard shelf because olive oil will congeal in refrigerator. Use within 1 week.

Mustard acts as an emulsifier, holding other ingredients in suspension.

Yield: ¾ cup

per 2 tablespoon (25 mL)	**calorie breakdown**
calories 71	% protein 0
g fat 7.7	% fat 93
g fibre 0	% carbohydrate 7

CRACKED WHEAT AND BULGUR

Both are derived by cracking whole wheat kernels. The difference is that bulgur is cooked and dried before being cracked, while cracked wheat is simply cracked. Bulk food stores usually carry both products. Supermarkets often carry only cracked wheat.

Bulgar needs only to be rehydrated with boiling water. Cracked wheat requires cooking. Blend one part cracked wheat with three parts boiling water or hot milk. Cook 5 to 6 minutes, stirring occasionally.

Mediterranean Salad

Broccoli is our most nutritious vegetable, and cauliflower is its cousin. What more can we say? Leftovers make a perfect box lunch.

½	head cauliflower, cut into florets	½
1	small head broccoli, cut into florets	1
3	tomatoes, cut into wedges	3
½ cup	pitted, whole black olives	125 mL
¼ lb	feta cheese, cut into small cubes	125 g

Dressing:

¼ cup	red wine vinegar	50 mL
1	clove garlic, minced	1
⅛ tsp	salt	0.5 mL
⅛ tsp	pepper	0.5 mL
1 tbsp	chopped fresh oregano *or* ½ tsp (2 mL) dried	15 mL
2 tbsp	olive oil	25 mL
	romaine leaves	

Cook cauliflower in boiling water for 5 minutes until tender crisp. Rinse with cold water, drain well, and pat dry. Repeat with broccoli. In large bowl, combine cauliflower, broccoli, tomatoes, olives, and cheese. In shaker, combine vinegar, garlic, salt, pepper, oregano, and oil. Pour over vegetables and toss gently. Marinate up to 2 hours at room temperature or overnight in refrigerator. Bring to room temperature and serve on romaine.

Yield: 6 servings

per serving	**calorie breakdown**
calories 149	% protein 16
g fat 10.2	% fat 57
g fibre 3.5	% carbohydrate 27

Opposite *(clockwise from centre bottom): Minted Red Potato Salad (page 79), Grilled Fish (shark steak, page 85), and Vegetable Pouch (page 86); Grilled Peaches and Blueberries (page 102); Tomato Bruschetta (page 68).*

MINTED RED POTATO SALAD

Marg's Yorkshire mother-in-law taught her to add a sprig of fresh mint when boiling new potatoes. It gives flavour to early new potatoes, which lack maturity.

4	medium, new red-skinned potatoes	4
1	sprig fresh mint	1
4	green onions, sliced	4

Dressing:

½ cup	plain skimmed milk yogurt	125 mL
1 tsp	Dijon mustard	5 mL
1 tbsp	granulated sugar	15 mL
½ tsp	salt	2 mL
¼ tsp	pepper	1 mL
1 tbsp	finely chopped fresh mint leaves	15 mL

Scrub new potatoes, leaving skins on. In medium, covered saucepan, simmer potatoes with mint until tender; drain, discard mint, cool, and cut into cubes. Place in bowl with green onions.

To make dressing: Combine yogurt, mustard, sugar, salt, pepper, and mint leaves. Pour over potato mixture and toss lightly.

Yield: 4 servings

per serving	calorie breakdown
calories 181	% protein 14
g fat 0.3	% fat 2
g fibre 3.1	% carbohydrate 85

Opposite (clockwise from centre bottom): Romaine and Watercress (page 18); Fire and Ice Tomatoes (page 80); Marinated Summer Vegetables (page 81); Carrot and Raisin Salad (page 136); Yogurt Slaw (page 9).

FIRE AND ICE TOMATOES

A salad for the deck that is made in the morning and keeps you warm all evening.

3	ripe tomatoes, sliced	3
1	sweet green pepper, cut into strips	1
1	medium red onion, sliced, separated into rings	1
¾ cup	rice vinegar	175 mL
1 tbsp	granulated sugar	15 mL
½ tsp	celery seed	2 mL
¼ tsp	salt	1 mL
⅛ tsp	cayenne	0.5 mL
3 tbsp	water	45 mL
1	cucumber, sliced	1

Place tomato slices in glass baking dish. Fill spaces with pepper strips. Top with onion rings. In 2-cup (500 mL) liquid measure, blend vinegar, sugar, celery seed, salt, cayenne, and water. Cover loosely, microwave on high for 3 minutes. Let stand 3 minutes. Pour over vegetables, cover and refrigerate at least 2 hours. To serve, arrange cucumber slices on plate, lift marinated vegetables from sauce and place on top of cucumber slices.

Yield: 4 servings

per serving	**calorie breakdown**
calories 91	% protein 10
g fat 0.8	% fat 7
g fibre 4.2	% carbohydrate 83

Marinated Summer Vegetables

Pick up a variety of summer vegetables at the roadside market; marinate them while at their peak of freshness. Stored in a jar in the refrigerator, they are ready for a picnic.

2 qts	prepared vegetables*	2 L

Marinade:

2 tbsp	oil	25 mL
¼ cup	vinegar (white, rice, *or* herbed)	50 mL
2 tbsp	lemon juice	25 mL
1	clove garlic, minced	1
½ tsp	salt	2 mL
⅛ tsp	pepper	0.5 mL
1 tbsp	chopped fresh basil *or* 1 tsp (5 mL) dried basil	15 mL
pinch	granulated sugar	

*A mixture of summer vegetables such as asparagus, zucchini, snow peas, green beans, wax beans, broccoli, cauliflower, green and red pepper.

Cut or slice vegetables into bite-size pieces. Leave snow peas whole. Blanch in boiling water for 1 or 2 minutes, depending on type; they should be crisp. Rinse in ice water to stop cooking. Drain well. Place in a large jar or container with a cover.

Whisk all ingredients for marinade. Pour over vegetables. Cover and refrigerate for 2 hours before serving. Will keep several days in refrigerator; turn over to distribute marinade. To serve, remove vegetables with a slotted spoon.

Yield: 2 quarts (2 L)

per serving (1 cup/250 mL)　**calorie breakdown**
calories 70　% protein 13
g fat 3.2　% fat 36
g fibre 2.2　% carbohydrate 51

Easy Brunch Squares

In recent years we've gone through quiche, frittata, and crustless quiche. While our brunch squares are not exactly low-fat, the fats in the egg yolks and cheese "keep good company," as both contain a number of vitamins and minerals.

6	eggs	6
¼ cup	all-purpose flour	50 mL
½ tsp	baking powder	2 mL
1 cup	low-fat creamed cottage cheese	250 mL
½ cup	grated Monterrey Jack cheese	125 mL
1 cup	sliced mushrooms	250 mL
3	green onions, sliced	3
pinch	pepper	

In medium bowl, whisk eggs lightly. Blend flour and baking powder; whisk into eggs. Fold in cheeses. Lightly oil an 8-inch (2 L) square or 9-inch (2 L) round baking dish. Distribute mushrooms and onions over bottom. Pour egg mixture on top; sprinkle with pepper. Bake in 325°F (160°C) oven for 35 minutes or until knife inserted in the centre comes out clean. Cut in squares or wedges and serve hot.

Yield: 6 servings

Variations:
For cocktail squares, cut into 25 pieces.
Substitute canned, chopped artichokes, raw broccoli florets, or cooked, drained, and chopped spinach for mushrooms.

per serving	calorie breakdown
calories 152	% protein 39
g fat 7.2	% fat 43
g fibre 8.5	% carbohydrate 18

BRIE, BASIL, AND TOMATO PASTA

A thoroughly modern dish, it is a cinch to prepare and a snap to clean up.
You cannot make it without brie and fresh basil.

4	servings (about ¾ lb) dry fettuccine	300 g
3	large tomatoes	3
2 tbsp	olive oil	25 mL
¼ lb	brie cheese, cut into cubes	125 g
¾ cup	quark or yogurt cheese	175 mL
2	cloves garlic, minced	2
1	cup chopped fresh basil	250 mL
½ tsp	salt	2 mL
¼ tsp	pepper	1 mL

In a large saucepan of boiling water, cook fettuccine until al dente (tender
but firm). Meanwhile, seed and chop tomatoes; set aside. In small bowl,
combine oil, brie, quark, garlic, basil, salt, and pepper. Drain cooked pasta
and return to saucepan. Add tomatoes and cheese mixture. Toss to blend
and serve immediately on hot plates. Garnish with a sprig of basil.

Yield: 4 servings

per serving	**calorie breakdown**
calories 512	% protein 20
g fat 16.2	% fat 28
g fibre 4.4	% carbohydrate 52

STORAGE OF FRESH HERBS

Whether harvesting herbs from the garden or purchasing them from the
food store, special care is required to retain shelf life. Wash in cold water
and shake off excess moisture. Wrap in a paper towel, seal in plastic bag,
and store in refrigerator crisper. Basil will only keep a few days before
turning brown. Some herbs will keep several weeks.

Hodge Podge

There isn't a better or more traditional way to celebrate the first harvest of new vegetables than with Hodge Podge. Because of new agricultural technology, the first harvest comes at least a month earlier than in the past. Enjoy a large soup plateful accompanied by fresh bread; don't ruin the experience by serving meat.

1 lb	new potatoes	450 g
½ lb	new carrots	225 g
½ lb	fresh wax beans	225 g
½ lb	fresh green beans	225 g
1 lb	new peas	450 g
1 tsp	salt	5 mL
⅛ tsp	pepper	0.5 mL
1 cup	cereal cream (10% m.f.)	250 mL

Scrub new potatoes, leave small potatoes whole but cut larger ones into halves or quarters. Scrub new carrots and cut into 2-inch (5 cm) pieces. Wash beans, remove tips, and break into 2-inch (5 cm) pieces. Shell peas. Steam vegetables until tender crisp. If steaming together, start with potatoes and carrots and add beans and peas after 5 minutes of cooking. Drain vegetables well, place in saucepan; add salt, pepper, and cream. Heat but do not boil. Serve immediately.

Yield: 4 servings

per serving	calorie breakdown
calories 315	% protein 18
g fat 7.3	% fat 20
g fibre 13.1	% carbohydrate 62

GRILLED FISH

There are many who barbecue only beef and chicken. Fish grills quickly and has that same unique grilled taste. If wrapped in aluminum foil, the fish steams whether cooked on the barbecue or in the oven.

½ cup	white wine	125 mL
1 tbsp	olive oil	15 mL
1 tbsp	Worcestershire sauce	15 mL
pinch	pepper	
1 lb	fish fillet *or* 1-¼ lb (550 g) fish steaks	450 g
4	slices lemon	4

In glass or china dish, blend wine, oil, Worcestershire sauce, and pepper. Rinse fish with cold water; lay in wine marinade, turn over, cover and refrigerate for 30 to 60 minutes (not longer).

Barbecue fish on mesh rack or in hinged basket. If unavailable, prepare aluminum foil sheet: Perforate with fork, lay on grill and brush with marinade. Place fish on grill, top each serving with lemon slice and grill over medium heat, allowing 12 minutes per inch of thickness. Baste with marinade while cooking. Fish is cooked when it turns opaque and flakes when tested with a fork. In small saucepan, reduce remaining marinade to serve with fish.

Yield: 4 servings

per serving	calorie breakdown
calories 171	% protein 68
g fat 4.7	% fat 29
g fibre 0.1	% carbohydrate 3

FISH OF THE FUTURE

The species of fish that are harvested and farmed are changing as are the names applied to them. We cannot know what will be on the fishmonger's counter in two years time. We do know that halibut, haddock, sea bass, winter and yellow-tailed flounder have potential for farming and may be on the market in the next few years. Be prepared to try new species such as shark or grenadier when selecting fillets or steaks.

Vegetable Pouch

When cooking outdoors, it's a nuisance to run back and forth to the kitchen to cook vegetables, so they are often omitted from the meal. This foil pouch of vegetables can be prepared ahead and refrigerated until cooking time.

1	large carrot	1
1	small zucchini	1
12	small green or wax beans	12
1	red or green sweet pepper	1
1 tsp	butter or soft margarine	5 mL
1 tbsp	lemon juice	15 ml
1 tbsp	chopped fresh parsley	15 mL
¼ tsp	salt	1 mL
⅛ tsp	pepper	0.5 mL

Scrub carrot and zucchini (leave peel on new vegetables), cut into julienne strips. Remove end from beans, leave whole. Core, seed, and slice pepper lengthwise. Place vegetables on shiny side of heavy-duty foil; add remaining ingredients. Fold foil to seal securely and prevent leakage. Place on shelf or outer edge of barbecue grill for about 15 minutes.

Yield: 4 servings

per serving	calorie breakdown
calories 60	% protein 13
g fat 1.3	% fat 17
g fibre 2.8	% carbohydrate 70

PORK KEBOBS

The sirloin of pork, often referred to as butt end of leg, is the leanest cut of pork. To have a supply, buy a pork butt roast, cut it into steaks and cubes. Package, label, and freeze in meal-size portions.

1 lb	lean boneless pork	450 g
¼ cup	apple *or* pineapple juice	50 mL
2 tbsp	Hoisin sauce	25 mL
1 tsp	Dijon mustard	5 mL
1 tsp	grated fresh ginger	5 mL
1	sweet green pepper	1
20	mushrooms	20

Cut pork into ¾-inch (2 cm) cubes. Place in a shallow dish. Whisk together apple juice, Hoisin, mustard, and ginger; add to pork and toss to coat. Cover and marinate in refrigerator for at least an hour. Core, seed, and cut green pepper into ¾-inch (2 cm) chunks. Cut mushroom stems to ½ inch (1 cm). Alternately, thread pork, green pepper, and mushrooms onto skewers.* Place on hot grill over medium-high heat. Cook, basting often with marinade and turning occasionally, for 15 to 18 minutes or until pork is no longer pink in centre.

*If using wooden skewers, soak in water for 10 minutes before threading.

Yield: 4 servings

per serving	**calorie breakdown**
calories 140	% protein 57
g fat 2.7	% fat 17
g fibre 2.1	% carbohydrate 26

Breaded Zucchini Parmesan

Once they start to produce, you can't keep up with zucchini. As a variation from salad, muffins, and bread, try this recipe.

2	medium zucchini	2
1 cup	dried bread crumbs	250 mL
¼ cup	grated Parmesan cheese	50 mL
¼ cup	chopped fresh basil *or* 1 tsp (5 mL) dried	50 mL
	pepper to taste	
1	egg white	1
	oil for grill	

Slice zucchini on diagonal, ½-inch (1 cm) thick. On a plate, combine bread crumbs, Parmesan, basil, and pepper. In small bowl, beat egg white until frothy. Dip zucchini slices in egg white, then crumb mixture to coat. Lay on a platter in single layer. Spray or brush oil on grill and cook over medium heat for 3 minutes per side until golden brown. Alternatively, broil in oven. Serve at once.

Yield: 4 servings

Variation:
Substitute thickly sliced green tomatoes for zucchini.

per serving	**calorie breakdown**
calories 90	% protein 24
g fat 2.3	% fat 21
g fibre 2.2	% carbohydrate 55

SEASONED POTATOES IN FOIL

Whole potatoes wrapped in foil for barbecuing take a long time to cook and result in a bland steamed vegetable, unless topped with sour cream or cheese. For a variety of quick, tasty potatoes from the grill try the following three recipes.

6	medium round potatoes	6
2	medium onions	2
1 tbsp	butter	15 mL
½ tsp	salt	2 mL
¼ tsp	pepper	1 mL
1	clove garlic, minced (optional)	1

For one pouch you will need the extra wide, heavy-duty foil; with regular foil, make 2 smaller pouches. Scrub and slice unpeeled potatoes, ¼-inch (0.5 cm) thick. Thinly slice onions. Spread half the butter on centre of shiny side of foil. Layer potatoes and onions, sprinkling each layer with salt, pepper, and garlic. Dot with remaining butter. Fold foil to seal securely and prevent leakage. Barbecue over medium heat until potatoes are tender, about 20 minutes. If well sealed, pouch may be carefully turned once or twice; avoid puncturing the foil.

Yield: 6 servings

per serving
calories 123
g fat 2.3
g fibre 5.8

calorie breakdown
% protein 14
% fat 15
% carbohydrate 71

Potato Fans

4	(8 oz/225 g) baking potatoes	4
1 tbsp	butter, melted	15 mL
½ tsp	paprika	2 mL
¼ tsp	pepper	1 mL

Scrub and prick potatoes several times with a fork. Microwave on high for 6 minutes. Make cuts at ½-inch (1 cm) intervals across potatoes to within ½-inch (1 cm) of bottom. Gently twist knife to make potato slices fan. Combine melted butter, paprika, and pepper. Carefully drizzle evenly over each potato (less than 1 tsp/5 mL per potato). Finish cooking on upper shelf or perimeter of barbecue, about 30 minutes.

Yield: 4 servings

per serving	calorie breakdown
calories 171	% protein 14
g fat 3.2	% fat 16
g fibre 8.3	% carbohydrate 70

Potato Kebobs

9	small new potatoes	9
1 tsp	oil	5 mL
½ tsp	paprika	2 mL
⅛ tsp	pepper	0.5 mL
¼ tsp	salt	2 mL

Scrub potatoes but do not peel. Rub with oil and thread on 3 skewers. Sprinkle with paprika, salt, and pepper. Barbecue over medium heat for 15 minutes or until fork tender, turning 2 or 3 times. Serve hot.

Yield: 3 servings

per serving	calorie breakdown
calories 101	% protein 15
g fat 1.7	% fat 15
g fibre 5	% carbohydrate 70

MIKE'S SIRLOIN STEAK

A family favourite at the Routledge house, Mike loved to prepare and serve this dish. It is the most economical steak to purchase when you want tender beef for the family. It will stretch to feed a crowd.

| 1 (2 lb) | 2-inch/5 cm thick slice top sirloin steak | 900 g |

Marinade:

¼ cup	orange juice	50 mL
¼ cup	sherry	50 mL
2 tbsp	soya sauce	25 mL
1	clove garlic, minced	1
2 tsp	grated fresh ginger	10 mL
1 tsp	dry mustard	5 mL
½ tsp	curry powder	2 mL

Remove any fat from beef. In an 8-inch (2 L) square glass dish, combine ingredients for the marinade. Lay steak in marinade, turn it over, cover and refrigerate at least 4 hours, turning meat twice. Remove from refrigerator 1 hour before cooking. Barbecue over hot coals to desired doneness, turning once. Medium-rare will require about 15 minutes per side. For medium-well or well done, lower heat so outside will not burn before inside is cooked. To serve, slice meat on the diagonal. Bring marinade to a boil and serve as sauce.

Yield: 8 servings

per serving	calorie breakdown
calories 124	% protein 67
g fat 3.5	% fat 28
g fibre 0.1	% carbohydrate 6

Broiled Tomatoes

Here is one more idea for getting a vegetable on the barbecued dinner plate.
It also gives the plate a shot of colour.

3	large, firm ripe tomatoes	3
¼ tsp	salt	1 mL
dash	pepper	
1 tbsp	chopped fresh thyme *or* ½ tsp (2 mL) dried	15 mL

Remove stem end and cut tomatoes in half horizontally. Place cut side down on oiled grill for about 3 minutes. Turn over and sprinkle with salt, pepper, and thyme. Grill 3 minutes longer or until tender.

Yield: 6 servings

Variation:
To broil in oven: Place cut side up on shallow pan. Sprinkle with salt, pepper, and thyme. Broil 3 inches (8 cm) from element until tender, about 6 minutes.

per serving	**calorie breakdown**
calories 26	% protein 14
g fat 0.4	% fat 12
g fibre 1.5	% carbohydrate 74

FLANK STEAK TERIYAKI

There are only two flank steaks on each beef carcass, so you may have to search for one at the meat counter. It has intense beef flavour and is tender when marinated and sliced on the diagonal.

8 oz	flank steak	225 g
3 tbsp	red wine vinegar	45 mL
2 tbsp	light soya sauce	25 mL
1 tsp	granulated sugar	5 mL
2	cloves garlic, minced	2
1 tbsp	peeled and thinly sliced fresh ginger	15 mL

Slice flank steak diagonally ¼ inch (1 cm) thick. Place in shallow glass dish. In small bowl, combine vinegar, soya sauce, sugar, garlic, and ginger. Pour over meat and toss to coat. Cover and marinate in refrigerator for at least 1 hour. Thread meat ribbons onto 6 skewers.* Place on hot grill over high heat. Cook, basting often with marinade and turning once until meat is cooked to desired doneness. Since meat is thinly sliced it will cook quickly. Bring remaining marinade to a boil and serve as sauce.

*If using wooden skewers, soak in water for 10 minutes before threading, to prevent burning.

Yield: 3 servings

Variation:
To broil in kitchen: Marinate flank steak unsliced. Remove from marinade; broil 5 to 10 minutes per side, depending on thickness, but not past medium doneness. To serve, slice on diagonal.

per serving
calories 136
g fat 5.4
g fibre 0.1

calorie breakdown
% protein 52
% fat 37
% carbohydrate 11

BARBECUED CORN ON THE COB

To obtain sweet tasting corn, buy only fresh-picked, well-chilled ears. Barbecue corn with the husks intact to preserve flavour.

1 or 2 ears corn per person

butter, salt, pepper

Pull back husks from ears, being careful not to detach from cob. Remove silks; fold husks back up around cobs. Soak in water for 20 minutes. Drain and cook on covered* grill over medium-high heat for 20 to 25 minutes, turning several times, until corn is tender. Remove husks and serve with a little butter, salt, and pepper.

*If cooking on open barbecue, wrap each cob in foil.

per ear with 1 tsp (5 mL) butter
calories 108
g fat 3.2
g fibre 3.4

calorie breakdown
% protein 11
% fat 23
% carbohydrate 65

QUICK SOAK METHOD FOR BEANS

In large saucepan, measure three parts water to each part dried beans. Bring to a boil. Reduce heat, cover and simmer for two minutes. Remove from heat, let stand one hour; drain. Proceed with recipe. Beans may be frozen after soaking.

Ross's Cowboy Beans

If you like baked beans and love a late supper that's ready whenever you decide to eat, this tangy, modern version of baked beans is for you.

3 cups	dried beans (soldier, Jacob's cattle, or navy beans)	750 mL
1	medium onion, chopped	1
2	cloves garlic, minced	2
1	large sausage, sliced (chorizo, if available)	1
2 tbsp	vinegar	25 mL
¼ cup	molasses	50 mL
1	small, dried red chili pepper	1
½ tsp	cumin	2 mL
½ tsp	dry mustard	2 mL
1½ tsp	salt	7 mL
1 (19 oz) tin	V-8 or tomato juice	540 mL

Wash beans and soak overnight in 2 quarts (2 L) tepid water. In the morning, drain beans, discarding water.* Place beans in large saucepan; add hot water to cover. Simmer for 1 hour, until skins burst when blown on. Blend all other ingredients together and pour into slow cooker or bean crock. Drain beans and add to crock. If baking in oven, add enough boiling water to cover beans. If using crockpot, add boiling water until you just see it. Bake in 300°F (150°C) oven for 6 hours, adding boiling water as necessary to keep beans covered.

Or cook on high in crockpot for 1 hour, then on low for 4 to 5 hours. You should not have to add water.

May be stored in refrigerator for 4 days or frozen.

*For quick soak method, see page 94.

Yield: 6–8 servings

per serving	**calorie breakdown**
calories 446	% protein 21
g fat 4.9	% fat 10
g fibre 23.3	% carbohydrate 69

CHICKEN SATAY

Satay is an Indonesian word for "skewered morsels of grilled meat served with a peanut sauce." The yogurt marinade and sauce keeps skinless poultry moist.

8	chicken thighs and/or drumsticks	8

Marinade:

1 cup	plain skimmed milk yogurt	250 mL
1 tbsp	minced fresh ginger	15 mL
½ tsp	ground cardamom	2 mL
½ tsp	ground coriander	2 mL
½ tsp	pepper	2 mL

Peanut Sauce:

⅓ cup	peanut butter	75 mL
2	cloves garlic, minced	2
2 tbsp	lime juice	25 mL
2 tbsp	light soya sauce	25 mL
1 tbsp	molasses	15 mL
¼ tsp	cayenne	1 mL
1 cup	hot water	250 mL

Remove skin and visible fat from chicken pieces and place in non-metal container. Blend marinade ingredients and pour over chicken. Cover and refrigerate at least 3 hours, preferably overnight. Simmer chicken in marinade in covered skillet for 30 minutes, turning once. Remove, discard marinade; refrigerate chicken pieces.

To prepare sauce, warm peanut butter in small saucepan. Blend seasonings into hot water and whisk into peanut butter. Continue whisking over medium heat until sauce thickens, about 2 minutes. Store in refrigerator in covered container. Dilute with water as required. Serve warm or cold.

Yield: 4 servings

per serving	calorie breakdown
calories 194	% protein 36
g fat 9.2	% fat 42
g fibre 8.8	% carbohydrate 20

BOILED LOBSTERS

A lobster boil sometime between May and September is an essential summer experience in the Maritimes. At the end of such a feast, a New Jersey guest said, "I'm not going to eat for a week because I don't want anything to interfere with the taste I have in my mouth."

| 1 | live lobster per person (1¼ to 1½ lbs/600 to 700 g) | 1 |
| | salt, preferably coarse | |

Fill a large pot with enough water to completely cover lobsters. Unless using sea water, add 2 tablespoons (25 mL) salt per 1 quart (1L) of water and bring to rolling boil. Grasp lobster by its back and quickly plunge head-first into water. Have a prod in hand. When all lobsters are in the pot, cover and return to boil. Then reduce to a bubbly simmer. Lobster of 1¼ to 1½ pounds (600 to 700 g) will cook in about 15 minutes. Two pounders (1 kg) take 20 minutes. Timing starts *after* water has returned to full boil. Antennae come out easily when lobster is done. Serve lobster on table or log covered with newspapers. With heavy, sharp knife or cleaver, split tail down centre and crack claws by giving a sharp chop opposite pincher joint. Arrange on plate for guests to do the rest.

Every part of lobster contains superb meat. Twist claw and knuckles off and crack shell with cutters. Remove meat with fork or pick. Break flippers from tail and push out meat. Remove and discard dark vein that runs along centre top of tail. The carapice (body) contains tasty bites of meat—the green liver (tomaelly) and sometimes red roe (cavier). Even legs contain tidbits; nibble and squeeze out meat.

Today, most of us eat lobster without any dipping sauce. Some locations use vinegar or lemon juice. Restaurants often serve melted butter. We like the taste of lobster on its own.

Lobster Seasons:
Coastal locations have different lobster seasons. Ask tourism for a lobster season map if planning a tour of an area.

per serving	calorie breakdown
calories 630	% protein 88
g fat 6.3	% fat 9
g fibre 0	% carbohydrate 2

Lobster Roll

In Paris, Chicago, and Vancouver, lobster rolls are a delicacy. Along the North Atlantic, lobster rolls are a special summertime sandwich served even at McDonald's restaurants. It's difficult to beat the original home-style recipe.

1 cup	cooked lobster meat	250 mL
½ cup	diced celery	125 mL
2	green onions, sliced	2
3 tbsp	Cheryl's salad dressing*	45 mL
2	hot dog rolls, toasted	2

*see page 15 or substitute low-fat salad dressing

Chop lobster, taking care to remove cartilage from claw meat. In small bowl, combine lobster with celery, onions, and salad dressing. Spoon into rolls. Serve immediately.

Yield: 2 servings

per serving	calorie breakdown
calories 264	% protein 32
g fat 4.3	% fat 15
g fibre 1.7	% carbohydrate 53

FRENCH VANILLA ICE CREAM

Making a custard sauce as the base for ice cream ensures that the eggs are safely cooked. The custard may be made ahead of time and chilled in the refrigerator.

2 cups	1% milk	500 mL
¾ cup	granulated sugar	175 mL
2	eggs, beaten	2
1½ tsp	pure vanilla extract	7 mL
1 cup	whipping cream	250 mL

Microwave Method:
In a 1 quart (1 L) glass dish, microwave milk and sugar on high for 3 minutes. Stir a little hot milk into beaten eggs; then stir eggs into milk mixture. Microwave on medium for 4 to 5 minutes, stirring twice, until custard coats the back of a metal spoon. Stir in vanilla and refrigerate to chill.

Stovetop Method:
In small saucepan, heat milk and sugar over medium heat, stirring constantly until almost boiling. Stir a little hot milk into beaten eggs; then stir eggs into remaining milk mixture. Return to heat and continue cooking until custard coats the back of a metal spoon. Stir in vanilla and refrigerate to chill.

To Make Ice Cream:
Stir whipping cream into chilled custard. Pour into ice-cream maker and follow manufacturer's instructions. Alternately, pour into shallow pan and freeze until crystals form. Remove and whisk to break up crystals. Return to freezer until frozen.

Yield: 8 servings

Variations:
This is a good base for any fruit ice cream. Add 1 cup (250 mL) whole berries or sliced or crushed fruit to custard mix. For a nut ice cream add 1 cup (250 mL) chopped nuts. May substitute extract (lemon, almond, rum, peppermint, etc.) for vanilla.

per serving	**calorie breakdown**
calories 167	% protein 10
g fat 6.9	% fat 37
g fibre 0	% carbohydrate 53

Strawberry Glazed Pie

Two-crust strawberry and raspberry pies became history years ago when Marg introduced this one-crust fresh, uncooked strawberry pie to her family—even before we were concerned about fat intake.

1	(9-inch/23 cm) cooked pastry crust*	1
1 qt	fresh strawberries, washed and hulled	1 L
¾ cup	water	175 mL
¼ cup	granulated sugar	50 mL
3 tbsp	cornstarch	45 mL
1 tbsp	lemon juice	15 mL

* see page 42

Reserving 1½ cups of the smaller strawberries for glaze, arrange the remainder, points up, in circles to cover pastry. In small saucepan, mash reserved berries; add water and cook until soft. Meanwhile, blend sugar and cornstarch; stir into berry mixture. Cook, stirring constantly until thick and clear. Remove from heat, stir in lemon juice. Cool slightly. Pour evenly over pie. Refrigerate until set.

Yield: 8 servings

Variations:
This pie may be made with fresh raspberries or blueberries. For raspberry, replace the lemon juice with ½ tsp (2 mL) almond extract.

per serving	calorie breakdown
calories 176	% protein 5
g fat 6.7	% fat 31
g fibre 3	% carbohydrate 64

Blue and Green Crisp

Gooseberries are tart and tangy, a fruit that is regaining space in our kitchens. You may use green or ripe gooseberries. If you love them, freeze them whole, with nothing added.

2 cups	wild blueberries, fresh or frozen	500 mL
1 cup	gooseberries, fresh or frozen	250 mL
½ cup	granulated sugar	125 mL
1 tbsp	lemon juice	15 mL
1 tsp	lemon rind	5 mL
½ cup	quick cooking oats	125 mL
½ cup	whole wheat flour	125 mL
½ cup	lightly packed brown sugar	125 mL
1 tsp	nutmeg	5 mL
2 tbsp	butter	25 mL

Combine blueberries and gooseberries in shallow baking dish. Sprinkle with sugar, lemon juice, and rind. In small bowl, combine oats, flour, brown sugar, and nutmeg. With pastry blender or fingertips, work in butter. Sprinkle evenly over fruit, press down lightly. Microwave, uncovered, on high for 7 minutes until topping is lightly browned. Let stand 5 minutes. Serve warm.

Or oven bake at 350°F (160°C) uncovered for 45 minutes, until topping is browned.

Yield: 6 servings

Variations:
Crisps may be made with different combinations of fruits e.g. blueberries with raspberries, sliced peaches, or rhubarb; strawberries with rhubarb; cranberries with pears, and so on. Adjust granulated sugar according to sweetness of fruits.

per serving	**calorie breakdown**
calories 258	% protein 5
g fat 7.1	% fat 24
g fibre 4.6	% carbohydrate 71

GRILLED PEACHES AND BLUEBERRIES

Peaches and blueberries are complementary in colour and flavour. Their harvest times coincide, making this easy outdoor dessert possible.

4	freestone peaches	4
½ cup	fresh blueberries	125 mL
1 tbsp	lemon juice	15 mL
1 tbsp	lightly packed brown sugar	15 mL
½ tsp	nutmeg	2 mL
	vanilla yogurt (optional)	

Wash peaches to remove fuzz. Cut peaches in half; remove pits. Arrange, with cut sides up, in two rows on 16-inch (40 cm) square of heavy-duty foil. Fill each cavity with 1 tablespoon (15 mL) blueberries. Sprinkle with lemon juice. Combine brown sugar and nutmeg; sprinkle over top. Fold foil to seal package. Grill over medium-high heat, without turning package over, for 15 minutes or until peaches are fork tender. Serve warm, with vanilla yogurt, if desired.

Yield: 4 servings

per serving
calories 63
g fat 0.2
g fibre 2.2

calorie breakdown
% protein 4
% fat 2
% carbohydrate 94

PEACH YOGURT POPS

When it's summer, everybody enjoys a frozen dessert on a stick.

1 cup	plain skimmed milk yogurt	250 mL
2 tbsp	corn syrup *or* honey	25 mL
¼ cup	frozen concentrated orange juice	50 mL
2	peaches, peeled and chopped	2
1	egg white	1
2 tsp	granulated sugar	10 mL

In blender or food processor, combine yogurt, corn syrup or honey, and orange juice. Add chopped peach and pulse (but do not purée). In small bowl, beat egg white until frothy. Sprinkle in sugar and continue beating until firm peaks form. Fold yogurt mixture into egg white. Pour into individual popsicle or yogurt containers. Insert flexible sticks and freeze.

Yield: 9 servings

Note:
In this case, the raw egg white is safe because it is frozen. See page 45.

per serving	**calorie breakdown**
calories 113	% protein 17
g fat 0.1	% fat 1
g fibre 0.9	% carbohydrate 82

Pavlova with Lemon Filling

Many cultures make meringues but only New Zealanders and Australians call them Pavlova, after the dancer Anna Pavlova. This recipe came from Timaru, New Zealand. Pavlova is usually served with fresh fruit (kiwi in New Zealand) and whipped cream. We have used lemon filling and suggest fresh seasonal fruit.

2	egg whites, at room temperature	2
1/8 tsp	salt	0.5 mL
1/8 tsp	cream of tartar	0.5 mL
1/2 cup	granulated sugar*	125 mL
1/2 tsp	pure vanilla	2 mL
1/2 tsp	cornstarch	2 mL
1/2 tsp	vinegar	2 mL

*If eggs seem small in size, reduce sugar by 2 tbsp (25 mL).

Prepare baking sheet by covering with foil or parchment paper. Using a round plate, trace an 8-inch (20 cm) circle in the middle of the paper. Lightly oil or spray the surface and sprinkle with water. In medium mixing bowl, sprinkle salt and cream of tartar over egg whites. Beat until soft peaks form. Gradually add sugar, a spoonful at a time, beating continually until stiff peaks form. Add vanilla, cornstarch, and vinegar and beat only to blend. Spoon onto circle and using back of a tablespoon, shape into a nest about 1½ inches (4 cm) high around edge. Bake in 325°F (160°C) oven for 15 minutes. Reduce oven temperature to 250°F (120°C) and bake for 45 minutes longer. If meringue starts to brown, reduce oven temperature. When done it should be firm to the touch. Remove from oven, let cool 10 minutes, carefully loosen from paper and place on serving plate.

Lemon Filling:

½ cup	granulated sugar	125 mL
1 tbsp	cornstarch	15 mL
2	egg yolks	2
1	egg	1
1	lemon, grated rind and juice	1
¼ cup	vanilla skimmed milk yogurt	50 mL

In 2-cup (500 mL) glass measure, blend sugar and cornstarch. Add yolks and egg; whisk to combine. Stir in lemon juice and rind. Microwave on high for 2 to 2½ minutes or until mixture bubbles and thickens, stirring after each minute. Cool to room temperature and fold in yogurt. Refrigerate.

To assemble and serve Pavlova:
Carefully spread lemon filling over meringue nest. Arrange 2 cups (500 mL) whole or sliced seasonal fruit over top. Cut into wedges with metal pizza cutter.

Yield: 6 servings

per serving (no fruit)
calories 188
g fat 2.7
g fibre 0.2

calorie breakdown
% protein 8
% fat 12
% carbohydrate 80

PEACH CUSTARD PIE

Peach Chiffon Pie was a longtime favourite of Marg's family. Since we no longer use egg whites in uncooked, gelatin products, we changed the recipe to a custard pie.

1	(9-inch/23 cm) baked pastry crust*	1
2 cups	peeled and chopped fresh peaches	500 mL
½ cup	granulated sugar	125 mL
2 tbsp	lemon juice	25 mL
¼ cup	cornstarch	50 mL
1 cup	1% milk	250 mL
2	eggs, beaten	2
½ cup	vanilla skimmed milk yogurt	125 mL
1	fresh peach for garnish	1

*see pages 42 and 229

Immediately toss peaches with sugar and lemon juice; let stand 20 minutes, then drain well, reserving liquid. In medium saucepan, combine cornstarch, milk, and drained juice. Cook, stirring constantly over medium heat until mixture thickens and bubbles. Whisk ¼ cup (50 mL) of the hot mixture into beaten eggs; then whisk egg mixture into saucepan. Return to heat and cook 1 minute longer, stirring constantly. Cool to room temperature and fold in peaches and yogurt. Spoon into pastry and refrigerate. To serve, garnish with fresh peach slices dipped in lemon water.

Yield: 8 servings

per serving	calorie breakdown
calories 276	% protein 8
g fat 10.1	% fat 32
g fibre 2.2	% carbohydrate 59

TO PEEL PEACHES

Immerse ripe peaches in boiling water for 30 seconds, then plunge into cold water. Peel off skin and slice or chop peaches into lemon water or orange juice. To prevent browning, work quickly with small batches of fruit.

WILD BLUEBERRY CAKE

In the past, commercially harvested, wild blueberries from Maine, Quebec, and the Maritimes were processed. If you wanted fresh ones, you either picked your own or bought them at a market during August and September. Some growers, understanding our desire for this wild berry as a fresh fruit, are marketing them in quart boxes and 5- and 10-pound containers. Freeze them (with nothing added) for winter baking.

2 cups	all-purpose flour	500 mL
1 tbsp	baking powder	15 mL
½ cup	soft margarine	125 mL
¾ cup	granulated sugar	175 mL
2	eggs	2
½ tsp	vanilla	2 mL
1	orange, grated rind and juice	1
	milk, to make ¾ cup (175 mL) with orange juice	
2 cups	wild blueberries, fresh or frozen	500 mL
2 tbsp	granulated sugar	25 mL
¼ cup	brown sugar	50 mL
½ tsp	cinnamon	2 mL

Sift flour with baking powder, set aside. In medium bowl, cream margarine and sugar until light. Add eggs, one at a time, beating after each addition. In liquid measure, combine vanilla, orange juice, and enough milk to make ¾ cup (175 mL). Reduce speed of mixer, add flour alternately with liquid ingredients, starting and ending with flour. Spread one half of batter in oiled 9-inch (2.5 L) square cake pan; cover with blueberries; sprinkle with orange rind and 2 tablespoons sugar. Spoon remaining batter evenly over berries, spreading carefully. Mix brown sugar and cinnamon; sprinkle over top. Bake in 350⁰F (180⁰C) oven for 45 to 50 minutes, until centre springs back when touched. Cool on wire rack. Serve warm or cold.

Yield: 12 servings

per serving	**calorie breakdown**
calories 252	% protein 6
g fat 8.9	% fat 31
g fibre 1.6	% carbohydrate 63

Wild Blueberry Muffins

We use the term "wild blueberries" to distinguish the native species, which grows on the Atlantic coastal barrens, from the high-bush, cultivated berries. In taste there is no comparison; the wild berries concentrate blueberry flavour.

1	medium orange	1
¼ cup	oil	50 mL
½ cup	1% milk	125 mL
1	egg	1
¾ cup	all-purpose flour	175 mL
¾ cup	whole wheat flour	175 mL
½ cup	granulated sugar	125 mL
2 tsp	cream of tartar	10 mL
1 tsp	baking soda	5 mL
1 cup	wild blueberries, fresh or frozen	250 mL

Cut orange (both peel and pulp) into 8 pieces, remove any seeds and place in food processor or blender with oil, milk, and egg. Process until quite smooth. In medium bowl, combine flours, sugar, cream of tartar, and soda. Stir in orange mixture, only until moistened. Fold in blueberries. Spoon into 12 medium paper-lined or nonstick muffin cups, filling ¾ full. Bake in 375°F (190°C) oven for 15 to 18 minutes or until firm to touch. Cool on wire rack. These freeze well.

Yield: 12 muffins

per muffin
calories 145
g fat 4.7
g fibre 1.7

calorie breakdown
% protein 8
% fat 28
% carbohydrate 64

GENUINE BRAN MUFFINS

Low in fat and full of wheat bran, this is a basic muffin to keep the digestive system regular.

1½ cups	natural wheat bran	375 mL
1 cup	whole wheat flour	250 mL
3 tbsp	granulated sugar	45 mL
1½ tsp	baking powder	7 mL
½ tsp	baking soda	2 mL
¼ cup	oil	50 mL
¼ cup	molasses	50 mL
1 cup	1% milk	250 mL
1	egg	1
½ cup	raisins	125 mL

In medium bowl, combine bran, flour, sugar, baking powder, and baking soda. In liquid measure, whisk oil, molasses, milk, and egg. Add to dry ingredients along with raisins, mixing only to moisten. Batter will be quite wet compared to other muffins. Spoon into 12 medium paper-lined or nonstick muffin cups, filling ¾ full. Bake in 400°F (200°C) oven for 15 minutes or until firm to touch. Cool on wire rack. These freeze well.

Yield: 12 muffins

Variations:
Substitute currants or chopped dates for raisins.

per muffin	**calorie breakdown**
calories 138	% protein 9
g fat 4.6	% fat 27
g fibre 5.2	% carbohydrate 64

CINNAMON COFFEE CAKE

This is a surprisingly wonderful cake for Sunday brunch or family dinner.

1 cup	whole wheat flour	250 mL
½ cup	all-purpose flour	125 mL
¾ cup	firmly packed brown sugar	175 mL
1 tsp	baking powder	5 mL
1 tsp	baking soda	5 mL
1 cup	buttermilk*	250 mL
2 tbsp	oil	25 mL
1 tsp	vanilla	5 mL
1	egg	1

Topping:

1 tbsp	butter	15 mL
⅓ cup	firmly packed brown sugar	75 mL
1 tbsp	cinnamon	15 mL

*May substitute equal parts of plain skimmed milk yogurt and 1% milk.

In medium bowl, combine flours, ¾ cup (175 mL) brown sugar, baking powder, and baking soda. In liquid measure, whisk buttermilk, oil, vanilla, and egg. Add liquid ingredients to dry ones and stir only to moisten.

For topping, in small bowl, work butter into ⅓ cup (75 mL) brown sugar and cinnamon. Spread half of batter in oiled 8-inch (2 L) square cake pan. Sprinkle with half the ⅓ cup (75 mL) brown sugar mixture. Spoon on remaining batter, spreading evenly and sprinkle with remaining brown sugar mixture. Bake in 350°F (180°C) oven for 30 to 35 minutes or until centre springs back when touched. Cool on wire rack. Serve warm or cold. Freezes well.

Yield: 12 servings

per serving	calorie breakdown
calories 171	% protein 7
g fat 3.8	% fat 19
g fibre 1.7	% carbohydrate 73

FLATBREAD WITH OLIVES

Flatbread is a North American version of Italian focaccia. It may be served as an appetizer, accompaniment for dinner, or may be split in half for a sandwich.

1 cup	hot water	250 mL
1 tsp	granulated sugar	5 mL
1 tbsp	olive oil	15 mL
½ tsp	salt	2 mL
1¼ cups	all-purpose flour	300 mL
1½ tsp	(½ pkg) instant yeast*	7 mL
1 cup	whole wheat flour	250 mL
½ cup	chopped firm black olives	125 mL
1 tbsp	chopped fresh rosemary *or* 1 tsp (5 mL) dried	15 mL
1 tsp	olive oil to brush top	5 mL

*see page 112

In medium bowl, combine hot water, sugar, olive oil, and salt. Blend 1 cup (250 mL) of the all-purpose flour with yeast. Add to hot water mixture; beat until smooth and elastic. Stir in whole wheat flour, olives, and rosemary (dough will be sticky). Turn onto floured surface and knead for 3 minutes, working in remaining cup (50 mL) all-purpose flour as required to achieve soft dough. Let rest 10 minutes. Roll dough to form circle ½ inch (1 cm) thick. Place on baking sheet. Brush top lightly with olive oil and let rise in warm place until double in size, 30 minutes. To give dimpled effect, press index and middle fingers into dough about 1 inch (2 cm) apart. Bake in 375°F (190°C) oven for 18 to 20 minutes until golden brown.

Yield: 8 servings

Variations:
Omit olives; sauté 1 thinly sliced medium onion in 1 tablespoon (15 mL) olive oil, cool, and scatter over dough just before baking. Substitute other herbs for rosemary. This recipe is suitable in quantity for a bread machine.

per serving	calorie breakdown
calories 155	% protein 11
g fat 3.2	% fat 18
g fibre 3	% carbohydrate 71

TRADITIONAL ACTIVE DRY YEAST VS INSTANT DRY YEAST:

There are two kinds of dry yeast. Active dry yeast is the standard product that is activated before being added to bread dough. Put ½ cup (125 mL) of 110°F (45°C) water in liquid measure. Stir in 1 teaspoon (5 ml) sugar and 1 package (1 tablespoon/15 ml) traditional dry yeast. Set aside for 10 minutes, then stir well and add to warm (commonly referred to as "baby bottle temperature") bread mixture.

The newer form of yeast is instant dry yeast (often sold under the brand name "Quick-Rise"). It is designed for a warmer environment—125°F (55°C)—and is stirred into 1 cup (250 ml) of flour, which is added to the warmer (commonly referred to as "bath water temperature") mixture .

The rising procedure is different for each kind of yeast. With regular dry yeast, the kneaded dough ball is placed in large, covered container and put in oven, with oven light on. A tray of hot water may be placed on lower rack to hasten rising. When dough ball has doubled in size, dough is punched down and allowed to rest 10 minutes. It is then shaped into rolls and/or loaves, placed in pans, covered with a tea towel, and returned to oven for second rising, about 1 hour.

With instant yeast, the kneaded dough ball is allowed to rest 10 minutes, after which it is shaped and placed in pans. The pans are placed in oven to rise, under same conditions. If a chewier bread is desired, follow rising procedure for regular dry yeast. Two risings strengthens texture of bread.

Baking procedure is the same in both cases. Loaves bake at 400° to 425°F (200° to 220°C) for 15 minutes of browning and then at 325°F (160°C) for 30 to 40 minutes, depending on loaf size. Rolls are baked at 375°F (190°C) for 20 to 30 minutes, depending on size and shape and whether rolls are separate or joined. Bread and rolls made with all-purpose flour require slightly higher temperature for browning than whole grain breads. When done, bread should have a hollow sound when rapped with knuckles.

DOOHICKIES

A chocolate lover may be able to satisfy that craving with this simple, no-bake cookie. Because this recipe is full of rolled oats, it got past the board of censors.

¾ cup	cocoa	175 mL
4 cups	quick cooking oats*	1 L
2 cups	granulated sugar	500 mL
½ cup	1% milk	125 mL
½ cup	soft margarine	125 mL
1 tsp	vanilla	5 mL

*For better taste, spread oats in large, heavy frying pan and toast over medium heat, stirring constantly for 5 to 8 minutes.

In large bowl, combine cocoa and oats. In 2 quart (2 L) saucepan, combine sugar, milk, and margarine. Bring to boil and cook for 2 minutes, stirring constantly. Remove from heat, add vanilla and drizzle over oat mixture. Quickly stir to combine. Drop by teaspoonfuls on waxed paper. When set, store in sealed container between layers of waxed paper.

Yield: 40

per cookie
calories 108
g fat 3.4
g fibre 1.5

calorie breakdown
% protein 7
% fat 27
% carbohydrate 66

Chocolate Crunchies

When children want chocolate cookies, this one fills the order.

1 cup	all-purpose flour	250 mL
1 cup	whole wheat flour	250 mL
¼ cup	cocoa	50 mL
1½ tsp	baking soda	7 mL
¼ tsp	salt	1 mL
1 cup	lightly packed brown sugar	250 mL
½ cup	soft margarine	125 ml
1	egg	1
¼ cup	corn syrup	50 mL
	granulated sugar	

Combine flours, cocoa, baking soda, and salt; set aside. In medium bowl, cream brown sugar and margarine; beat in egg and corn syrup until light. Add dry ingredients, mixing well. Shape dough into 1-inch (2 cm) balls. Dip half of each ball in water, then in granulated sugar. Place sugar side up, 2 inches (5 cm) apart on ungreased baking sheets. Bake in 350⁰F (180⁰C) oven for 13 to 15 minutes. Remove from baking sheets, cool on wire rack. These freeze well.

Yield: 3 dozen

per cookie
calories 81
g fat 2.9
g fibre 0.8

calorie breakdown
% protein 5
% fat 31
% carbohydrate 63

ITALIAN CRUSTY BREAD

Italian and French breads contain no fat, hence their chewy texture. These are the breads to eat with higher-fat entrées, but don't smother them with butter and cheese.

2 cups	hot water	500 mL
5 cups	all-purpose flour	1250 mL
1 tbsp	instant yeast*	15 mL
1 tbsp	sugar	15 mL
2 tsp	salt	10 mL
	milk for brushing loaves	

*see page 112

In large bowl, measure hot water. Blend 2½ cups (625 mL) of the flour and yeast. Add to water and beat until smooth and elastic. Add sugar, salt, and enough of remaining flour to make soft dough. Turn on floured surface; knead 5 minutes, adding flour as required. Dough ball should be smooth and firmer than dough of other yeast breads. Return to bowl; cover and let rise in warm place until double in bulk, 1 to 1½ hours. Punch down and let rest 10 minutes. Divide and shape into 2 long loaves, tapered at ends. Place on lightly oiled baking sheet. Cut 5 or 6 diagonal slits on top and brush with milk. Let rise until double in size, 1 hour. Brush with milk again. Bake in 400°F (200°C) oven 25 to 30 minutes, until loaves are crusty and golden brown. To increase crustiness, place shallow pan of hot water on bottom shelf of oven.

Yield: 2 loaves (24 slices)

Variation:
Use half whole wheat flour.

per slice	**calorie breakdown**
calories 104	% protein 12
g fat 0.3	% fat 3
g fibre 1	% carbohydrate 85

JIFFY ROLLS

This recipe provides fresh rolls in a hurry. Extra yeast speeds the rising, giving rolls in 2 hours.

¼ cup	granulated sugar	50 mL
1 tsp	salt	5 mL
¼ cup	oil	50 mL
2 cups	hot water	500 mL
2 tbsp	(2 pkgs) instant yeast*	25 mL
4 cups	all-purpose flour	1 L
2	eggs, lightly beaten	2
3 cups	whole wheat flour	750 mL

*see page 112

In large bowl, stir sugar, salt, and oil into hot water. Blend and beat 3 cups (750 mL) of the all-purpose flour and the yeast into water mixture until smooth and elastic. Add eggs, whole wheat flour, and enough of remaining all-purpose flour to make a soft, slightly sticky dough. Turn on floured surface and knead 5 minutes. Place a pan of hot water on lower shelf of oven. Turn oven light on. Return dough to bowl, cover and place in oven for 15 minutes. Remove, punch down, shape rolls, and place in oiled pans. Cover with tea towel, return to oven and let rise until double in size, about 30 minutes. Remove rolls and water; preheat oven to 350°F (180°C). Bake at least 20 minutes until golden brown; time depends on whether rolls are separate or joined. Remove from pans and cool on wire racks.

Yield: 4½ dozen

per roll	**calorie breakdown**
calories 73	% protein 13
g fat 1.3	% fat 15
g fibre 1.3	% carbohydrate 72

CORNBREAD

A neglected quick bread that meets all the modern health requirements, it's whole grain, low in fat and sugar, and quick to make.

1 cup	whole wheat flour	250 mL
1 cup	cornmeal	250 mL
¼ cup	granulated sugar	50 mL
¼ tsp	salt	1 mL
2 tsp	baking powder	10 mL
1 cup	1% milk	250 mL
3 tbsp	oil	45 mL
1	egg	1

In medium bowl, combine flour, cornmeal, sugar, salt, and baking powder. In liquid measure, whisk milk, oil, and egg. Add liquid ingredients to dry and stir only to combine. Turn into lightly oiled 8-inch (2 L) square cake pan. Bake in 350°F (180°C) oven 20 to 25 minutes or until centre springs back when touched. Let rest in pan 10 minutes, then invert on wire rack. Serve warm or cold. Freezes well.

Yield: 12 servings

Variations:
Stir ¼ cup finely chopped red or green sweet pepper into batter.
For piquant bread, add seeded and diced jalapeño pepper.

per serving	**calorie breakdown**
calories 135	% protein 10
g fat 4.7	% fat 30
g fibre 2.5	% carbohydrate 60

CASSEROLE RYE BREAD

Casserole breads are for cooks who don't like to knead dough. The gluten is developed by vigorously beating the batter. Because it's a small recipe, this bread can be made with stand mixer or food processor.

2 cups	hot water	500 mL
¼ cup	lightly packed brown sugar	50 mL
1 tsp	salt	5 mL
2 tbsp	oil	25 mL
2½ cups	all-purpose flour	625 mL
1 tbsp	instant yeast*	15 mL
2 tbsp	caraway seeds (optional)	25 mL
2½ cups	rye flour	625 mL

*see page 112

In Large Bowl: Combine hot water, sugar, salt, and oil. Blend and add all-purpose flour and yeast. Stir vigorously for 5 minutes until batter is smooth and very elastic. Add caraway seeds, if using, and enough rye flour to make soft dough (softer than for dough of kneaded breads). Turn on floured surface, cover and let rest 10 minutes. Shape into round loaf and place in oiled 1½-quart (1.5 L) straight-sided casserole. Cover with tea towel and let rise until double in size, 1 to 1½ hours. Bake in 350⁰F (180⁰C) oven for 50 minutes until hollow sounding when rapped with knuckles. Remove from dish and cool on wire rack.

In Food Processor: Insert plastic dough blade. Add all-purpose flour, yeast, brown sugar, and salt to container. Process 20 seconds. With machine running, pour hot water and oil through feed tube in steady stream. Process 1 minute until batter is smooth and elastic. Add 2 cups (500 mL) rye flour, process until surface of dough is smooth and barely sticky. Add more rye flour, if required, until dough cleans side of bowl. Pulse in caraway seeds, if using. Turn dough on floured surface. Follow remaining directions above.

Yield: 1 round loaf (20 slices)

per slice	calorie breakdown
calories 129	% protein 10
g fat 1.6	% fat 11
g fibre 2.7	% carbohydrate 79

PRUNE BROWNIES

We found that replacing the fat with a fruit purée works in some baked products but not others. Marg got approval on this one from her university students; in fact, in a blind test most chose the prune sample.

¼ cup	cocoa	50 mL
1 cup	granulated sugar	250 mL
½ cup	prune purée (recipe follows)	125 mL
2	eggs	2
1 tsp	vanilla	5 mL
¾ cup	all-purpose flour	175 mL

In medium bowl, blend cocoa and sugar. Whisk in prune purée, eggs, and vanilla. Stir in flour. Spread batter evenly in greased 8-inch (2 L) square baking pan. Bake in 350⁰F (180⁰C) oven 20 to 25 minutes or until centre springs back when touched.

Prune Purée:
Combine 4 ounces (125 g) pitted prunes—about ⅔ cup (150 mL)—with 3 tbsp (45 mL) water in blender or food processor. Process until prunes are finely chopped. Makes about ½ cup (125 mL).

Yield: 25 squares

per square	calorie breakdown
calories 63	% protein 7
g fat 0.6	% fat 9
g fibre 0.7	% carbohydrate 85

ALMOND BISCOTTI

We discovered biscotti at Starbuck's coffee kiosks on the west coast and have since been turned into biscotti lovers. A true biscotti (Italian for "biscuit") usually contains nuts and is otherwise free of added fat and eggs. It allows us to dunk again (for who can chew biscotti without), a habit we haven't indulged since doughnuts went on the abstinence list.

2 cups	whole wheat flour	500 mL
¾ cup	granulated sugar	175 mL
¾ cup	(100 g pkg) ground almonds	175 mL
2 tsp	baking powder	10 mL
⅓ cup	corn syrup	75 mL
⅓ cup	water	75 mL

In medium bowl, combine flour, sugar, almonds, and baking powder. In liquid measure, combine corn syrup and water; add to dry ingredients, working with wooden spoon to form stiff dough. Divide and shape into two long logs, about 1 inch (2 cm) in diameter. Line baking sheet with parchment or brown paper (to prevent burning) and bake in 350°F (180°C) oven 35 minutes, until firm and golden. Be careful not to underbake. Remove from paper and place on wire rack until cool enough to slice. Cut on diagonal into ½-inch (1 cm) slices. Stand slices on paper-lined baking sheet. Bake in 350°F (180°C) oven 20 minutes, until dry. Cool on wire rack; store in sealed container. Keeps for weeks. Biscuits should be difficult to chew without dunking in coffee, tea, or hot chocolate.

Yield: 40 biscuits

per biscuit
calories 48
g fat 0.6
g fibre 0.9

calorie breakdown
% protein 8
% fat 10
% carbohydrate 82

RHUBARB JUICE

What to do with all the rhubarb growing in the garden is an ongoing dilemma. This recipe for rhubarb juice is the answer. Make it, freeze it, and enjoy it all year.

Wash and cut rhubarb into 3-inch (7 cm) slices. Place in large soup pot, leaving 5-inches (12 cm) to top of pot. Add water just until you see it. Bring to boil, reduce heat and simmer, stirring occasionally until mushy, about 10 minutes. Strain through a fine sieve. To each cup of hot juice add ⅓ cup (75 mL) granulated sugar, stirring to dissolve. Cool juice and store in refrigerator for 1 week or freeze for up to 1 year.

RHUBARB PUNCH

1 qt	sweetened rhubarb juice	1 L
1 (12½ oz)	can frozen lemonade (undiluted)	355 mL
2 cups	cold water	500 mL
1 qt	chilled ginger ale or soda water	1 L
24	ice cubes	24
1	lemon, sliced	1
1	orange, sliced	1

In punch bowl, combine rhubarb juice, lemonade, and water. To serve, add ginger ale and ice cubes. Garnish with lemon and orange slices.

Yield: 16 (6 oz) servings

per serving	calorie breakdown
calories 85	% protein 2
g fat 0.1	% fat 1
g fibre 0.8	% carbohydrate 97

Sparkling Berry Punch

Punch making is a cinch now that we have so many delicious fruit juice concentrates.

1 (12 oz) can	frozen raspberry cocktail (undiluted)	340 mL
1 (12½ oz) can	frozen lemonade (undiluted)	355 mL
½ (12½ oz) can	frozen orange juice (undiluted)	175 mL
1 qt	cold water	1 L
2 qts	chilled ginger ale *or* soda water	2 L
24	ice cubes	24
1	lemon, sliced	1
1 cup	fresh or frozen raspberries	250 mL

In large punch bowl, combine raspberry cocktail, lemonade, orange juice, and water. Just before serving, add ginger ale or soda water and ice cubes. Garnish with lemon slices and raspberries.

Yield: 25 (6 oz) servings

Variations:
Cranberry or strawberry cocktail concentrate may be substituted for raspberry and/or limeade for lemonade.

per serving	**calorie breakdown**
calories 113	% protein 2
g fat 0.2	% fat 1
g fibre 0.6	% carbohydrate 97

Welcome to Autumn

Autumn is a riot of jewel colours, an explosion of fall chores, and then there's all those green tomatoes.

If there's one word for autumn, it must be "busy." A squirrel is our mentor. He finds and hides everything in preparation for winter; we try to follow his example. We harvest fall vegetables; we pick apples, pears, grapes, and plums. We find and dry nuts and seeds. We cover and dig and repot plants. We fill jars with pickles, jams, and relishes.

The autumn menus are designed to take advantage of this harvest. The meals centre around thick soups and vegetarian dishes; suppers include make-ahead and one-pot dishes; the desserts are cobblers, puddings, and apple dumpling. These meals turn attention back to the kitchen, the dining room, and indoor gatherings of friends and family. Naturally, there's a Thanksgiving feast and novel suggestions for using leftover turkey. Since autumn's the time for buckling down to business and starting new things following the leisurely days of summer, we've introduced ethnic meals. Some will challenge the cook; others challenge tastebuds; a few will challenge the meat-and-potatoes attitude of some family members. Ethnic meals provide innovative ways to incorporate dried beans and whole grains in menus. We hope you find them fun.

These meals will take you back to roadside and farm markets, unless you have an enormous garden. They will taste better if you start an indoor kitchen garden. Thyme, tarragon, rosemary, parsley, and mint are easy to keep on the windowsill through winter; basil's more difficult; oregano, coriander, summer savoury, and dill are impractical.

Autumn is a time of thanksgiving for the harvest, and of reckoning with the long winter that lies ahead. Autumn is a time of preparation, as if for a long journey. Relish its tranquility. Let its vibrant colours and strong flavours pervade the kitchen and be displayed at your table.

BRUNCH (6)*
Grapefruit
Broiled Back Bacon
Buckwheat Pancakes with
   Maple Syrup 139
Cran-apple Compote 162

SCHOOL LUNCH (1)
Nutritious Sandwich 181
Zucchini and Carrot Sticks
Molasses Drop Cookies 176

SPECIAL LUNCH (2)
Scallops Fettuccine 140
Oatcakes 177
Applesauce

QUICK SUPPER (2)
Swiss Chard with Lemon and Pepper
Fish Fillet with Vegetables
   Julienne 141
Boiled Potato
Lemon Bread 174

MAKE-AHEAD SUPPER (UP TO 10)
Autumn Soup 132
Maritime Tea Biscuits 175
Gwen's Raisin Squares 163

MAKE-AHEAD SUPPER (4)
Mulligatawny Soup 130
Anadama Bread 178
Rice and Raisin Pudding 164

SUPPER (5)
Stuffed Sweet Peppers 142-43
Multi-Grain Bread 53
Salad Greens with Vinaigrette 77
Pear Gingerbread 165

FAMILY DINNER (4)
Carrot and Raisin Salad 136
Brussels Sprouts with Ham 144
Potato Scallop au Gratin 146
Cranberry Cobbler 166

*indicates number served

SUPPER (4)
Caesar Salad with Croutons 134-35
Barley Pilaf 145
Apple Squares 167

SUPPER (4)
Rice with Chicken 148
Cole Slaw 137
Wine Poached Pears 168

MEDITERRANEAN DINNER (4)
Hummus and Pita Bread 126
Lamb Marrakesh 152
Steamed Rice
Eggplant and Red Pepper Stir-fry 147
Molly's Pompadour Pudding 169

NEW MEXICAN DINNER (4)
Green Chili Soup 133
Mexican Rice 149
Refried Bean Burritos 150-51
Tomato Salsa 151
Apple Dumplings 170

SPECIAL DINNER (6)
Tuna Pate and Pita Crisps 127-28
Stuffed Pork Loin, Applesauce
   Glaze 153
Oven Roasted Red Potatoes
Ratatouille 154
Raspberry Rhubarb Crumble 171

PLAN-OVER SUPPER (2)
Cold Roast Pork
Microwaved Sweet Potatoes
Hot Sauerkraut
Molasses Drop Cookies 176

THANKSGIVING DINNER (4)
Filled Poached Pears 129
Roasted Half Turkey with Spratt
   Dressing 156-57
Garlic Mashed Potatoes 158
Easy Squash 159
Broccoli Amandine 155
Debbie's Cranberry Chutney 182
Mom Signer's Pumpkin Pie 172

PLAN-OVER LUNCH (4)
Turkey Creole 160
Buttermilk Scones 179
Cantaloupe and Blueberries

PLAN-OVER LUNCH (4)
Turkey Salad with Kiwi Lime
   Dressing 138
Wild Blueberry Tea Bread 180

CANDLELIGHT DINNER (2)
Fiddlehead Soup 8
Citrus Salmon 161
Basmati Rice
Steamed Pole Beans
Cherry Galettes 173

STARTERS
Filled Poached Pears
Hummus
Pita Crisps
Tuna Paté

Stuffed Pork Loin, Applesauce
   Glaze
Stuffed Sweet Peppers
Turkey Creole

SOUPS AND SALADS
Autumn Soup
Caesar Salad with croutons
Carrot and Raisin Salad
Cole Slaw
Green Chili Soup
Mulligatawny Soup
Turkey Salad with Kiwi Lime
   Dressing

MAIN COURSE FOODS
Barley Pilaf
Broccoli Amandine
Brussels Sprouts with Ham
Buckwheat Pancakes
Citrus Salmon
Easy Squash Cookery
Eggplant and Red Pepper Stir-fry
Fish Fillet with Vegetables Julienne
Garlic Mashed Potatoes
Lamb Marrakesh
Mexican Rice
Potato Scallop au Gratin
Ratatouille
Refried Bean Burritos
Rice with Chicken
Roasted Half Turkey with Spratt
   Dressing
Scallops Fettuccine

DESSERTS
Apple Dumplings
Apple Squares
Cherry Galettes
Cran-apple Compote
Cranberry Cobbler
Gwen's Raisin Squares
Molly's Pompadour Pudding
Mom Signer's Pumpkin Pie
Pear Gingerbread
Raspberry Rhubarb Crumble
Rice and Raisin Pudding
Wine Poached Pears

BAKED GOODS
Anadama Bread
Buttermilk Scones
Lemon Bread
Maritime Tea Biscuits
Molasses Drop Cookies
Oatcakes
Wild Blueberry Tea Bread

MISCELLANEOUS
Debbie's Cranberry Chutney
Nutritious Sandwich

HUMMUS (CHICK PEA DIP)

It is so pale in colour, you might pass it by. Once you taste it on pita bread we're quite sure you will come back for more. Hummus comes to us from the Eastern Mediterranean and is a nutritious, fibre-rich starter.

1 (19 oz)	can chick peas, drained	540 mL
	or 2 cups (500 mL) cooked chick peas	
2	lemons, juice of (about ⅔ cup)	150 mL
¼ tsp	salt	1 mL
3	cloves garlic, quartered	3
1 tsp	ground cumin	5 mL
⅓ cup	tahini paste* (ground sesame seeds)	75 mL

*may substitute smooth peanut butter

In blender or food processor, blend all ingredients until smooth. Refrigerate 2 hours before serving. Serve with pita wedges. Will keep up to 2 weeks.

Yield: 10 servings

per ¼ cup (50 mL)   **calorie breakdown**
calories 114   % protein 14
g fat 4.3   % fat 32
g fibre 3.6   % carbohydrate 54

TUNA PATÉ

How many times in our years of home-making has a can of tuna been a life-saver when unexpected guests knock on the door?

Sizes of tuna cans vary; the average is 6 ounces (165 g). Size variance won't affect this recipe.

1 (6 oz)	can solid white tuna, packed in water	165 g
¼ cup	quark or yogurt cheese	50 mL
¼ cup	thinly sliced green onion	50 mL
2 tbsp	seafood cocktail sauce	25 mL
pinch	cayenne	

Drain tuna in sieve. In small bowl, break up tuna and blend in remaining ingredients. Pack in ramekin (small container); refrigerate 2 hours before serving. Serve on pita crisps or crackers.

Yield: ¾ cup (175 mL)

per 2 tablespoons	**calorie breakdown**
calories 53	% protein 79
g fat 0.2	% fat 4
g fibre 0.3	% carbohydrate 17

QUARK AND OTHER FRESH CHEESES

A fresh cheese has not been ripened; it is ready to eat when formed.
Cottage cheese is the most common. Made from skim milk, its curd is a drawback for cooking.
Cream cheese has distinctive flavour. Creaminess makes it a cook's favourite. High fat content, about 38%, is its drawback.
Ricotta, a mild-flavoured, low-fat, curded cheese, is used in Italian dishes.

Two low-fat, mild flavoured, fresh cheese have been revived because they are excellent substitutes for cream cheese:
Quark cheese is thick, mild-flavoured and desirable for cooking. Fat content, which varies, is on the label. Markets and upscale dairy cases carry it.
Yogurt cheese, easily made by straining plain yogurt (see page 49), is equally smooth and thick but has stronger flavour.

Pita Crisps

Many commercial crackers are high in fat and salt. Our crisps are a wise alternative. They may also replace chips.

3	pita bread (whole wheat best)	3
1	clove garlic, finely minced	1
2 tbsp	oil	25 mL

Cut each pita bread in half and split open. In small bowl, combine garlic and oil. Lightly brush the rough side of each pita quarter with oil mixture. Cut each half into 4 wedges. Place on baking sheet; bake in 400°F (200°C) oven 5 to 6 minutes, until crisp and lightly browned. Cool and store in covered container.

Yield: 48 crisps

Variation:
Replace pita bread with six 6-inch (15 cm) flour tortillas, each cut in half and then each half cut into 4 wedges.

per 3 crisps	calorie breakdown
calories 44	% protein 10
g fat 1.6	% fat 33
g fibre 0.1	% carbohydrate 57

Roasting Garlic

Select large bulb of garlic. Remove outer paper covering. Leaving bulb intact, cut off top to expose tips of cloves. Place in lightly oiled baking dish and brush top of bulb with oil. Sprinkle with pepper. Cover and roast in medium oven about 30 minutes, until cloves are soft. Remove and separate cloves from peeling. Mash with fork and, if desired, add herbs to taste. Spread on pita crisps, whole grain bread or crackers.

FILLED POACHED PEARS

An unusual combination of ingredients, served at an unexpected time in the meal—as a starter. It was introduced by Anne at Marg's gourmet group.

¼ cup	lemon juice	50 mL
1 cup	water	250 mL
2	large, firm, ripe pears (Bartlett best)	2
½ cup	finely chopped cooked ham	125 mL
4	green onions, sliced	4
½ cup	quark or yogurt cheese	125 mL

Set aside 2 tsp (10 mL) lemon juice for the filling. In small saucepan, combine water and lemon juice. Peel pears, halve them lengthwise, core, and drop into lemon water to prevent browning. Bring to boil, reduce heat and poach 2 to 3 minutes, until tender crisp. Remove with slotted spoon and drop into ice water to stop cooking; drain. Combine ham, green onions, cheese, and reserved lemon juice and mound in pear halves. Broil 4 inches (10 cm) from element, 3 to 4 minutes. Serve warm.

Yield: 4 servings

per serving
calories 138
g fat 4.7
g fibre 2.9

calorie breakdown
% protein 30
% fat 25
% carbohydrate 45

Mulligatawny Soup

The word "mulligatawny" is the eighteenth-century English derivative from the Tamil word, "milakutanni" for "pepper-water." We found two versions of this soup in our files; one made with chicken, onions, and curry and another made with vegetables and curry.

4 cups	coarsely chopped vegetables*	1 L
6 cups	chicken broth	1.5 L
1 tbsp	butter	15 mL
	curry seasoning (recipe follows)	
1 tsp	salt	5 mL
1¼ cups	plain, skimmed milk yogurt	300 mL
	fresh coriander *or* parsley for garnish	

*e.g. 2 parsnips, 2 carrots, 1 medium potato, 1 stalk celery, 1 medium onion, 6 mushrooms

In deep saucepan, bring vegetables and broth to boil; reduce heat and simmer 30 minutes. Cool slightly. Purée in blender or food processor until smooth. Return to saucepan and heat to boiling. In small skillet over medium heat, melt butter, add curry seasoning; cook and stir 1 minute. Add to soup. At this point, soup may be kept in refrigerator for up to 3 days or frozen. To serve, heat soup and stir in 1 cup (250 mL) yogurt. Do not boil. Garnish with remaining yogurt and chopped coriander or parsley.

Yield: 6 as main course; 8 as starter

CURRY SEASONING

1 tbsp	finely chopped onion	15 mL
1	clove garlic, minced	1
1 tsp	ground turmeric	1
½ tsp	ground ginger	2 mL
½ tsp	ground coriander	2 mL
¼ tsp	cayenne	1 mL
¼ tsp	ground cumin	1 mL

Using mortar and pestle, combine all ingredients to make a paste.
Alternatively, add 1 clove garlic, minced, and 1 tablespoon (15 mL)
curry powder.

per serving (main course)
calories 102
g fat 2.6
g fibre 1.5

calorie breakdown
% protein 15
% fat 22
% carbohydrate 62

CHILIES

Native to the Americas, chilies come in the same colours and have the same
nutritive value as bell peppers. There the similarity ends. They are used to
flavour foods and may replace salt, onions, and garlic. Chilies vary in
hotness by variety and by soil and climatic conditions in which they were
grown. Mild to medium include Mexi-Bell, Anheim, Poblano, Pasilla, and
Hungarian. The hotter ones include Fresno, Jalapeño, Serrano, Yellow, and
Cayenne. Most of these hot ones are deceptively small in size.

A Cautionary Note:
Chili peppers, no matter how mild, contain volatile oils that may cause a
painful burning sensation on your skin. It is best to wear rubber gloves
when chopping them. Don't touch your face, lips, or eyes. Wash hands
thoroughly with soap and water after handling. The veins and seeds are
"hotter" than the flesh; discard these unless you want "hair-raising" fieriness.

131

Autumn Soup

This soup makes a large batch, some to eat right away and some for the freezer. The vegetables can be varied according to what is on hand.

1 tbsp	oil	15 mL
1 (8 oz)	beef shank, marrow bone	250 g
9 cups	water or vegetable cooking water	2.25 L
1 (13 oz)	can tomato paste	369 mL
2	cloves garlic, minced	2
2 tsp	salt	10 mL
¼ tsp	pepper	1 mL
1 tsp	dried basil	5 mL
¼ tsp	chili powder	1 mL
1	bay leaf, crushed	1
½ cup	red lentils	125 mL
2 cups	chopped cabbage	500 mL
2	large onions, chopped	2
2	large carrots, sliced	2
1	sweet green pepper, cored and chopped	1
1	stalk celery, sliced	1
1	cup peeled and chopped broccoli stems	250 mL

In large soup pot, heat oil and brown beef shank. Add remaining ingredients; bring to boil. Reduce heat, cover and simmer 1 hour. Remove soup bone, cut meat into cubes and return to soup. Discard bone. Taste and adjust seasonings—no more salt though! Freezes well.

Yield: 10 servings

per serving	calorie breakdown
calories 130	% protein 22
g fat 2.5	% fat 16
g fibre 5.6	% carbohydrate 62

GREEN CHILI SOUP

*A specialty soup of the southwestern United States is not exactly what you
expected to find in a Maritime cookbook. It's here for a number of reasons.
Mexican food is popular; it's often vegetarian; and it uses seasonings other
than salt and cured meats.*

1 tsp	olive oil	5 mL
1	clove garlic, minced	1
1	small onion, diced	1
2	long green chilies* *or* 2 poblano chilies, seeded and chopped	2
1	large tomato, peeled, seeded, and chopped	1
4 cups	chicken broth	1 L
3	medium potatoes, peeled and diced	3
1 tsp	dried oregano	5 mL
½ tsp	salt (if broth unsalted)	2 mL
¼ cup	grated Monterey Jack cheese	50 mL

*see page 131

In medium saucepan, heat oil; sauté garlic and onion 1 minute. Add chilies,
tomato, broth, potatoes, oregano, and salt. Bring to boil, reduce heat,
cover and simmer until potatoes are cooked, about 10 minutes. Taste and
adjust seasonings. Serve hot, garnished with cheese.

Yield: 8 servings

per serving	calorie breakdown
calories 160	% protein 38
g fat 5.4	% fat 30
g fibre 1.4	% carbohydrate 32

Caesar Salad

Many people are mistaken in thinking this salad is a good diet food to order in restaurants. Most contain too many bacon bits (not a part of the original Caesar) and more dressing than romaine. Raw egg yolk in the dressing creates the potential risk of salmonella infection. Our recipe minimizes the amount of olive oil, tells you how to sterilize a raw egg (a trick learned on CBC Radio's "Quirks & Quarks"), and still tastes like a Caesar.

1	large head romaine	1
1 cup	croutons (recipe follows)	250 mL

Blender Dressing:

1	clove garlic, split	1
½ tsp	salt	2 mL
⅛ tsp	pepper	0.5 mL
1 tsp	anchovy paste *or* 2 anchovy fillets	5 mL
1 tsp	Dijon mustard	5 mL
1 tsp	Worcestershire sauce	5 mL
dash	hot pepper sauce	
1	sterilized egg*	1
⅓ cup	olive oil	75 mL
2 tbsp	grated Parmesan cheese	25 mL

*see page 135

In blender or food processor, blend garlic, salt, pepper, anchovy paste *or* fillets, mustard, Worcestershire sauce, hot pepper sauce, and egg. With machine running, add oil in slow steady stream, blending until smooth. Add Parmesan cheese and pulse to mix. Separate romaine leaves from head, breaking off tough ends and veins. Rinse in cold water; dry in salad spinner or on tea towel. Tear into bite-size pieces and place in large salad bowl. Sprinkle with croutons. To serve, add dressing and toss.

Yield: 4 servings

*To Sterilize a Raw Egg

(for any use where raw egg is required in combination with lemon)

1	raw egg	1
3 tbsp	lemon juice	45 mL
1 tbsp	water	15 mL

In liquid measure, whisk egg until frothy. Add lemon juice and water. Cover and microwave on high 45 seconds. It will bubble. Remove and stir with clean fork. Cover and microwave on high 30 seconds. Remove and beat with clean fork or whisk one minute to prevent coagulation. Mixture should be smooth and creamy.

To Make Croutons

2 cups	French bread cubes (½ inch/1 cm)	500 mL
1 tbsp	olive oil	15 mL

Sprinkle bread cubes with olive oil; toss and spread in single layer on baking sheet. Bake in 400°F (200°C) oven 5 minutes, until crisp and golden brown. For flavoured croutons, add 1 tsp (5 mL) garlic powder and/or dried herbs to oil.

per serving	calorie breakdown
calories 309	% protein 9
g fat 22.7	% fat 66
g fibre 1.8	% carbohydrate 25

SAFE EGGS ARE COOKED ONES

The only safe egg is a well-cooked egg. This has become so important that delightful dishes such as mousse, egg nog, Caesar salad, and eggs Benedict are in danger of becoming extinct.

The problem is salmonella, a bacteria that is known to be present in 40 per cent of chickens and on the outside of egg shells. In recent years salmonella bacteria have been found in the interior of eggs, transferred from infected hens before the shell is formed. For most of us, salmonella infection is merely an inconvenience; for the young, the elderly, pregnant women, and people whose immune system is compromised, salmonella is a serious health risk. Salmonella grows quickly at room temperature. It is readily killed at 160°F (85°C) or by holding a temperature of 140°F (60°C) for three minutes. Pasteurized eggs are safe to use in uncooked dishes. Cracked eggs are never safe to use. Buy only clean, undamaged eggs from refrigerated cases. Take them home directly and refrigerate immediately.

If you want a room temperature egg white for whipping, take the egg from the refrigerator as you begin making the product, separate it and place the white in a warm bowl.

Carrot and Raisin Salad

Donna's family ate this salad weekly, in combination with various Maritime supper dishes.

2 tsp	sesame seeds	10 mL
1 tbsp	low-fat salad dressing	15 mL
1 tsp	vinegar	5 mL
1 tsp	honey	5 mL
1	large carrot, peeled and grated	1
¼ cup	raisins	50 mL

Toast sesame seeds in small skillet until lightly browned. Set aside to cool. Blend salad dressing, vinegar, and honey. In salad bowl, combine carrot, raisins, and sesame seeds. Add dressing and toss.

Yield: 4 servings

per serving	calorie breakdown
calories 82	% protein 6
g fat 3.2	% fat 32
g fibre 2.0	% carbohydrate 62

Cole Slaw

Cole slaw is a wholesome salad associated with family restaurants and fried entrées. There is no set rule for ingredients as long as cabbage is the star. To maintain crispness, add as little dressing as possible; it will keep for a couple of days in the refrigerator.

3 cups	chopped cabbage	750 mL
½ cup	diced celery or green pepper	125 mL
½ cup	chopped red or green onion	125 mL
¼ tsp	salt	1 mL
⅛ tsp	pepper	0.5 mL
2 tbsp	chopped fresh parsley (optional)	25 mL

Dressing:

3 tbsp	low-fat salad dressing	45 mL
1 tbsp	vinegar	15 mL
2 tsp	sugar	10 mL

Blend cabbage, celery, and onion in salad bowl. Sprinkle with salt, pepper, and parsley. Add dressing, toss and serve.

Yield: 4 servings

per serving
calories 44
g fat 0.7
g fibre 1.6

calorie breakdown
% protein 12
% fat 13
% carbohydrate 75

Turkey Salad with Kiwi Lime Dressing

In the Maritimes, turkey salad is traditionally served at tea time. We have added a modern kiwi fruit dressing. This fruit originated in China, where it was called "gooseberry." New Zealand renamed it kiwi fruit and created an international market. Now it is grown in many countries, including western Canada.

1 tbsp	lime juice	15 mL
1 small	apple, quartered, cored, and sliced	1
2 cups	diced cooked turkey *or* chicken	500 mL
1 cup	pineapple tidbits, fresh *or* canned	250 mL
1	small stalk celery, sliced	1
½ cup	pecan halves	125 mL
¼ tsp	white pepper	1 mL

Dressing:

2 tbsp	canola oil	25 mL
¼ cup	honey	50 mL
1 tbsp	lime juice	15 mL
1	ripe kiwi fruit, peeled and sliced	1
1 tsp	grated fresh ginger	5 mL

In salad bowl, toss lime juice with apple slices. Add remaining salad ingredients. In blender or food processor, blend all dressing ingredients until smooth. Pour dressing over turkey mixture, toss and serve.

Yield: 4 servings

per serving	calorie breakdown
calories 300	% protein 40
g fat 6.9	% fat 21
g fibre 2.3	% carbohydrate 39

BUCKWHEAT PANCAKES

Acadians were famous for their buckwheat pancakes, a simple, thin cake made of buckwheat and white flour blended with salt, a rising agent, and water or milk. Our recipe has more ingredients and makes a light, tender pancake.

¾ cup	all-purpose flour	175 mL
¾ cup	buckwheat flour	175 mL
¼ cup	granulated sugar	50 mL
1 tsp	baking powder	5 mL
1 tsp	baking soda	5 mL
¼ tsp	salt	1 mL
1½ cups	buttermilk*	375 mL
2 tbsp	oil	25 mL
2	eggs	2
1 cup	wild blueberries, fresh or frozen (optional)	250 mL

*May substitute equal parts of plain skimmed milk yogurt and 1% milk.

In mixing bowl, preferably with spout, combine flours, sugar, baking powder, baking soda, and salt. In liquid measure, whisk buttermilk, oil, and eggs. Add liquid ingredients to dry and mix only to blend (batter will be lumpy). Let rest 5 minutes. Pour batter on hot non-stick griddle or skillet using about ¼ cup (50 mL) for each pancake. Sprinkle a heaping spoonful of blueberries, if using, over each pancake. Cook over medium heat until bubbles form on surface. Turn and cook until browned. Overlap pancakes on serving platter and keep warm while cooking the remainder. Serve warm with maple syrup or a fruit sauce.

Yield: 4 servings, 12 (5-inch/12 cm) pancakes

Variations:
Ratio of all-purpose and buckwheat flour may be changed to suit personal taste, as long as total flour equals 1½ cups (375 mL). Other flours or meals may be used. For children, make pancakes in favourite shapes: apples, bunnies, turtles, cats, and even dinosaurs!

per serving (3 pancakes) **calorie breakdown**
calories 328 % protein 14
g fat 10.0 % fat 27
g fibre 2.2 % carbohydrate 59

Scallops Fettuccine

A complete meal on a plate, this is as beautiful to look at as it is to eat. It's difficult to believe it contains so little fat.

2	servings (¼ lb/125 g) dry fettuccine	2
6 cups	boiling water	1.5 L
1 tsp	salt	5 mL
8 oz	scallops (if large cut in half)	225 g
2 tbsp	olive oil	25 mL
2	cloves garlic, minced	2
½	sweet red pepper, seeded and cut in strips	½
¼ lb	snow peas	125 g
1	medium carrot, cut julienne	1
¼ cup	vermouth or sherry	50 mL
1 tbsp	oyster sauce	15 mL
1 tsp	grated fresh ginger	5 mL
⅛ tsp	white pepper	0.5 mL

Prepare all vegetables and have pasta cooking before starting to cook scallops as this dinner happens quickly. Cook fettuccine in boiling, salted water 10 to 12 minutes, until al dente. Meanwhile, in heavy skillet, heat oil, stir-fry scallops and garlic 2 to 3 minutes, until scallops become opaque. Remove with slotted spoon to hot plate. Add red pepper, snow peas, and carrot to skillet; stir-fry 2 minutes, until tender crisp. Return scallops, stir in vermouth, oyster sauce, ginger, and pepper. Cover and turn off heat. Pour fettuccini into colander; shake to drain and put on hot plates. Spoon scallops and vegetables over top. Reduce broth, if necessary, and pour over each serving. Serve immediately.

Yield: 2 servings

per serving	calorie breakdown
calories 493	% protein 25
g fat 11.8	% fat 22
g fibre 4.2	% carbohydrate 52

FISH FILLET WITH VEGETABLES JULIENNE

This is a fast, simple fish dinner that is certain to bring rave reviews. It's no more work than broiling or microwaving a fillet, but it's in the gourmet class.

1	leek	1
1	small carrot	1
½	sweet red pepper	½
1 tbsp	olive oil	15 mL
1 (8 oz)	fish fillet	225 g
½	lemon, juice of	½
pinch	white pepper	

Cut leek in half lengthwise, flush out soil under running water. Slice leek (white and light green part), carrot, and red pepper into thin slivers, 3 inches (7 cm) long. In medium skillet, heat oil, add fish fillet, with rough inside down. Sear quickly, lift and invert onto hot plate. Add vegetables to skillet and stir-fry 1 minute. Return fillet (uncooked side down), centreing over vegetables. Squeeze lemon juice over fish and sprinkle with pepper. Cover, reduce heat and steam just until fish is opaque, about 5 minutes. Serve fish and vegetables on hot plates. Reduce dripping, if necessary, and pour around fish. Serve immediately.

Yield: 2 servings

Variations:
Celery, zucchini sticks, mushrooms, and/or green onions may be used in place of listed vegetables.

per serving	calorie breakdown
calories 228	% protein 45
g fat 7.9	% fat 31
g fibre 1.8	% carbohydrate 24

STUFFED SWEET PEPPERS

In the fall, we could live on sweet peppers stuffed with brown rice and vegetables. Donna generally makes up several large batches for the freezer. Microwaved, they provide an instant, nutritionally balanced meal. Green peppers may be substituted when red pepper prices are out of reach.

5	large sweet red peppers	5
2 cups	water (*or* vegetable *or* chicken stock)	500 mL
1 cup	brown rice	250 mL
½ tsp	salt	2 mL
1 tbsp	dried summer savoury	15 mL
1	medium carrot, diced	1
1	large stalk celery, diced	1
½ cup	frozen peas	125 mL
1 tsp	oil	5 mL
1	medium onion, diced	1
2	cloves garlic, minced	2
1 lb	ground turkey *or* chicken	450 g
¼ tsp	pepper	1 mL
1 cup	grated Mozzarella *or* Gouda cheese	250 mL

Cut peppers in half lengthwise, remove seeds and stems, keeping halves intact. In medium saucepan, add peppers to enough boiling water to cover; simmer 3 minutes. Remove and plunge into cold water to stop cooking process. Drain well.

Bring 2 cups (500 mL) water or broth to boil in 2 quart (2 L) microwave dish. Add rice, salt, and summer savoury. Microwave on high 10 minutes. Stir in carrot and celery, microwave on high 10 minutes longer, until rice is cooked. Stir in frozen peas and fluff rice with a fork.

In medium skillet heat oil, add onion, garlic, turkey or chicken and stir-fry until meat is cooked. Add to cooked rice along with pepper and cheese. Taste and adjust seasonings.

Fill pepper halves with rice mixture, rounding tops. Place in shallow pan and bake in 400⁰F (200⁰C) oven 15 minutes. Serve hot.

May be frozen before baking.

Yield: 10 servings for lunch; 5 servings for dinner

Variations:
May use leftover, finely chopped turkey or chicken or omit meat altogether. May vary vegetables and/or reserve cheese for topping.

per half pepper	calorie breakdown
calories 212	% protein 27
g fat 6.9	% fat 29
g fibre 1.6	% carbohydrate 43

BELL PEPPERS

Red and green ones are common; yellow, orange, and purple are hybrids developed in recent years. Green peppers are less sweet so they keep longer; they are also much cheaper. Bell peppers are high in fibre and Vitamin C; red, yellow, and orange varieties are also high in Vitamin A.

Eat them raw or cooked. Remove stem, core, and seeds. Seeds may be added to salads.

Skin may be removed, if desired. Place whole peppers on broiler pan; roast 4 inches from heat. Turn with tongs until charred on all sides. Place peppers in brown paper bag. Close and let stand 15 minutes. Pull off skins. Roasted peppers taste sweeter.

Brussels Sprouts with Ham

Brussels sprouts are neglected, except by the English. We now know that sprouts are one of the best vegetables for inhibiting the development of certain cancers.

¾ lb	fresh Brussels sprouts	340 g
1 tbsp	butter	15 mL
¾ cup	sliced fresh mushrooms	175 mL
½ cup	diced cooked ham	125 mL
1 tbsp	lemon juice	15 mL
¼ tsp	salt	1 mL
pinch	pepper	

Cook Brussels sprouts in ½ cup (125 mL) boiling water 15 to 18 minutes, until tender crisp.* Meanwhile, in small skillet melt butter; sauté mushrooms 2 minutes. Add ham, lemon juice, salt, and pepper; heat through. Drain Brussels sprouts, place in hot serving dish; top with ham mixture. Serve immediately.

*Alternatively, microwave Brussels sprouts on high, in vented container 6 to 7 minutes.

Yield: 4 servings

per serving	calorie breakdown
calories 102	% protein 29
g fat 4.5	% fat 36
g fibre 0.2	% carbohydrate 35

Barley

Barley is a tough grain. Each kernel has three layers of protection, all very fibrous. The refining process removes these husks, leaving the endosperm, which we call pot barley. If the barley is further steamed and polished, it is called pearl barley. Hulled barley, with only the outer husk removed, is the most nutritious form of the grain, but its fibrous texture and long cooking time reduces its appeal for most people.

Barley Pilaf

This dish can stand by itself as a meatless meal. It is an ideal dish to take to a pot luck supper and an excellent accompaniment to cold roasted meat. The wild rice adds colour and texture.

4 cups	broth (meat *or* vegetable)	1 L
1 tsp	celery seed	5 mL
1 tsp	salt (if broth unsalted)	5 mL
⅛ tsp	pepper	0.5 mL
½ tsp	dried thyme	2 mL
1 cup	pearl barley	250 mL
2 tbsp	wild rice (optional)	25 mL
1 tbsp	olive oil	15 mL
1	clove garlic, minced	1
½ cup	chopped celery	125 mL
½ cup	chopped green pepper	125 mL
1	medium onion, chopped	1
1 cup	sliced mushrooms	250 mL

In medium saucepan, bring broth to boil; add celery seed, salt, pepper, thyme, and barley. Reduce heat, cover and simmer 10 minutes. Stir in wild rice and continue to simmer 35 minutes, until barley is tender, adding boiling water as required to prevent burning. Drain off any remaining water. In medium skillet, heat oil and sauté garlic, celery, green pepper, onion, and mushrooms over medium heat 3 minutes. Stir vegetables into barley mixture. Taste and adjust seasonings. Serve hot.

May be made ahead, refrigerated, and reheated in the microwave.

Yield: 4 servings

per serving
calories 416
g fat 6.3
g fibre 6.6

calorie breakdown
% protein 18
% fat 13
% carbohydrate 69

Potato Scallop au Gratin

We all make potato scallop (scalloped potatoes is the heart of North America) but not many make this recipe. Marg shares her secret on this one.

1 tbsp	butter	15 mL
2 tbsp	all-purpose flour	25 mL
½ tsp	salt	2 mL
¼ tsp	pepper	1 mL
1 tsp	Dijon mustard	5 mL
1 cup	1% milk	250 mL
1 cup	low-fat cottage cheese	250 mL
4 cups	peeled, thinly sliced potatoes	1 L
1 cup	thinly sliced onions	250 mL
	chopped fresh parsley for garnish	

In the Microwave:

In 2 quart (2 L) casserole, microwave butter on high, 30 seconds, until melted. Work in flour, salt, pepper, and mustard. Gradually whisk in milk. Microwave on high 2½ to 3 minutes, stirring 2 or 3 times, until thick. Stir in cottage cheese; sauce will be lumpy. Toss potatoes and onions together and stir into sauce. Cover and vent casserole; microwave on high 15 to 18 minutes, until potatoes are cooked. Let stand 5 minutes. To serve, garnish with chopped parsley.

In the Oven:

In medium skillet, melt butter; work in flour, salt, pepper, and mustard. Gradually whisk in milk. Continue to cook and stir until thick. Add cottage cheese and remove from heat. In 2 quart (2 L) shallow casserole, layer potatoes and onions. Distribute sauce over potatoes. Bake, covered, in 350⁰F (180⁰C) oven 30 minutes. Remove cover and continue baking 30 minutes, until potatoes are tender. Garnish with chopped parsley.

Yield: 6 servings

per serving	calorie breakdown
calories 217	% protein 19
g fat 3.1	% fat 13
g fibre 3.1	% carbohydrate 68

Eggplant and Red Pepper Stir-Fry

This is a modern presentation of vegetables we have in our fall gardens thanks to scientists who developed early maturing varieties.

2 tsp	olive oil	10 mL
1	small eggplant, chopped	1
1	sweet red pepper, seeded and chopped	1
1	clove garlic, minced	1
pinch	black pepper	

In heavy skillet, heat oil and add vegetables, garlic, and black pepper. Stir-fry 1 minute. Reduce heat, cover, and steam 2 minutes. Serve hot.

Yield: 4 servings

Variations:
May substitute sweet green pepper or seeded tomato for sweet red pepper.

per serving	calorie breakdown
calories 35.1	% protein 6
g fat 2.4	% fat 56
g fibre 0.7	% carbohydrate 38

Vegetable Variety Awareness

Eggplant and red bell peppers are not unusual vegetables, yet they are not often on dinner plates. Here are other vegetables to grow and serve.
Celery root: a homely brown root vegetable that looks like a mis-shapen hairy turnip. The flesh is creamy white and has a nutty, celery taste. Shred for salad; slice thinly for relish tray; chop or cut in sticks to cook.
Jicama (hic-ah-muh): a globular brown-skinned tuber with crisp, sweet, juicy flesh. Common in Mexico and California, it is moving eastward. Shred for salad; slice for relish tray; substitute for water chestnuts.
Kohlrabi (coal-rob-ee) a German cabbage, it is actually a swollen stem with leaves jutting out on all sides. Kohlrabi has a mild turnip flavour and may be used in similar ways. The stems and leaves are tasty when cooked.
Salsify: Topped with leafy shoots, it looks like a thin parsnip covered with grassy sprouts. The shoots are good in salads; the roots may be used as parsnips or carrots.

RICE WITH CHICKEN (ARROZ CON POLLO)

Marg has enjoyed versions of this dish in every Latin American country visited. It's a meal in a pot, using ingredients available in any market.

3 lb	broiler chicken	1.5 kg
2 tbsp	oil	25 mL
2	cloves garlic, minced	2
1	large onion, sliced	1
1	green or red pepper, cut in strips	1
1	stalk celery, sliced	1
1 (19 oz) can	tomatoes, including juice	540 mL
1½ cups	chicken broth	375 mL
1 tsp	salt (if broth unsalted)	5 mL
¼ tsp	freshly ground pepper	1 mL
½ tsp	turmeric	2 mL
¼ tsp	ground cumin	1 mL
1 cup	long grained rice	250 mL
1 cup	frozen peas	250 mL
2 tbsp	finely chopped parsley	25 mL

Remove skin and visible fat from chicken. Cut into pieces (drumsticks, thighs, 4 breast pieces). Use back, neck, and wings to make broth. Heat oil in large, heavy saucepan. Add chicken and brown quickly on both sides. Remove chicken and sauté garlic, onion, pepper, and celery. Return chicken; add tomatoes, chicken broth, salt, pepper, turmeric, cumin, and rice. Bring to boil, reduce heat, cover and simmer 15 minutes. Add peas; cook 5 minutes longer, until chicken is cooked. Serve immediately, sprinkled with parsley.

Yield: 4 to 5 servings

per serving	calorie breakdown
calories 710	% protein 44
g fat 16.1	% fat 21
g fibre 3.6	% carbohydrate 35

MEXICAN RICE

A combination dish that turns a burrito or enchilada into dinner.

¾ cup	long grain *or* converted white rice	175 mL
1	small onion, chopped	1
1	clove garlic, minced	1
¼ cup	chopped green pepper	50 mL
½ tsp	salt	2 mL
¼ tsp	pepper	1 mL
½ cup	tomato juice	125 mL
1 cup	water	250 mL

Wash rice, drain, and place in 2 quart (2 L) casserole. Add onion, garlic, green pepper, salt, and pepper. In liquid measure, microwave tomato juice and water on high, 2 minutes or until hot. Pour over rice, stir to blend. Cover, vent and microwave on high 12 minutes, stirring once. Alternatively, cover and bake in 350°F (180°C) oven 40 minutes. Fluff with fork and serve.

Yield: 4 servings

per serving	**calorie breakdown**
calories 151	% protein 9
g fat 0.3	% fat 2
g fibre 1.5	% carbohydrate 89

TO MAKE CHICKEN BROTH

Place chicken back, neck, and wings in medium saucepan; add coarsely chopped, unpeeled carrots, broccoli stems, cabbage core, onion, celery leaves, bay leaf, and other herbs to taste. Cover with water and bring to boil; remove foam. Reduce heat, cover and simmer 1 hour. Strain and refrigerate. When cold, skim and discard solid fat.

Refried Bean Burritos

A tortilla filled with beans makes a low-calorie, low-fat, high-fibre main course food. Add too much cheese and it becomes high-calorie and high-fat, as well as high-fibre.

8	(6-inch/15 cm) flour tortillas	8
2 cups	refried beans (recipe follows)	500 mL
1 cup	grated Monterey Jack cheese	250 mL

On centre of each tortilla, spoon ¼ cup (50 mL) refried beans. Roll up and place seam side down in 9 x 13 inch (3.5 L) baking pan. Sprinkle with cheese. Bake in 350⁰F (180⁰C) oven 25 to 30 minutes to heat through and melt cheese. Serve with tomato salsa.

Yield: 8 burritos

Refried Beans:

2 cups	dried pinto beans	500 mL
2 tbsp	oil	25 mL
1	large onion, diced	1
1	jalapeño pepper, seeded and diced	1
2 tsp	ground cumin	10 mL
3	cloves garlic, minced	3
1 tsp	salt	5 mL
1 tsp	granulated sugar	5 mL
½ tsp	pepper	2 mL
5	drops hot pepper sauce	5
1 can	(5½ oz) tomato paste	156 mL
¼ cup	water	50 mL

Wash beans and soak overnight in 6 cups (1.5 L) tepid water.* Drain, cover with fresh water, and simmer 2 hours, until tender.** Drain. In large, heavy skillet, heat oil and sauté onion 1 minute. Add drained pinto beans and remaining ingredients. Simmer, stirring frequently, until beans have absorbed sauce. Extra water may be required to keep beans moist. Taste and adjust seasonings. Store in refrigerator. Freezes well.

*May use short soak method from Ross's Cowboy Beans, see page 95.

**Alternatively, on rack in pressure cooker, cook 25 minutes under 15 pounds pressure.

Yield: about 4 cups

per burrito	**calorie breakdown**
calories 277	% protein 17
g fat 2.7	% fat 9
g fibre 6.5	% carbohydrate 75

Tomato Salsa:

3	large tomatoes, peeled, seeded, and chopped	3
4	green onions, sliced	4
¼ cup	sweet green pepper, diced	50 mL
1	clove garlic, minced	1
1 tbsp	lemon or lime juice	15 mL
pinch	granulated sugar	
2 tbsp	chopped fresh coriander	25 mL
	hot peppers to taste (jalapeño)	

Combine ingredients. Store covered in refrigerator.

Yield: about 1 cup (250 mL)

per 2 tablespoons salsa	**calorie breakdown**
calories 28	% protein 14
g fat 0.4	% fat 10
g fibre 1.7	% carbohydrate 76

Lamb Marrakesh

Everyone wants the leg and the chops. This means the shoulder of lamb,
which is just as flavourful, is left. Use it to make this hearty Moroccan meal.

3 lb	lamb shoulder (*or* 1.5 to 2 lb boneless)	1.4 kg
½ cup	seedless raisins	125 mL
¼ cup	sherry	50 mL
1 tbsp	oil	15 mL
2	onions, sliced	2
2	cloves garlic, minced	2
1 (28 oz) can	plum tomatoes	796 mL
1 tsp	ground cumin	5 mL
¼ tsp	cayenne	1 mL
¼ tsp	cinnamon	1 mL
½ tsp	allspice	2 mL
½ tsp	dried coriander	2 mL
¼ tsp	dried tarragon	1 mL

Separate meat from bone, remove all visible fat, and cut into 1-inch (2 cm)
cubes. In small bowl, combine raisins and sherry. In large, heavy saucepan,
heat oil, sauté onion and garlic 1 minute. Add lamb and sauté 2 minutes,
until brown. Add tomatoes (including liquid), spices, herbs, and raisin
mixture. Bring to boil, scraping to loosen bits. Cover, reduce heat and
simmer 1 hour. Taste and adjust seasoning. Serve with rice, pasta, or
couscous.

Yield: 4 to 5 servings

To Cook in Slow Cooker:
Use skillet to brown meat, etc.; transfer to slow cooker. Cook on high until
mixture starts to simmer, reduce heat and cook covered, 2 hours.

per serving	**calorie breakdown**
calories 360	% protein 38
g fat 13.5	% fat 34
g fibre 3.4	% carbohydrate 28

Stuffed Pork Loin with Applesauce Glaze

Marg's butcher knew whenever she taught this recipe to her gourmet cooking class because he would get a flood of requests to remove the bone from pork loins.

| 3 lb | pork loin butt roast (bone removed) | 1.35 kg |

Prune Stuffing:

½ cup	chopped prunes	125 mL
2 tbsp	red wine *or* apple juice	25 mL
1 cup	bread crumbs	250 mL
1	small apple, peeled, cored, and diced	1
¼ cup	diced onion	50 mL
½ tsp	salt	2 mL
dash	pepper	
½ tsp	dried sage	2 mL

Applesauce Glaze:

½ cup	applesauce	125 mL
1 tsp	dry mustard	5 mL
¼ tsp	cloves	1 mL

Pour wine or apple juice over prunes. Combine remaining ingredients for stuffing; add soaked prunes, mix well. Slit meat if necessary to make it lie flat; spread stuffing evenly down centre of meat. Roll and tie firmly with string at 2-inch (5 cm) intervals. Place roast on rack in shallow roasting pan. Insert meat thermometer. Roast, uncovered, in 325°F (160°C) oven until thermometer reads 140°F (60°C). Blend applesauce, mustard, and cloves. Spread on roast and continue roasting until thermometer reads 165°F (75°C). Allow meat to rest 15 minutes before carving. Remove strings and carve. To keep stuffing intact, serve with wide, flat spatula.

Yield: 10 servings

per serving	calorie breakdown
calories 254	% protein 49
g fat 8.2	% fat 30
g fibre 1.4	% carbohydrate 21

RATATOUILLE

Standard fare along the Mediterranean Sea, ratatouille became a popular vegetarian dish in our homes after we ate it in Greek restaurants. We like this version made in layers and baked in the oven. For a quick family supper, make it on top of the stove.

1 tbsp	olive oil	15 mL
1	small eggplant, sliced ⅜ inch (1 cm) thick	1
2	small zucchini, sliced ⅜ inch (1 cm) thick	2
1	large onion, sliced	1
2	cloves garlic, minced	2
1	sweet red or green pepper, seeded, and sliced	1
2	large tomatoes, peeled, seeded, and chopped	2
8	mushrooms, sliced	8
1 tbsp	chopped fresh basil *or* ½ tsp (2 mL) dried	15 mL
1 tbsp	chopped fresh thyme *or* ½ tsp (2 mL) dried	15 mL
½ tsp	salt	2 mL
¼ tsp	pepper	1 mL

Spread half of oil in 9-inch (2.5 L) baking dish or casserole and layer half the eggplant, zucchini, onion, garlic, red pepper, tomatoes, mushrooms, and seasonings. Repeat with second layer of everything. Sprinkle with remaining oil. Cover and bake in 350°F (180°C) oven 1 hour. Serve hot or cold.

Stovetop method: Coarsely chop vegetables, combine with oil and seasonings in heavy saucepan. Cover and simmer 20 minutes, until fork tender.

Yield: 6 servings

per serving	calorie breakdown
calories 66	% protein 11
g fat 2.8	% fat 34
g fibre 2.5	% carbohydrate 55

Broccoli Amandine

Broccoli, dressed up and determined to please, even for the person who says, "No more broccoli."

1	small stalk fresh broccoli	1
1 tbsp	butter	15 mL
2	green onions, thinly sliced	2
2 tbsp	slivered almonds, toasted	25 mL
2 tbsp	lemon juice	25 mL
⅛ tsp	salt	0.5 mL
⅛ tsp	pepper	0.5 mL

Wash broccoli in cold water. Trim off heavy stalks.* Cut lengthwise through remaining stem up to flower buds to hasten cooking. Place in steamer over boiling water. Cover, reduce heat, and steam 5 minutes, until tender crisp. Drain and keep warm. Meanwhile, in a small skillet, melt butter, add onions and almonds; stir over medium heat until nutty brown, 2 minutes. Add lemon juice, salt, and pepper. Serve over hot broccoli.

*Reserve heavy stalks to peel, chop, and add to stir-fries and soups.

Yield: 4 servings

per serving	**calorie breakdown**
calories 65	% protein 15
g fat 4.6	% fat 57
g fibre 2.0	% carbohydrate 28

Roasted Half Turkey with Spratt Dressing

For small families, this is an excellent way to have Thanksgiving turkey with both dark and light meat, and still have some for plan-overs. Ask your butcher to cut the bird in half. Wrap one half well, label with date and weight, and freeze. Marg's mom was a Spratt, one of a family of thirteen. The recipe for "Spratt dressing" (not stuffing) has been handed down for at least four generations. Of course we had to take out the large slice of butter. Grandma Spratt, a dairy farmer, would not be pleased.

½	broiler turkey (half wt 5 lb)*	2.5 kg
1 tbsp	oil	15 mL
½ tsp	dry mustard	2 mL
½ tsp	Worcestershire sauce	2 mL

Dressing:

1 tbsp	oil	15 mL
1	small onion, diced	1
3 cups	day-old bread cubes	750 mL
½ cup	raisins	125 mL
2 tbsp	dried summer savoury	25 mL
¼ tsp	salt	1 mL
⅛ tsp	pepper	0.5 mL

*see page 225

Rinse turkey with cold water, drain well. Place on rack, skin side up, in shallow roasting pan. Skewer leg to tail and wing flat against breast. Combine oil, mustard, and Worcestershire sauce; brush over both sides of turkey. Insert meat thermometer into middle of thick thigh muscle (parallel to but not touching bone) and next to body. Make a foil tent (dull side out) and place loosely over turkey. Roast in 325⁰F (160⁰C) oven 1 hour. Meanwhile, prepare dressing. In small skillet, heat oil, sauté onion 2 minutes. In a medium bowl, combine bread cubes, raisins, savoury, salt, pepper, and onion mixture. Cut 12-inch (30 cm) square of foil. Remove turkey from oven and rack; place foil on rack, shiny side up, poke a few holes with fork so juices will run through. Mound on sufficient dressing to fill cavity. Place turkey over dressing. Replace foil tent, return to oven and continue cooking until meat thermometer reads 185°F (90°C), about 1 hour. Baste several times. Remove foil tent if not browning well. When done, remove and let rest 15 minutes before carving. Place dressing in serving dish and keep hot.

Gravy:

For those who must have it! Drain drippings from roasting pan into liquid measure, let settle, skim fat and discard. Return drippings to pan. Sprinkle with 2 tablespoons (25 mL) flour; stir over medium heat until blended and bubbling. Add 1 cup (250 mL) turkey broth, vegetable cooking water, or water. Stir and scrape pan to deglaze, cooking until smooth and thick. Taste and adjust seasoning. If too thick, add more liquid.

Yield: 8 servings

Note:

While small turkeys require about 25 minutes roasting time per pound, large turkeys need only 20 minutes per pound. Basted birds tend to roast more quickly.

per serving (no skin, with stuffing)
calories 348
g fat 9.8
g fibre 0.6

calorie breakdown
% protein 53
% fat 26
% carbohydrate 22

per serving (with skin and stuffing)
calories 476
g fat 21.8
g fibre 0.6

calorie breakdown
% protein 42
% fat 42
% carbohydrate 16

COOKING POULTRY—WITH OR WITHOUT SKIN?

The reduction in fat from cooking chicken or turkey without the skin is small, according to a recent pilot study reported in the *Journal of the American Dietetic Association*. The results support the theory that poultry fat does not migrate between cells. Cooking poultry with the skin on does reduce cooking time and increase moisture retention. Author Ellen Chambers Hurley concluded that one way to make low-fat diets pleasurable is to cook poultry with the skin on and remove it before serving. The difficult part is discarding that attractive, crispy skin.

GARLIC MASHED POTATOES

Garlic has a 5000-year history as a food and as a cure for everything from depression to cancer and cardiovascular disease. What is not so well known is that the longer you cook it, the milder and sweeter it becomes, as in this potato dish. If its the sharper, pungent quality of garlic you desire, eat it raw.

4	medium potatoes, peeled	4
2	cloves garlic	2
⅓ cup	1% milk	75 mL
½	tsp salt	2 mL
⅛	tsp pepper	0.5 mL
¼	cup breadcrumbs	50 mL
1 tbsp	butter (optional)	15 mL

Cut potatoes and garlic in half and add to 1 inch (2 cm) boiling water in medium saucepan. Return to boil, cover, reduce heat, and simmer until potatoes are easily pierced with fork. Drain, return to warm element to dry off. Add milk, salt, and pepper. Mash potatoes and garlic, adding more milk if necessary and whip until light and fluffy. Taste and adjust seasoning. Spoon into lightly oiled 6-cup (1.5 L) baking dish. Sprinkle with bread crumbs and dot with butter. Bake, uncovered in 350ºF (180ºC) oven 15 minutes or until hot. *Or* refrigerate up to 3 days and reheat in oven, covered for 15 minutes, then uncovered for 15 minutes or until hot. Alternatively, reheat in microwave on high for 12 to 15 minutes.

Yield: 4 servings

per serving
calories 166
g fat 0.6
g fibre 2.6

calorie breakdown
% protein 12
% fat 3
% carbohydrate 85

The Merit of Potatoes

There's nothing wrong with pasta, rice, or couscous. But there are a lot of things right about a potato on the dinner plate. A potato is full of nutrients, including a small amount of readily digestible protein. It is a good source of Vitamin C (ascorbic acid). Potato skin provides fibre. The carbohydrate in a potato is complex; it makes you feel full and satisfied. All are reasons why a potato is a good food for every age, from toddler to teenager to senior. Our meals include a great number of potato dishes, representative of the Maritimes' largest agricultural crop.

To Buy, Store, and Cook Potatoes

Because we cook potatoes so frequently, we feel it's important to do it well. Select potatoes that have been protected from light. In food stores this means potatoes stored in areas protected from fluorescent lights, preferably in paper bags. It prevents them from "greening"—developing a greenish colour near the skin which tastes bitter. It follows that at home potatoes require a dry, dark storage location. Short-term storage under the kitchen sink is all right; longer term storage demands a cooler, dark location. Refrigerator temperature is too cold; it turns the potato starch to sugar. Wash potatoes just before preparing them. To remove only a thin layer of skin, use a vegetable peeler. Certain nutrients are lost by soaking potatoes in cold water or cooking in a large quantity of water. To boil potatoes, place in saucepan containing 1 inch of boiling water. Cut larger potatoes to make even-sized pieces. To rush-cook them, put a saucepan with water on to boil while you microwave the potatoes on high for 3 minutes. You can rush-bake potatoes in the same manner. While the oven is pre-heating, micro-wave a pair of scrubbed, pricked bakers for 4 minutes. It cuts baking time in half. Pre-baking 4 potatoes in the microwave will take 7 minutes. If potatoes are varied in size, microwave larger ones first.

Easy Squash Cookery

The easiest way to cook a winter squash is to microwave it. It cooks quickly and you avoid all that difficult chopping and peeling.

For a squash of approximately 1 pound (450 g), scrub, pierce with a fork, and place on a plate or rack. Microwave on high for 6 to 8 minutes, rotating if required. Rest for 5 minutes, cut into wedges, remove and discard seeds, and serve.

Larger winter squash may be halved or sectioned. Remove and discard seeds, place on tray or rack, skin side up; cover loosely and microwave on high, testing at 8 minutes and then every 3 minutes until done. For mashed squash, scrape flesh away from skin, put into bowl, and mash.

TURKEY CREOLE

Cajun Creole may not be maritime, but this Louisiana style cooking is based on a mixture of Acadian, German, and Spanish influences and blends meats, fruits, and vegetables. Throw away those turkey casserole recipes calling for creamed sauces and canned soups.

1 tbsp	oil	15 mL
1	medium onion, coarsely chopped	1
1	stalk celery, sliced	1
1	clove garlic, minced	1
1	small sweet green pepper, chopped	1
2 cups	chopped tomatoes (fresh tomatoes, peeled and seeded or canned tomatoes, seeded)	500 mL
½ tsp	dried thyme	2 mL
1	bay leaf	1
½ tsp	salt	2 mL
dash	cayenne (¼ tsp/1 mL for mild burn)	
2 cups	cooked turkey, cut into bite-size pieces	500 mL
6	mushrooms, sliced	6
1 tbsp	cornstarch	15 mL
2 tbsp	water	25 mL
2 tbsp	chopped fresh parsley	25 mL

In large saucepan, heat oil; sauté onion, celery, and garlic, 2 minutes. Add green pepper, tomatoes, thyme, bay leaf, salt, and cayenne. Cover and simmer 15 minutes. Add turkey and mushrooms; return to boil. Remove and discard bay leaf. Combine cornstarch and water; add to Creole and simmer, stirring, 1 minute. Serve over steamed rice garnished with parsley.

Yield: 4 to 5 servings

Variation: substitute leftover fish for the turkey.

per serving	calorie breakdown
calories 213	% protein 46
g fat 7.7	% fat 32
g fibre 2.6	% carbohydrate 22

CITRUS SALMON

Aquaculture is the strongest, most productive and financially viable segment of the east coast fishery. To date, salmon is the most successful species being farmed. Cages anchored in tidal waters and cottage industries that produce smoked and processed foods are an example of what the future may hold for other species.

½ cup	dry red wine*	125 mL
¼ cup	orange juice	50 mL
¼ cup	fresh lime juice (*or* juice of 1 lime)	50 mL
½ tsp	sugar	2 mL
1 tsp	fresh tarragon, chopped *or* ½ tsp (2 mL) dried	5 mL
2	salmon fillets (½ lb/250 g)	2
1	leek, cut into ¼-inch (0.5 cm) slices	1
2	tangerines, peeled, sectioned	2

* Use white wine if you don't have a bottle of red open.

In a shallow, stovetop-safe casserole, combine wine, orange juice, lime juice, sugar, and tarragon. Lay salmon fillets in marinade and refrigerate 1 hour. Remove salmon, add leek to casserole, bring to boil, reduce heat and simmer, covered, 10 minutes, taking care liquid does not evaporate. Lay salmon on top of leeks and simmer 5 to 10 minutes, until fish is opaque. Add tangerine sections and heat through. With wide spatula, carefully transfer to hot plates; pour sauce over. Serve immediately.

Yield: 2 servings

per serving	**calorie breakdown**
calories 278	% protein 44
g fat 8.2	% fat 31
g fibre 1.1	% carbohydrate 25

CRAN-APPLE COMPOTE

As a fruit compote with pancakes, a topping for vanilla yogurt,
or a sauce with a whole grain roll, this simple recipe offers sparkling flavour.

1½ cups	cranberries, fresh or frozen	375 mL
¾ cup	water	175 mL
4	apples, peeled, cored, and cut in eighths	4
¾ cup	granulated sugar	175 mL

In medium saucepan, cook cranberries and water until skins burst. Blend or process to make smooth purée. Put sliced apples in same saucepan, cover with sugar and cranberry sauce. Over medium heat, simmer gently until apples are translucent and have absorbed liquid. Serve warm or cold. Keeps in refrigerator 2 weeks.

Yield: 6 servings

per serving
calories 155
g fat 0.3
g fibre 2.7

calorie breakdown
% protein 1
% fat 2
% carbohydrate 98

Gwen's Raisin Squares

This is a nice variation on date squares, not as sweet but just as tasty.

1½ cups	raisins	375 mL
¾ cup	orange juice	175 mL
⅓ cup	granulated sugar	75 mL
1 tsp	cinnamon	5 mL
1 tsp	nutmeg	5 mL
2 tbsp	flour	25 mL
1 cup	lightly packed brown sugar	250 mL
⅔ cup	butter or soft margarine	150 mL
2 cups	quick cooking oats	500 mL
1 cup	whole wheat flour	250 mL

In small saucepan, heat raisins and orange juice. Blend sugar, spices, and flour and stir into hot raisin mixture. Cook over medium heat, stirring constantly until thick. Set aside to cool.

In medium bowl, with pastry blender or fingers, blend brown sugar, butter, oats, and flour. Pack half in 9-inch (2.5 L) square cake pan. Spread raisin mixture over, cover with remaining crumb mixture, and press lightly. Bake in 350^{0}F (180^{0}C) oven 30 minutes, until brown on top. Cool pan on wire rack. These freeze well.

Yield: 25 squares

per square	calorie breakdown
calories 159	% protein 5
g fat 4.5	% fat 24
g fibre 1.8	% carbohydrate 70

Rice and Raisin Pudding

There are oodles of rice pudding recipes, few of which meet the test. Rice pudding must contain cooked rice and soft raisins, must have a satin smooth sauce, and must taste of cinnamon and vanilla.

¼ cup	granulated sugar	50 mL
1 tbsp	cornstarch	15 mL
1½ cups	1% milk	375 mL
1 cup	(more or less) cooked rice	250 mL
2 tbsp	raisins	25 mL
1-inch	cinnamon stick	2.5 cm
1	egg	1
½ tsp	pure vanilla extract	2 mL

In medium saucepan, blend sugar and cornstarch. Stir in 1¼ cups (325 mL) milk, rice, raisins, and cinnamon stick. Cook over medium heat, stirring constantly until mixture thickens, 4 to 5 minutes. Remove from heat. In liquid measure, combine remaining ¼ cup (50 mL) milk and egg. Stir some hot pudding into egg; then egg mixture into pudding. Return to medium heat and stir constantly for 1 minute to cook egg. Remove from heat; add vanilla. Pour into serving dish, cover and cool. Remove cinnamon stick before serving.

Yield: 4 servings

per serving
calories 156
g fat 1.2
g fibre .4

calorie breakdown
% protein 11
% fat 7
% carbohydrate 82

PEAR GINGERBREAD

*Along the Atlantic seaboard, centuries of trade with the West Indies assured a
steady supply of molasses, used as the everyday sweetener for breads and desserts.*

Topping:

1 tbsp	butter, melted	15 mL
¼ cup	brown sugar	50 mL
2 tbsp	preserved ginger, finely chopped	25 mL
4	firm ripe pears, peeled and sliced	4

Gingerbread:

¼ cup	soft margarine	50 mL
¼ cup	lightly packed brown sugar	50 mL
1	egg	1
½ cup	molasses	125 mL
¾ cup	all-purpose flour	175 mL
½ cup	whole wheat flour	125 mL
1 tsp	baking soda	5 mL
1 tsp	cinnamon	5 mL
1 tsp	ground ginger	5 mL
⅓ cup	hot water	75 mL

Spread butter in 9-inch (2.5 L) square baking pan; sprinkle with brown
sugar and ginger. Cover with overlapping rows of pear slices. In medium
bowl, cream margarine and brown sugar; beat in egg and molasses until
batter is light. Combine flours, baking soda, cinnamon, and ginger. Add to
molasses mixture alternately with hot water, beginning and ending with
flour, stirring after each addition. Spoon batter over pears. Bake in 350⁰F
(180⁰C) oven 30 to 40 minutes, until centre springs back when touched.
Cool on rack 10 minutes; then invert on serving plate. Serve warm or cold.

Yield: 12 servings

per serving	**calorie breakdown**
calories 189	% protein 5
g fat 4.9	% fat 22
g fibre 2.6	% carbohydrate 73

CRANBERRY COBBLER

A cobbler could successfully be baked in the makeshift ovens of yesteryear. So long as you could get it hot at the outset, the biscuit would rise and then the oven could not ruin the dessert. Cranberry makes a tart cobbler. However, rhubarb, raspberry, cherry, blueberry, or any combination of these fruits makes a tasty cobbler.

1 (12 oz) pkg	cranberries, fresh or frozen	340 g
1½ cups	water	375 mL
¾ cup	granulated sugar	175 mL
1 tsp	soft margarine	5 mL

Topping:

½ cup	all-purpose flour	125 mL
½ cup	whole wheat flour	125 mL
2 tsp	baking powder	10 mL
¼ cup	granulated sugar	50 mL
2 tbsp	soft margarine	25 mL
½ cup	raisins	125 mL
½ cup	1% milk	125 mL

In medium saucepan, combine cranberries, water, and sugar; cook until skins burst, about 5 minutes. Remove, stir in margarine and transfer to 2 quart (2 L) shallow baking dish.

To prepare topping, in medium bowl, combine flours, baking powder, and sugar. Cut in margarine; and stir in raisins. Add milk, mix only to moisten. Drop by large spoonfuls on cranberry mixture. Bake in 350°F (180°C) oven 30 minutes, until topping is golden brown and cooked through. Serve warm.

Yield: 8 servings

per serving	**calorie breakdown**
calories 244	% protein 5
g fat 3.3	% fat 12
g fibre 3.4	% carbohydrate 84

Apple Squares

Great for dessert, a box lunch, or after school break, this recipe can be doubled to provide some for the freezer.

1 cup	whole wheat flour	250 mL
2 tsp	baking powder	10 mL
1 tsp	cinnamon	5 mL
½ tsp	nutmeg	2 mL
1 cup	lightly packed brown sugar	250 mL
¼ cup	oil	50 mL
1	egg	1
2	medium apples	2
½ cup	chopped nuts	125 mL

In medium bowl, combine flour, baking powder, cinnamon, nutmeg, and brown sugar. Put oil and egg in blender or food processor. Peel, core, and quarter apples; add to oil and egg. Pulse to finely chop apple. Pour into dry ingredients, add nuts, and stir to combine. Spread in oiled 9-inch (2.5 L) square baking pan. Bake in 350⁰F (180⁰C) oven 35 minutes, until centre springs back when touched. Serve warm or cold.

Yield: 20 servings

per serving
calories 122
g fat 4.6
g fibre 1.5

calorie breakdown
% protein 7
% fat 32
% carbohydrate 61

Fruit Desserts

Overly sweet desserts of the past needed whipped cream or ice cream to cut the sweetness. Increasing the fruit and decreasing the sugar negates the need to add topping.

Wine Poached Pears

With improved storage facilities, Bartlett pears have become a staple fall and winter fruit. They grow in many parts of the country and are a specialty of the Annapolis Valley of Nova Scotia.

½ cup	dry red wine	125 mL
¼ cup	brown sugar	50 mL
8	whole cloves	8
2	large pears	2

In skillet large enough to hold 4 pear halves in a single layer, combine wine, sugar, and cloves. Cut pears in half (do not peel); remove stem and core. Make 4 or 5 fanlike slits through bulb of each pear half, carefully spreading each slit slightly. Over medium heat, warm sauce to dissolve sugar, add pears, cut side down, and simmer for 5 minutes, basting frequently. Transfer pears to dessert plates and reduce sauce by half. Remove cloves and pour sauce around pears. Serve hot or cold.

Yield: 4 servings

per serving	**calorie breakdown**
calories 108	% protein 2
g fat 0.4	% fat 4
g fibre 2.6	% carbohydrate 95

MOLLY'S POMPADOUR PUDDING

Donna's mother-in-law was famous for this blancmange pudding with chocolate floating island. It is a sophisticated pudding compared to the milk and Irish moss desserts made by early settlers. The moss is still harvested from tidal waters. It is dried in the autumn sun for processing into a nourishing, vegetarian gelatin used as a commercial thickening agent.

2 cups	1% milk	500 mL
¼ cup	granulated sugar	50 mL
3 tbsp	cornstarch	45 mL
pinch	salt	
1	egg yolk	1
½ tsp	vanilla	2 mL
2 tsp	butter	10 mL

Topping:

2	egg whites	2
¼ cup	granulated sugar	50 mL
2 tsp	cocoa	10 mL

In medium-sized, heavy saucepan over medium heat, bring 1½ cups (375 mL) milk to near boiling. In liquid measure, combine sugar, cornstarch, salt, and remaining ½ cup (125 mL) milk. Whisk into hot milk and cook over low heat, stirring constantly until mixture thickens. Remove from heat. Whisk egg yolk; stir some hot pudding into egg yolk, then whisk yolk mixture into hot pudding. Return to low heat, stir 1 minute to cook yolk. Remove, add vanilla and butter; pour into 1 quart (1 L) casserole.

For topping, beat egg whites until soft peaks form. Blend sugar and cocoa; gradually beat into egg whites, 1 spoonful at a time, beating until stiff peaks form. Spoon on pudding and bake in 325°F (160°C) oven 20 minutes, until meringue sets and browns. Serve warm or cold.

Yield: 4 servings

per serving	**calorie breakdown**
calories 223	% protein 125
g fat 4.8	% fat 19
g fibre 0.4	% carbohydrate 69

Apple Dumplings

During Donna's first year in the Maritimes, a rural homemaker served this dessert to her family and to her. The family made no comment; Donna thought she'd died and gone to heaven. This version has one third as much fat and sugar, but we guarantee it's just as delightful.

½ cup	all-purpose flour	125 mL
1 tsp	baking powder	5 mL
⅛ tsp	salt	0.5 mL
2 tbsp	cold soft margarine	25 mL
3 tbsp	1% milk	45 mL
2	apples, peeled, halved, and cored	2
1 tsp	cinnamon	5 mL

Sauce:

¾ cup	apple cider or juice	175 mL
¼ cup	brown sugar	50 mL
1 tbsp	butter	15 mL
¼ tsp	cinnamon	1 mL

In medium bowl, combine flour, baking powder, and salt. Cut in margarine until size of small peas. Using fork, stir in milk only to moisten. Press dough into ball and place on floured surface. Roll to make a 12-inch (30 cm) square, thin sheet of pastry. Cut into four 6-inch (15 cm) squares, patching if necessary. Place apple halves, cavity up, on squares. Sprinkle with cinnamon. Dampen edges of pastry and pull around apple halves, pressing edges to seal. Place with folded edges down, in 8-inch (2 L) square baking pan.

In liquid measure, combine sauce ingredients; microwave on high until bubbly hot, about 1½ minutes. Pour over dumplings and bake in 350⁰F (180⁰C) oven 40 minutes. Serve warm. May be reheated.

Yield: 4 generous servings

per serving	**calorie breakdown**
calories 239	% protein 4
g fat 8.0	% fat 29
g fibre 1.9	% carbohydrate 67

RASPBERRY RHUBARB CRUMBLE

This is a special dessert that brings July to your table all year.

2 cups	finely chopped frozen rhubarb	500 mL
1 pkg	(2 cups) unsweetened frozen raspberries	425 g
⅓ cup	granulated sugar	75 mL
2 tbsp	all-purpose flour	25 mL
1 cup	whole wheat flour	250 mL
1 cup	brown sugar	250 mL
pinch	salt	
⅓ cup	butter	75 mL
¼ tsp	nutmeg	1 mL

Layer fruit in shallow 2 qt (2 L) casserole. Combine granulated sugar and all-purpose flour; sprinkle over fruit. In food processor or with pastry blender, combine whole wheat flour, brown sugar, salt, and butter. Sprinkle evenly over fruit, pack lightly and bake in 350⁰F (180⁰C) oven 40 minutes. Serve warm.

Yield: 8 servings

per serving	**calorie breakdown**
calories 324	% protein 4
g fat 7.4	% fat 20
g fibre 5.2	% carbohydrate 77

Mom Signer's Pumpkin Pie

This recipe started in Donna's mother's kitchen but has evolved so that she may no longer recognize it. We think it's a winner; afterall, anything made with a vegetable, milk, and eggs has much nutritive value.

1	(9-inch/23 cm) unbaked pastry crust*	1
¾ cup	brown sugar	175 mL
2 cups	canned pumpkin	500 mL
½ tsp	cinnamon	2 mL
½ tsp	nutmeg	2 mL
¼ tsp	cloves	1 mL
¼ tsp	allspice	1 mL
3	eggs	3
1 cup	evaporated skimmed milk	250 mL

**see page 42

For a more attractive pie, flute pastry edge. Refrigerate pastry crust while preparing filling. In blender or food processor, combine all filling ingredients; process until smooth. Pour into pastry shell. Bake in 425°F (220°C) oven 15 minutes. Reduce heat to 325°F (160°C) and bake 45 to 50 minutes longer, until top loses stickiness when touched with dry finger.

Yield: 8 servings

Variations: For a larger pie, add an extra ½ cup (125 mL) pumpkin and bake in 10-inch (25 cm) pastry shell. Serves 10.For special Thanksgiving pie, place plain yogurt in small funnel, keeping index finger over bottom. Centre over uncooked pie; allowing a thin stream to flow, rotate funnel in spiral manner making concentric circles. Take a sharp knife and pull across top of pie from centre to edge at 3, 6, 9, and 12 o'clock positions. Reverse direction of knife and make shallow markings between each line from edge to centre of pie. When baked you will have a weblike pattern.

per serving	calorie breakdown
calories 277	% protein 12
g fat 8.6	% fat 28
g fibre 1.9	% carbohydrate 60

CHERRY GALETTES

Sour cherries are a special crop of the Annapolis Valley. They are synonymous with cherry pie. Galettes offer an alternative dessert that's just as tasty and more attractive.

2	egg whites	2
⅓ cup	icing sugar	75 mL
¼ cup	quick cooking oats	50 mL
¼ cup	all-purpose flour	50 mL
2 tbsp	butter, melted and cooled	25 mL

Filling:

2 tbsp	granulated sugar	25 mL
1 tbsp	cornstarch	15 mL
⅓ cup	water	75 mL
1 cup	frozen sour cherries	250 mL
1 tbsp	kirsch or other cherry liqueur (optional)	15 mL

Line a baking sheet with parchment or brown paper. Beat egg whites until frothy. Gradually add icing sugar, beating until stiff peaks form. Fold in oats and flour. Drizzle butter over batter; fold in. Drop batter by teaspoonfuls on covered baking sheet, 4 inches (10 cm) apart. With thin metal spatula spread batter to make 3-inch (7 cm) circles, ¼ inch (0.5 cm) thick. Bake in 400°F (200°C) oven 5 to 6 minutes until golden brown at edges. Let rest 1 minute. With thin, metal spatula, loosen galettes and transfer to wire rack to cool. Reuse same paper for remaining batter. Store in sealed container or freeze. Makes about 15 galettes.

For filling: In small saucepan, blend sugar and cornstarch. Over medium heat, stir in water and cook, stirring constantly until mixture thickens. Remove from heat and fold in cherries and kirsch.

To assemble: Spoon filling between layers of 3 galettes; top with cherry from filling and lightly dust with icing sugar.

Yield: 2 servings

per serving	calorie breakdown
calories 227	% protein 6
g fat 4.5	% fat 19
g fibre 1.5	% carbohydrate 75

LEMON BREAD

The "queen" of fruit breads, reserved for afternoon tea; lemon bread is higher in fat than other sweet breads. Do use a big fresh lemon.

¼ cup	butter	50 mL
¾ cup	granulated sugar	175 mL
2	eggs	2
1½ cups	all-purpose flour	375 mL
1 tsp	baking powder	5 mL
½ cup	1% milk	125 mL
1	lemon, grated rind	1

Topping:

1	lemon, juice of	1
¼ cup	granulated sugar	50 mL

In medium bowl, cream butter and sugar until fluffy. Beat in eggs, one at a time. Sift together flour and baking powder. Reduce speed, add half the flour to creamed mixture, then milk and remaining flour. Fold in lemon rind. Turn into oiled 8 x 4 x 2½ inch (1.5 L) loaf pan. Let rest 15 minutes. Invert another pan over top and bake in 325⁰F (160⁰C) oven 30 minutes. Remove inverted pan and bake 25 to 30 minutes, until toothpick inserted in centre comes out clean. Mix lemon juice and sugar, drizzle over top of hot bread. Cool on wire rack 15 minutes before removing from pan. Store in refrigerator or freezer.

Yield: 16 slices

per slice
calories 126
g fat 3.3
g fibre 0.4

calorie breakdown
% protein 7
% fat 23
% carbohydrate 70

Opposite *(clockwise from centre bottom): Broccoli Amandine (page 155), Roasted Half Turkey with Spratt Dressing (page 156), Debbie's Cranberry Chutney (page 182), Microwaved Squash (page 159), Garlic Mashed Potatoes (page 158); Mom Signer's Pumpkin Pie (page 172); Filled Poached Pears (page 129).*

MARITIME TEA BISCUITS

Old-fashioned tea biscuit recipes contain ¾ cup (175 mL) of butter and 2½ cups (625 mL) of flour. Some cooks think that much butter is required to make a biscuit flaky and tender; not true. The flakiness and tenderness result from using proper method.

2 cups	all-purpose flour*	500 mL
1 tbsp	granulated sugar (optional)	15 mL
2 tsp	cream of tartar	10 mL
1 tsp	baking soda	5 mL
½ tsp	salt	2 mL
¼ cup	cold butter	50 mL
¾ cup	1% milk	175 mL

*May use half (1 cup/250 mL) whole wheat flour

In medium bowl, combine flour, sugar, cream of tartar, baking soda, and salt. With pastry blender or two knives, cut in butter to size of small peas. Gradually add milk, stirring with fork, and adding only enough to moisten. (Don't over mix.) Turn on floured surface, form dough into a ball and knead 5 times. Using rolling pin, flatten to 1-inch (2 cm) thick round. Cut into 1½ inch (4 cm) square or round biscuits. Place on baking sheet and bake in 400°F (200°C) oven 12 to 15 minutes, until golden brown. Remove and cool on wire rack.

Yield: 20 small biscuits

per biscuit	**calorie breakdown**
calories 72	% protein 9
g fat 2.2	% fat 27
g fibre 0.4	% carbohydrate 63

Opposite *(clockwise from centre bottom): Pear Gingerbread (page 165); Raspberry Rhubarb Crumble (page 171); Strawberry Parfait (page 49); Apple Dumpling (page 170); Cranberry Cobbler (page 166).*

MOLASSES DROP COOKIES

To live anywhere in eastern Canada is to make and eat molasses cookies. From rolled to dropped to refrigerated sliced to ginger and brandy snaps, the cookies are sweetened with molasses. We were delighted to find one that met our guidelines. Originally, the recipe would have listed lard.

2 tsp	baking soda	10 mL
½ cup	sour milk	125 mL
1 cup	soft margarine	250 mL
⅔ cup	brown sugar	150 mL
1½ cups	molasses	375 mL
2	eggs	2
2 cups	all-purpose flour	500 mL
2 tsp	ground ginger	10 mL
2 tsp	cinnamon	10 mL
2 cups	whole wheat flour	500 mL

Add soda to sour milk; set aside. In medium bowl, beat margarine, brown sugar, molasses, and eggs until smooth and fluffy. Blend in all-purpose flour, ginger, and cinnamon. Add milk mixture, then whole wheat flour; mix well. Drop by tablespoonful 2 inches (5 cm) apart on cookie sheets. Bake in 375°F (190°C) oven 12 to 14 minutes, until centre springs back when touched. Remove from cookie sheet and cool on wire rack. To store, layer with waxed paper. These freeze well.

Yield: 5 dozen

per cookie	**calorie breakdown**
calories 91	% protein 6
g fat 3.4	% fat 33
g fibre 0.7	% carbohydrate 61

TO SOUR MILK

Add 1 tablespoon (15 mL) of vinegar per 1 cup (250 mL) of milk. Stir and allow to sit for 10 minutes.

OATCAKES

These traditional Scottish biscuits are free of sweeteners but were served with butter. Although we prefer them plain, they may be eaten with peanut butter or cheese.

1 cup	lightly packed brown sugar	250 mL
2 cups	oatmeal* (coarsely ground oats)	500 mL
2 ¼ cups	whole wheat flour	550 mL
1 tsp	baking soda	5 mL
½ tsp	salt	2 mL
1 cup	cold lard	250 mL
½ cup	cold water	125 mL

* Available in bulk food stores; if unavailable, pulverize quick cooking oats in food processor.

In medium bowl, combine brown sugar, oatmeal, flour, baking soda, and salt. Cut in lard using pastry blender or two knives. Drizzle water over dough, while mixing with a fork. Squeeze dough into ball; cut in half. Roll ¼ inch (0.5 cm) thick. Cut and place oatcakes 1 inch (2 cm) apart on baking sheets. Bake in 375⁰F (190⁰C) oven 10 to 12 minutes, until lightly browned. Transfer immediately to wire racks to cool. These freeze well.

Yield: 7 to 8 dozen

per 2 oatcakes	calorie breakdown
calories 78	% protein 9
g fat 2.4	% fat 27
g fibre 1.2	% carbohydrate 64

ROLLED OATS AND OATMEAL

Food stores carry several types of rolled oats; the usual labels are coarse rolled oats, quick cooking oats, and instant oats. All are made by the same process; quick cooking and instant oats are subjected to more processing, so the rolled flakes of oats are thinner, smaller, and more powdery. Our oatcakes use oatmeal; oats that are mechanically ground in a manner similar to cornmeal. It gives a baked product with the texture of whole wheat flour and the nourishment of oats.

Oats, dried peas, beans, and lentils are good sources of soluble fibre, the kind of fibre, if eaten regularly, that may help to lower blood cholesterol.

Anadama Bread

This Maritime bread is supposed to have derived its unusual name from a fisherman's description of his lazy wife. It has a nutlike taste and is high in fibre.

5 cups	*boiling* water	1.25 L
1 cup	molasses	250 mL
½ cup	oil	125 mL
2 tbsp	salt	25 mL
2 cups	cornmeal	500 mL
6 cups	all-purpose flour	1.5 L
6 cups	whole wheat flour	1.5 L
½ cup	lukewarm water	125 mL
1 tsp	granulated sugar	5 mL
2 tbsp	(2 pkgs) active dry yeast	25 mL

In large bowl, combine boiling water, molasses, oil, salt, and cornmeal. Add 4 cups (1 L) all-purpose flour and 2 cups (500 mL) whole wheat flour. Beat hard for 3 minutes until elastic. Cover and let rest 10 minutes. Meanwhile, dissolve 1 tsp (5 mL) sugar in ½ cup (125 mL) lukewarm water; stir in yeast and set aside for 10 minutes, until frothy. Stir yeast mixture into batter. Add remaining 4 cups (1 L) whole wheat flour and enough of the remaining all-purpose flour to make a soft dough. Turn on floured surface and knead 6 minutes. Return to bowl, cover and let rise in warm place until double in bulk, about 1½ hours. Punch down and let rest 10 minutes. Divide dough and shape into 5 loaves. Place in oiled bread pans. Cover and let rise until double in size, 1 hour. Bake in 400°F (200°C) oven 15 minutes; reduce heat to 325°F (160°C) and bake about 35 minutes longer (depending on loaf size), until loaves sound hollow when rapped with knuckles. Remove from pans immediately and cool on wire racks.

Yield: 5 loaves

Variations:
In place of cornmeal, use natural wheat bran or chopped sunflower seeds.

per slice	calorie breakdown
calories 104	% protein 10
g fat 1.8	% fat 16
g fibre 1.9	% carbohydrate 74

BUTTERMILK SCONES

Some say "scon" and others say "scone." In either case, the product is a layered, flaky, quick bread, similar to a tea biscuit.

1 cup	whole wheat flour	250 mL
¾ cup	all-purpose flour	175 mL
1 tbsp	granulated sugar	15 mL
1 tsp	baking powder	5 mL
½ tsp	baking soda	2 mL
¼ cup	cold butter	50 mL
¾ cup	buttermilk	175 mL

In medium bowl, blend flours, sugar, baking powder, and baking soda. Using a pastry blender or two knives, cut in butter. Add buttermilk and stir with fork, only to moisten. Turn on floured surface and knead 5 times. Form into ball and flatten to 1-inch (2.5 cm) thickness. Place on baking sheet, cut into 8 wedges and separate slightly. Bake in 425⁰F (220⁰C) oven 15 minutes, until golden brown. Remove from pan and cool on wire rack. Serve warm. Freeze well.

Yield: 8 servings

Variations:
May add ½ cup (125 mL) currants or raisins and 1 tsp (5 mL) cinnamon, if being served as dessert, with honey or maple syrup.

per scone
calories 155
g fat 5.2
g fibre 2.4

calorie breakdown
% protein 11
% fat 30
% carbohydrate 59

WILD BLUEBERRY TEA BREAD

Here's an old chestnut, probably an adaptation of an English or Irish scone. It's not a fancy bread, but it is great with a robust mug of tea.

1 cup	all-purpose flour	250 mL
1 cup	whole wheat flour	250 mL
1 tbsp	cream of tartar	15 mL
1 tsp	baking soda	5 mL
¼ tsp	salt	1 mL
¼ cup	granulated sugar	50 mL
¼ cup	oil	50 mL
¾ cup	buttermilk*	175 mL
1	egg, separated	1
¾ cup	wild blueberries, fresh or frozen	175 mL

*may substitute equal parts plain yogurt and 1% milk

Topping:

1 tbsp	granulated sugar	15 mL
1 tsp	cinnamon	5 mL
1 tbsp	grated orange rind	15 mL

In medium bowl, blend flours, cream of tartar, baking soda, salt, and sugar. In liquid measure, whisk oil, buttermilk, and egg yolk. Add liquid ingredients to dry, mixing with fork, only to moisten. Fold in blueberries. Dough will be wet. Turn onto floured surface and knead 5 times. Place on oiled, 9-inch (23 cm) round pie plate and pat to 1-inch (2 cm) thickness. Whip egg white with fork and brush over dough. Combine topping ingredients; sprinkle over egg white. Bake in 375°F (190°C) oven 30 to 35 minutes, until toothpick inserted in centre comes out clean. Serve warm.

Yield: 8 servings

per serving
calories 78
g fat 2.4
g fibre 1.2

calorie breakdown
% protein 9
% fat 27
% carbohydrate 64

NUTRITIOUS SANDWICH

If there's a person in your house who eats a peanut butter sandwich everyday, there may be ways to change the sandwich without withdrawing peanut butter. Here's one possibility.

2	slices whole grain or oatmeal bread	2
1 tbsp	honey or jam	15 mL
2 tbsp	peanut butter	25 mL
1 tbsp	raisins	15 mL
1	small carrot, peeled and grated	1

Spread 1 slice bread with honey or jam. Spread peanut butter on other slice, top with raisins and carrot. Place honey or jam slice on top and press together. Cut in half and package for lunch box.

Yield: 1 serving

Variation:
Add chopped celery, cabbage, or sweet green pepper instead of carrot.

per serving	calorie breakdown
calories 477	% protein 11
g fat 16.1	% fat 29
g fibre 7.7	% carbohydrate 61

Debbie's Cranberry Chutney

Debbie served this for our gourmet's 1985 Christmas dinner, and Marg has been making it ever since. The original recipe called for apricot preserves, which she doesn't usually have on the shelf, and walnuts, which she doesn't care for in chutneys. It is a great accompaniment to poultry, game, or pork.

½ cup	cider vinegar	125 mL
1 cup	lightly packed brown sugar	250 mL
1 tsp	curry powder	5 mL
½ tsp	ground ginger	2 mL
¼ tsp	ground cloves	1 mL
1 3-inch	cinnamon stick	7 cm
1½ cups	water	375 mL
1	lime, peeled, seeded, and finely chopped	1
2	firm pears, cored and diced	2
2	firm apples, peeled, cored, and diced	2
1 (12 oz) pkg	cranberries, fresh or frozen	340 g
½ cup	raisins, preferably white	125 mL

Combine vinegar, sugar, curry, ginger, cloves, cinnamon, and water; bring to boil, stirring until sugar is dissolved. Add lime, pears, and apples; simmer 10 minutes. Add cranberries and raisins; simmer 20 minutes, stirring occasionally, until thick. Discard cinnamon stick. Cool and refrigerate. Will keep for weeks.

Yield: about 4 cups

Variation:
May substitute lemon for lime.

per serving	**calorie breakdown**
calories 104	% protein 1
g fat 0.2	% fat 2
g fibre 2.3	% carbohydrate 98

WELCOME TO WINTER

Winter colours are those of a log cabin quilt: a glowing hearth at the centre, surrounded by neatly fitted building blocks of darker tones and richer shades. Even though the outdoors is cold and nature is pared down to white, grey, and black, indoor activities create their own warmth and bring out a palette of colours. Most of these activities involve food and friends, combined with crafts, arts, and sports.

This season includes winter solstice, a time when the sun is farthest south of the equator. Combined with the religious celebrations associated with the shortest days of the year, we love to gather with family and friends for good food and conversation around the hearth.

The difficulty in winter meal planning is the desire to incorporate fresh food. Fresh fruits include imported oranges and bananas, and local stored apples and pears. We have made good use of these. Imported fresh vegetables with crisp texture are preferred; local stored root vegetables, winter squashes, and members of the cabbage family are the economical ones. They are not subject to floods and frosts of the sun belt in the United States.

We include novel ways to prepare and serve stored vegetables; we have a number of potato dishes. Because broccoli, Brussels sprouts, romaine, and cabbage are among the best vegetables we can eat, we give them extra attention. There aren't many tossed salads, snow peas, or red peppers in our winter meals. However, in deference to our heritage, there are stews, chowders, and puddings.

Winter is long in many parts of Canada and cold in most of the country. It's no wonder many people become snow birds and leave for awhile. For those who stay along with the chickadees, winter offers time for reflection, for writing, for quilting and crafts, and for projects like this book.

This long season does contain weeks of brilliant sunshine reflected off glazed snow and absorbed by south facing glass. May your kitchen have a sunny window, a potted herb and a cozy quilt to curl up in at a warm red hearth.

BREAKFAST (2)*
Baked Rhubarb 255
Microwaved Porridge 256
Banana Poppy Seed Muffins 247

CHRISTMAS BREAKFAST (4)
Orange or Tangerine
Christmas Bread 248-49

BRUNCH OR SPECIAL SUPPER (4)
Mulled Cran-apple Cider 259
Anne's Sunday Pancakes with
    Cinnamon Syrup 204-05
Lemon Meringue Pie 228

RECOVERY MEAL (2)
Thai Chicken Soup 196
Pita Crisps 128
Mandarin Oranges

SPECIAL LUNCH (4)
Corn and Shrimp Chowder 197
Flatbread with Olives 111
Mom's Oatmeal Cookies 250

FAMILY DINNER (4)
Clamato Juice
Curried Shepherd's Pie 203
Winter Vegetable Stir-fry 206
Fudge Sauced Pudding 230

FAMILY DINNER (6)
Leanne's Tomato Basil Soup 198
Didi's Baked Salt Cod 207
Harvard Beets 208
Fresh Fruit Cup

FAMILY SUPPER (4)
Cole Slaw 137
Baked Liver 209
Potato Puff 210
Quick Rhubarb Pudding 231

FAMILY DINNER (4)
French Beef Stew 211
Assorted Winter Vegetables
The Working Cook's Rolls 61
Bananas Foster 232

QUICK SUPPER (4)
Macaroni and Cheese 212
Maritime Brown Bread 251
Smorgasbord Bean Salad 202
Date Bread 252

SATURDAY NIGHT SUPPER (6)
Maritime Baked Beans 213
Steamed Brown Bread 253
Mustard Pickles, Chow Chow
Wild Blueberry Grunt 233

OVEN DINNER (4)
Salsa Meatloaf 214
Baked Potato 159
Rutabaga and Apple Scallop 215
Date Pudding Cake 234

VEGETARIAN SUPPER (4)
Vegetarian Chili 216
Cornbread 117
Apple Bread Pudding 235

ACADIAN SUPPER (6)
Pickled Herring, Crackers
Chicken Fricot 217
Acadian Fruit Tart 238

PARTY DINNER (6)
Salmon Paté 187
Baked Ham, Sweet Mustard
    Sauce 218
Squash Risotto 219
Steamed Broccoli
Blueberry Cheesecake 236

PLAN-OVER LUNCH (4)
Split Pea Soup 199
Potato Bannock 56
Fresh Fruit

*indicates number served

PARTY DINNER (6)
Seafood Chowder 200
Spiced Eye of Round 220
Oven Browned Potatoes
Creamed Onions 221
Oriental Vegetable Stir-fry 222
Pickled Beets, Horseradish
Pumpkin Roll 239

PLAN-OVER DINNER (2)
Sliced Roast Beef
Potato Pancakes 223
Steamed Brussels Sprouts
Cranberry Orange Bread 254

CHRISTMAS DINNER (6)
Lobster Cocktail 189
Stuffed Roasted Chicken 224
Cranberry Relish 257
Duchess Potatoes 226
Fiddleheads, Squash
Good For You Pudding,
   Brandy Sauce 242-43

CHRISTMAS EVE SUPPER (4)
Winter Vegetables, Donna's
   Dip 188
Mussel Stew 201
Granary Rolls 58-59
Dark Fruitcake 240-41

NEW YEAR'S EVE COCKTAIL-
STYLE DINNER (12)
Oysters on the Half Shell 190
Lobster Bouchées 191
Chicken Pinwheels 192
Crab Cheesecake, Crackers 193
Sweet and Sour Meatballs 194
Baked Vegetable Pickups 195
Anadama Bread 178
Trifle 244

VALENTINE DINNER (2)
Leaf Lettuce Vinaigrette 77
Mussel Cataplana 227
Italian Crusty Bread 115
Divinity Fudge 258
Spanish Coffee 260

STARTERS
Baked Vegetable Pickups
Chicken Pinwheels
Crab Cheesecake
Donna's Dip
Lobster Bouchées
Lobster Cocktail
Oysters on the Half Shell
Salmon Paté
Sweet and Sour Meatballs

SOUPS AND SALADS
Corn and Shrimp Chowder
Leanne's Tomato Basil Soup
Mussel Stew
Seafood Chowder
Smorgasbord Bean Salad
Split Pea Soup
Thai Chicken Soup

MAIN COURSE FOODS
Acadian Chicken Fricot
Anne's Sunday Pancakes,
   Cinnamon Syrup
Baked Ham, Sweet Mustard Sauce
Baked Liver
Chicken Fricot
Creamed Onions
Curried Shepherd's Pie
Didi's Baked Salt Cod
Duchess Potatoes
French Beef Stew
Harvard Beets
Macaroni and Cheese
Maritime Baked Beans
Mussel Cataplana
Oriental Vegetable Stir-fry
Potato Pancakes
Potato Puff
Rutabaga and Apple Scallop
Salsa Meatloaf
Spiced Eye of Round
Squash Risotto
Stuffed Roasted Chicken
Vegetarian Chili
Winter Vegetable Stir-fry

DESSERTS
Acadian Fruit Tart
Apple Bread Pudding
Bananas Foster
Blueberry Cheesecake
Dark Fruitcake
Date Pudding Cake
Fudge Sauced Pudding
Good For You Pudding,
   Brandy Sauce
Lemon Meringue Pie
Pumpkin Roll
Quick Rhubarb Pudding
Trifle, Sponge Cake
Wild Blueberry Grunt

BAKED GOODS
Banana Poppy Seed Muffins
Christmas Bread
Cranberry Orange Bread
Date Bread
Maritime Brown Bread
Mom's Oatmeal Cookies
Steamed Brown Bread

MISCELLANEOUS
Baked Rhubarb
Cranberry Relish
Divinty Fudge
Microwaved Porridge
Mulled Cran-apple Cider
Spanish Coffee

SALMON PATÉ

A seasoned paté free of gelatin and butter, this one is quick and easy to make.

¼ cup	quark or yogurt cheese	50 mL
1 (7¾ oz) can	sockeye salmon, drained	213 g
1 tbsp	lemon juice	15 mL
1 tsp	horseradish	5 mL
pinch	cayenne	
¼ cup	finely chopped green onions	50 mL
1 tbsp	chopped fresh dill *or* ½ tsp (2 mL) dried dill	15 mL

In small bowl, blend quark, salmon, lemon juice, horseradish, and cayenne. Stir in green onions and dill. Pack in ramekin (small dish), cover and refrigerate. Serve surrounded with crackers or melba toast.

Yield: 6 servings

Variation:
For a special treat, add ¼ cup (50 mL) chopped smoked salmon.

per serving	**calorie breakdown**
calories 74	% protein 51
g fat 2.6	% fat 32
g fibre 0.2	% carbohydrate 17

CRACKERS ARE GETTING BETTER

Saltines, commonly called soda biscuits, used to be the standard cracker. We ate them with soup and decorated them with tidbits of tasty food for starters to dinner. The fat content was reasonable; they could be purchased in salted and unsalted versions. We moved on to a myriad of crisp, browned, fried crackers that contained more calories from fat than anything else.

  If you haven't read the cracker shelf lately, you are in for a surprise. A revolution is taking place. Nutrient analysis appears on many boxes. Baked crackers are in. Cracker surfaces are pale and seasoned with spicy ingredients other than salt. It is possible to buy a healthy, ready-to-eat cracker at the food store.

Donna's Dip

Spice Island has a blended seasoning called Beau Monde, which can now be purchased at bulk food stores. It's tasty but salty.

½ cup	low-fat mayonnaise	125 mL
½ cup	quark or yogurt cheese	125 mL
2 tsp	Beau Monde spice	10 mL
1 tsp	dried dill	5 mL

Mix all ingredients together. Refrigerate 1 hour before serving to allow flavours to blend. Serve with seasonal raw vegetables. Store in refrigerator.

Yield: 1 cup (250 mL)

per 2 tablespoons
calories 69
g fat 6
g fibre 0

calorie breakdown
% protein 13
% fat 77
% carbohydrate 11

LOBSTER COCKTAIL

Along the Atlantic coast, a seafood starter is mandatory for feast days. We have chosen an elegant, effortless, lobster cocktail to begin Christmas dinner.

1 (11.3 oz) can	frozen whole lobster*	320 g
1 head	butterhead lettuce	1
½ cup	seafood sauce with horseradish	125 mL

*or knuckles and claws, *not* salad

Thaw and drain lobster; cut into bite-size chunks. Line cocktail or sherbet glasses with torn lettuce. Spoon about 1½ tablespoons (20 mL) seafood sauce in centre and top with lobster. Chill until serving time.

Yield: 6 servings

per serving	**calorie breakdown**
calories 67	% protein 55
g fat 0.4	% fat 5
g fibre 1.5	% carbohydrate 40

OYSTERS ON THE HALF SHELL

Donna loves oysters. To her there are only two ways to eat them: on the half shell or in a milk stew.

12	fresh oysters in the shell	12
	hot pepper sauce	
3 tbsp	fresh lemon juice	45 mL
	crushed ice	

Scrub oysters with bristle brush, taking care to clean seams well. Discard any that are not tightly closed. Place 6 oysters in a ring, large half down, on microwave dish. Microwave on high watching carefully until shells start to spread, about 2 minutes. Remove oysters individually and continue cooking a few seconds at a time until each one has loosened sufficiently to be opened fully with an oyster knife. Repeat with remaining 6 oysters. Open shells carefully so as not to spill liquor and slide knife along top half of shell to cut foot loose. Arrange on bed of crushed ice. Shake 2 drops sauce on each one and drizzle with fresh lemon juice. Chill and serve.

Yield: 12 oysters

per oyster	**calorie breakdown**
calories 15	% protein 39
g fat 8.5	% fat 31
g fibre 0	% carbohydrate 30

LOBSTER BOUCHÉES

Chou pastry made into small bouchées creates elegant cases for lobster. In larger units, the same pastry has the name cream puff.

Bouchées:

½ cup	water	125 mL
¼ cup	butter	50 mL
½ cup	all-purpose flour	125 mL
⅛ tsp	salt	0.5 mL
2	eggs	2

Filling:

1 cup	cooked lobster, fresh, frozen, or canned	250 mL
½ cup	diced celery	125 mL
¼ cup	low-fat salad dressing	50 mL
1 tbsp	lemon juice	15 ml
pinch	white pepper	

In medium saucepan, bring water and butter to a boil. Add flour and salt all at once and beat with wooden spoon until mixture leaves side of pan and forms a ball. Remove from heat and cool slightly. Add eggs, one at a time, beating after each addition until batter is smooth, creamy, and thick. Drop by teaspoonful (ball should be no more than ¾ inch/2 cm in diameter) on baking sheet, 2 inches (5 cm) apart. Bake in 375⁰F (190⁰C) oven 25 to 30 minutes, until golden brown and crisp. Cool on wire rack.

For filling, finely dice lobster, removing any cartilage in claw meat. Combine with remaining ingredients. At serving time, cut top off bouchées; fill and replace tops.

Yield: 24 bouchées

per bouchée	calorie breakdown
calories 37	% protein 22
g fat 2.1	% fat 52
g fibre 0.1	% carbohydrate 26

Chicken Pinwheels

At a cocktail style dinner several dishes need to contain plain food. In that category, this is a winner.

3	boneless chicken breasts (12 oz/400 g)	3
1	large clove garlic, minced	1
¼ tsp	salt	1 mL
¼ tsp	black pepper	1 mL
3	thin slices cooked ham	3
2 tbsp	freshly squeezed lemon juice	25 mL
¼ tsp	paprika	1 mL

Flatten chicken breasts by rolling between two sheets of waxed paper. Blend together garlic, salt, and pepper; sprinkle over chicken. Top each with ham slice and roll tightly. Place seam side down on baking dish. Drizzle with lemon juice and sprinkle with paprika. Bake in 350⁰F (180⁰C) oven 20 minutes. Cover and refrigerate. At serving time, slice into pinwheels. Serve with a satay sauce or salsa.

Yield: 15 to 18 slices

per slice
calories 77
g fat 1.5
g fibre 0

calorie breakdown
% protein 79
% fat 18
% carbohydrate 2

CRAB CHEESECAKE

This sounds like New Year's Eve to us. It's from a most reliable, suberb cook in Maine.

1	egg	1
1 tbsp	all-purpose flour	15 mL
¼ tsp	salt	1 mL
pinch	white pepper	
¼ lb	ricotta cheese	115 g
¼ cup	1% milk	50 mL
1 (6 oz) can	crab meat, drained	170 g
1	clove garlic, minced	1
¼ cup	sliced green onion	50 mL
2 tbsp	grated Parmesan cheese	25 mL
1 tbsp	chopped fresh thyme or tarragon *or* 1 tsp (5 mL) dried	15 mL
5	drops hot pepper sauce	5

In medium bowl, beat egg until thick. Beat in flour, salt, and pepper. Break up ricotta and beat into egg mixture along with milk. Fold in crab meat, garlic, onions, Parmesan, thyme, and hot pepper sauce. Turn into lightly oiled 6-inch (15 cm) springform or other straight-sided baking dish. Bake in 350⁰F (180⁰C) oven 30 minutes or until a knife inserted in centre comes out clean. Cool on wire rack 10 minutes, loosen edges and remove. Cool and refrigerate. Serve with crackers or Italian bread.

Yield: 10 servings

per serving
calories 44.7
g fat 1.9
g fibre 0.1

calorie breakdown
% protein 44
% fat 39
% carbohydrate 16

Sweet and Sour Meatballs

North Americans want meatballs on top of spaghetti; Italians eat meatballs in sandwiches; the Dutch put meatballs in their tomato soup; the Chinese put tiny sausage balls on Brussels sprout leaves. It verifies that the world loves meatballs, even if they taste exactly the same as crumbled ground meat with seasoning.

1 lb	lean ground beef	450 g
1 cup	dry bread crumbs	250 mL
¼ cup	1% milk	50 mL
½ tsp	salt	2 mL
⅛ tsp	black pepper	0.5 mL
½ tsp	ground allspice	2 mL
1	egg	1

Sauce:

2 tbsp	lightly packed brown sugar	25 mL
1 tsp	minced fresh ginger	5 mL
1	clove garlic, minced	1
⅔ cup	orange juice	150 mL
¼ cup	vinegar	50 mL
1 tbsp	light soya sauce	15 mL
1 tbsp	Worcestershire sauce	15 mL
1 tbsp	cornstarch	15 mL

Mix together beef, bread crumbs, milk, salt, pepper, allspice, and egg. Form into ¾-inch (2 cm) balls and place on cookie sheet. Bake in 350°F (180°C) oven for 20 minutes. Meanwhile, in liquid measure, combine sauce ingredients. Transfer meatballs to 2-quart (2 L) casserole; add sauce and bake covered in 325°F (160°C) oven 30 minutes. Serve hot with toothpicks as starter or over rice as entrée. Will keep in refrigerator 4 days. Freezes well.

Yield: 40 meatballs

per meatball	**calorie breakdown**
calories 43	% protein 26
g fat 2	% fat 42
g fibre 0	% carbohydrate 33

Baked Vegetable Pick-Ups

When serving a "pick-up" meal, it's easy to find all kinds of meat, fish, poultry, and cheese dishes that are suitable. However, it's almost impossible to get genuine vegetables on that table. This recipe handles the challenge.

¼ cup	grated Parmesan cheese	50 mL
½ cup	bread crumbs	125 mL
2 tbsp	chopped fresh basil *or* 1 tsp (5 mL) dried	25 mL
4 cups	assorted vegetables (carrots and sweet pepper strips, whole mushrooms, cauliflower, and broccoli florets)	1 L
¼ cup	low-fat salad dressing	50 mL

In plastic bag, combine cheese, crumbs, and basil; set aside. In bowl, toss vegetables with salad dressing; cover well. In small batches, shake vegetables in crumb mixture to coat. Arrange in single layer on ungreased cookie sheet. Bake in 425°F (220°C) oven 15 minutes until golden brown. Serve hot.

Yield: 3 dozen pieces

per 3 pieces	**calorie breakdown**
calories 50	% protein 17
g fat 1.1	% fat 19
g fibre 1	% carbohydrate 63

Thai Chicken Soup

This is Donna's all-time favourite soup. She makes it when she has a cold and when winter blahs strike.

1 (10 oz)	chicken leg quarter	300 g
2 qts	water	2 L
¾ cup	short grain white rice	175 mL
1 tbsp	olive oil	15 mL
2 tbsp	chopped onion	25 mL
2 tsp	grated, fresh ginger	10 mL
2	cloves garlic, minced	2
¼ tsp	white pepper	1 mL
3 tbsp	fish sauce*	45 mL
1	small hot red pepper, seeded and chopped (optional)	1
2	green onions, sliced	2

*Available in oriental foods section; may substitute 1 tbsp (15 mL) oyster sauce.

Remove skin, bone, any fat, and tendons from chicken leg, reserving bones. Cut meat into thin slices 2 inches (5 cm) long and refrigerate. Rinse rice in cold water and place in large saucepan with 2 quarts (2 L) cold water and chicken bones. Bring to boil, cover, reduce heat, and simmer until rice is cooked, 20 minutes. Remove bones and discard. Meanwhile, in small skillet, heat oil and sauté onion and chicken pieces until lightly browned. Add to rice broth, using cup of broth to deglaze skillet. Add ginger, garlic, pepper, fish sauce, and red pepper, if using. You may want to start with half a pepper depending on "hotness" desired. Simmer 5 minutes to cook chicken. Serve hot, garnished with green onion.

Yield: 6 servings

per serving	calorie breakdown
calories 170	% protein 29
g fat 4.6	% fat 25
g fibre 0.4	% carbohydrate 46

CORN AND SHRIMP CHOWDER

Corn chowder is one of those quick family suppers that can stretch to feed extra guests. Adding small shrimp makes it a company dish.

1 tbsp	butter	15 ml
1	large onion, diced	1
1	stalk celery including leaves, diced	1
1	large potato, peeled and diced	1
1 cup	water	250 mL
½ tsp	salt	2 mL
¼ tsp	pepper	1 mL
1 (19 oz) can	kernel corn, including liquid	540 mL
½ cup	Matane shrimp, frozen (optional)	125 mL
2½ cups	1% milk	625 mL

In medium saucepan, melt butter; sauté onion and celery, 2 minutes. Add potato, water, salt, and pepper; bring to a boil, cover, reduce heat and simmer 6 to 8 minutes until potato is almost cooked. Add corn and shrimp; return to boil. Add milk, heat to just below boiling point. Serve hot.

Yield: 4 servings

per serving	**calorie breakdown**
calories 218	% protein 17
g fat 5.2	% fat 20
g fibre 2.9	% carbohydrate 63

Leanne's Tomato Basil Soup

This is a wonderful modern recipe. "Modern" meaning it combines a few prepared foods rather than mixing, stirring, chopping, and cooking a list of ingredients. It came to us from Leanne, who found it at a B & B in California.

1 (28 oz) can	plum tomatoes	796 mL
¼ cup	lightly packed fresh basil leaves	50 mL
1 cup	chicken broth	250 mL
1 tbsp	granulated sugar	15 mL
½ tsp	salt (less if broth salted)	2 mL
¼ tsp	pepper	1 mL
dash	cayenne (optional)	
	plain yogurt for garnish	

Place half the tomatoes and juice and all of basil in blender or food processor. Process until smooth and transfer to medium saucepan. Repeat with remaining tomatoes. Add chicken broth, sugar, salt, and pepper; bring to boil, reduce heat, cover and simmer 30 minutes. Taste and add cayenne, as desired. Serve hot, garnished with teaspoonful of plain yogurt. Freezes well.

Yield: 6 servings

Variation:
During gardening season, 2½ pounds (1 kg) fresh, peeled and seeded tomatoes may be used.

per serving	calorie breakdown
calories 98	% protein 33
g fat 2.4	% fat 21
g fibre 2.2	% carbohydrate 47

SPLIT PEA SOUP

Some people say the best thing about having roasted ham is the pea soup that follows.

2 cups	dried split peas	500 mL
10 cups	water	2.5 L
1	ham bone or ham hock	1
3	medium carrots, diced	3
5	medium onions, diced	5
2	large potatoes, diced	2
2	large stalks celery, including leaves, diced	2
1 tbsp	dried summer savoury	15 mL
1	large bay leaf, crushed	1
1 tsp	salt	5 mL
¼ tsp	pepper	1 mL

In a sieve, wash peas under cold running water, drain. Place water and ham bone in large saucepan. Bring to boil. Add peas and remaining ingredients; return to boil. Reduce heat, cover and simmer for 3 hours, stirring occasionally. Remove bone from soup, cut off any meat, chop finely, and return to soup. Taste and adjust seasonings. If soup is too thick, add water. Serve hot. Freezes well.

Yield: 8 servings

per serving
calories 287
g fat 1.4
g fibre 3.1

calorie breakdown
% protein 24
% fat 4
% carbohydrate 71

Seafood Chowder

When the temperature is sub-zero and the wind's blowing, nothing warms you better than a bowl of steaming chowder.

2 tbsp	butter	25 mL
1	medium onion, diced	1
1 cup	water	250 mL
1	bay leaf	1
1	medium potato, diced	1
½ tsp	salt	2 mL
¼ tsp	white pepper	1 mL
¼ lb	scallops or scallop pieces	115 g
¼ lb	Matane shrimp, frozen	115 g
½ lb	white fish fillet	225 g
3 cups	homogenized milk	750 mL
2 tsp	dulse powder (optional)	10 mL
	chopped parsley for garnish	

In medium saucepan, melt butter and sauté onion until translucent. Add water, bay leaf, and potato; cover and simmer, 6 minutes. Remove bay leaf. Add salt, pepper, scallops, shrimp, and lay fish fillet on top. Simmer 5 minutes longer. Add milk, heat thoroughly but do not boil. Sprinkle with dulse flakes. Serve hot, garnished with parsley.

Yield: 6 servings as starter, 4 as main course

Variation:
For a creamier chowder replace homogenized milk with 2 (385 mL) cans evaporated 2% milk.

per serving	calorie breakdown
calories 256	% protein 40
g fat 6.7	% fat 24
g fibre 0.7	% carbohydrate 36

MUSSEL STEW

This is a variation on the long-time New Brunswick yuletide favourite, Oyster Stew. Cultivated mussels are inexpensive to buy and easy to steam and shuck. When family and friends gather on Christmas Eve, enjoy a meal of mussel stew and homemade bread, a combination that offers the same warmth and nourishment for the body as the evening does for the spirit.

2 lbs	cultivated mussels	1 kg
½ cup	white wine *or* water	125 mL
1	medium onion, diced	1
½ cup	celery, diced	125 mL
2	medium potatoes, cubed	2
2	medium carrots, diced	2
1 tsp	salt	5 mL
¼ tsp	pepper	1 mL
	few drops hot pepper sauce	
1 qt	homogenized milk	1 L
2 tbsp	chopped, fresh parsley or coriander *or* 2 tsp (5 mL) dried	25 mL

Scrub mussels, discarding any that don't close when touched and remove beards. Pour wine or water into large saucepan, add mussels and bring to boil; cover and steam until shells open, 3 to 4 minutes. Drain, reserving liquid. Set aside 20 mussels in shell for garnishing and remove those remaining from the shell, discarding any that did not open. Bring reserved liquid to a boil, add onion, celery, potatoes, and carrots. Simmer covered for 10 minutes. Add salt, pepper, pepper sauce, milk, and cooked mussels. Heat, stirring constantly, until almost boiling. Serve at once, topping each bowl with reserved mussels in shell and sprinkling with parsley or coriander.

Yield: 4 servings as a main course; 6 as starter

per serving	**calorie breakdown**
calories 549	% protein 37
g fat 15.9	% fat 27
g fibre 3	% carbohydrate 35

SMORGASBORD BEAN SALAD

In the '60s and '70s, the Parish Church in Fredericton held an annual smorgasbord dinner that included a three-bean salad. We have replaced the lima beans with today's more popular chick peas and have reduced the fat, sugar, and salt in the dressing.

1 (10 oz) can	cut wax beans	284 mL
1 (10 oz) can	cut green beans	284 mL
1 (14 oz) can	red kidney beans	398 mL
1 cup	cooked chick peas	250 mL
2	stalks celery, sliced	2
1	small onion, thinly sliced and separated into rings	1
½	sweet green pepper, cut in 1-inch (2 cm) strips	½
¼ cup	oil	50 mL
½ cup	cider vinegar	125 mL
2 tbsp	granulated sugar	25 mL
1 tsp	Dijon mustard	5 mL
½ tsp	salt	2 mL
¼ tsp	pepper	1 mL

Drain all beans, rinse with cold water to remove salt, drain again. Place in glass container with chick peas (if using canned, drain and rinse), celery, onion rings, and green pepper. In liquid measure, whisk oil, vinegar, sugar, mustard, salt, and pepper; pour over bean mixture, cover and refrigerate at least overnight. Keeps 2 weeks in refrigerator; invert periodically to distribute dressing.

Yield: 10 to 12 servings

per serving	calorie breakdown
calories 124	% protein 13
g fat 5.3	% fat 36
g fibre 4	% carbohydrate 51

CURRIED SHEPHERD'S PIE

Shepherd's pie is a standard Maritime supper dish. Unusual seasoning of the ground beef makes this one distinctively different.

¼ cup	cooking sherry	50 mL
½ cup	raisins	125 mL
3	large potatoes, peeled and quartered	3
1 lb	lean ground beef	450 g
1	medium onion, diced	1
2 tsp	cornstarch	10 mL
2 tsp	curry powder	10 mL
¼ tsp	salt	1 mL
¼ tsp	pepper	1 mL
2 tbsp	water	25 mL
1	large apple, peeled, cored, and chopped	1
2 tbsp	1% milk	25 mL
1	clove garlic, minced	1
1 tbsp	butter	15 ml
¼ tsp	pepper	1 mL

Pour sherry over raisins and set aside. In small, covered saucepan, simmer potatoes in small amount of boiling water, until tender. Meanwhile, in medium skillet, lightly brown beef and onion. Sprinkle cornstarch, curry, salt, pepper, and water over meat and stir to blend. Cover and simmer until sauce thickens. Stir in apple and raisin mixture. Drain potatoes, mash and whip in milk, garlic, butter, and pepper. Spread meat mixture in 9-inch (2.5 L) square or 10-inch (2.5 L) round baking pan and cover with potatoes. Bake in 400⁰F (200⁰C) oven 20 minutes, until potatoes are lightly browned. May be made ahead and refrigerated; cooking time will increase 15 minutes.

Yield: 4 servings

per serving	calorie breakdown
calories 581	% protein 20
g fat 22.5	% fat 35
g fibre 6.0	% carbohydrate 45

Anne's Sunday Pancakes

Anne is a young professional woman with a special flair for low-cost, delicious dishes. Neither she nor we know its source, but this is a Sunday morning recipe.

½ cup	all-purpose flour	125 ml
1 cup	whole wheat flour	250 mL
½ cup	quick cooking oats	125 mL
1 tsp	baking powder	5 mL
1 tsp	baking soda	5 mL
2 tbsp	cold butter	25 mL
2 cups	buttermilk*	500 mL
¼ cup	corn syrup	50 mL
2	eggs	2
½ cup	chopped pecans	125 mL
1 cup	plain or vanilla skimmed milk yogurt	250 mL
2	bananas	2
	cinnamon·syrup (recipe follows)	

*May substitute equal parts of plain skimmed milk yogurt and 1% milk.

In medium bowl, preferably with spout, combine flours, oats, baking powder, and baking soda. Cut in butter. In liquid measure, whisk buttermilk, corn syrup, and eggs. Add liquid ingredients to dry ones, stirring only to moisten. Stir in pecans and let batter rest 5 minutes. Pour batter on medium-hot, nonstick griddle or skillet to form 5-inch (12 cm) pancakes. When bubbles appear on top, turn and cook until brown on underside. Overlap pancakes on hot plate while cooking remainder of batter. Serve with yogurt, sliced bananas, and cinnamon syrup.

Yield: 4 servings (12 pancakes)

Cinnamon Syrup:

½ cup	water	125 mL
4-inch	stick cinnamon	10 cm
½ cup	brown sugar	125 mL
½ cup	granulated sugar	125 mL

In medium saucepan, combine ingredients, bring to boil, reduce heat and simmer 5 minutes. Remove cinnamon stick and serve hot over pancakes.

per serving complete
calories 785
g fat 20.1
g fibre 7.5

calorie breakdown
% protein 10
% fat 22
% carbohydrate 68

Winter Vegetable Stir-Fry

Stir-frying is an easy way to dress up local, stored winter vegetables. It helps you avoid expensive, imported fresh vegetables and may surprise fussy family members, who would otherwise turn down rutabaga and cabbage.

1 tbsp	oil	15 mL
1 cup	diagonally sliced carrots	250 mL
1 cup	julienne rutabaga strips	250 mL
½ cup	sliced onion	125 mL
1 cup	thinly sliced cabbage (savoy, if available)	250 mL
½ tsp	granulated sugar	2 mL
1 tbsp	oyster sauce*	15 mL

*May substitute 2 tsp (10 mL) light soya sauce.

Prepare and measure all ingredients before starting to cook. To cook quickly, carrot slices should be ⅛ inch (4 mm) thick, rutabaga strips ¼ inch (8 mm) thick and 2 inches (5 cm) long. Heat oil in wok or large skillet over high heat. Add carrots and rutabaga; reduce heat to medium and stir-fry 3 minutes. Add onion and cabbage; stir-fry 2 minutes. Sprinkle sugar and oyster sauce over vegetables, stir and cover. Reduce heat to low, steam vegetables for 1 to 2 minutes. They should be quite crisp. Serve immediately.

Yield: 4 servings

per serving
calories 87
g fat 3.7
g fibre 3.3

calorie breakdown
% protein 8
% fat 36
% carbohydrate 56

Opposite (clockwise from centre bottom): Rhubarb Chutney (page 64); Curried Shepherd's Pie (page 203); Leanne's Tomato Basil Soup (page 198); Fudge Sauced Pudding (page 230); Winter Vegetable Stir-fry (page 206).

DIDI'S BAKED SALT COD

This recipe came into Donna's sailing gang, via Didi, many years ago, when each family had boats full of children. It could be made in advance, frozen, and taken to the boat. For a couple of days it helped keep the ice chest cold, and then it could be baked and eaten.

1 lb	salt cod, soaked overnight in cold water	450 g
6	medium potatoes, peeled, boiled, drained, and mashed	6
1	medium onion, chopped	1
2	cloves garlic, minced	2
¼ cup	butter	50 mL
½ cup	1% milk	125 mL
½ tsp	nutmeg	2 mL
¼ tsp	pepper	1 mL
½ cup	coarse bread crumbs	125 mL

Drain cod, add 1 quart (1 L) fresh water, bring to boil and simmer 5 to 7 minutes, until it flakes. Drain and add to mashed potato. Add onion, garlic, butter, milk, nutmeg, and pepper. Blend and taste to see if dish needs salt. Heap into large casserole and top with bread crumbs. Bake in 375°F (190°C) oven 40 minutes, until hot and puffy. Serve hot.

Yield: 6 servings

Note: You may divide mixture in half; have one casserole for dinner and put one in the freezer.

per serving	calorie breakdown
calories 556	% protein 46
g fat 11	% fat 18
g fibre 3.6	% carbohydrate 35

Opposite (clockwise from centre bottom): Prune Brownies (page 119); Christmas Bread (page 248); Steamed Brown Bread (page 253); Almond Biscotti (page 120); Wild Blueberry Tea Bread (page 180); Cranberry Orange Bread (page 254); Lemon Bread (page 176); Cranberry Orange Gift Loaves (page 254).

Harvard Beets

While it is more work to buy and cook fresh beets than to open a can, there is a world of difference in taste.

4	medium beets	4
1 tbsp	granulated sugar	15 mL
1 tbsp	cornstarch	15 mL
¼ tsp	salt	1 mL
¼ tsp	pepper	1 mL
⅔ cup	beet cooking water	150 mL
¼ cup	vinegar	50 mL
½ tsp	horseradish	2 mL
1 tsp	butter	5 mL

Scrub beets, leaving roots and 1 inch (2 cm) of tops; cook in 1 inch (2 cm) of water in covered saucepan 20 to 30 minutes, until tender. Alternatively, place on rack in 1 inch (2 cm) of water in pressure cooker and cook 8 minutes under 15 pounds pressure. Drain, reserving juice. Cool and slough off skins, roots, and tops. Slice beets into casserole. In small saucepan, blend sugar, cornstarch, salt, and pepper; stir in beet cooking water and vinegar. Cook over medium heat, stirring constantly, until sauce thickens and becomes clear. Remove, add horseradish and butter. Pour sauce over beets. Reheat in microwave at serving time. Freezes well.

Yield: 4 servings

per serving
calories 62
g fat 1.1
g fibre 2.3

calorie breakdown
% protein 7
% fat 15
% carbohydrate 79

BAKED LIVER

Liver is out of fashion, mostly because of its cholesterol content. Nevertheless, it is low in fat and packed with minerals, most notably iron.

2 tbsp	all-purpose flour	25 mL
¼ tsp	salt	1 mL
¼ tsp	pepper	1 mL
1 tsp	dried summer savoury	5 mL
1 tbsp	oil	15 mL
12 oz	beef liver, outer skin and channels removed	375 g
1	large onion, sectioned	1
½	sweet green pepper, cut into strips	½
½	jalapeño pepper, finely chopped (optional)	½
1	large carrot, sliced	1
1 (19 oz) can	kernel corn	540 mL
¼ cup	chili sauce *or* salsa	50 mL

On plate, blend flour, salt, pepper, and savoury. Dredge liver on both sides. In medium skillet, heat oil, brown liver quickly. Remove to casserole dish. Sauté onion and peppers for 2 minutes; add carrot, corn, and chili sauce, stirring to mix. Pour vegetables over liver. Bake, covered, in 350°F (180°C) oven 30 minutes.

Yield: 4 servings

per serving
calories 311
g fat 8
g fibre 3.8

calorie breakdown
% protein 28
% fat 22
% carbohydrate 50

CHOOSING LIVER

For maximum iron content, select calf or pork liver, because they contain twice as much iron as beef liver. Calf liver is highest in fat content while pork liver is lowest.

POTATO PUFF

When you have leftover mashed potatoes or when dinner guests are late and you planned to serve mashed potatoes, a potato puff saves the day and rejuvinates the potatoes.

2 cups	mashed potatoes	500 mL
1 tbsp	butter	15 ml
½ cup	1 % milk	125 mL
1	egg	1
¼ tsp	pepper	1 ml

Place mashed potatoes in medium bowl. In liquid measure, melt butter in microwave. Whisk in milk, egg, and pepper. Pour over potato and whip until well mixed. Turn into 1-quart (1 L), lightly oiled casserole. Bake in 375⁰F (190⁰C) oven 30 to 40 minutes until puffed and golden brown. Serve hot.

Yield: 4 servings

per serving
calories 168
g fat 4.6
g fibre 2.1

calorie breakdown
% protein 13
% fat 24
% carbohydrate 63

FRENCH BEEF STEW

It's possible to make a beef stew that includes vegetables. However, it's almost impossible to have both the meat and vegetables done, without one or the other being overdone. This stew avoids the problem.

2 tbsp	oil	25 mL
2 lbs	(1-inch/2 cm thick) round steak	900 g
1 tbsp	all-purpose flour	15 mL
1	chorizo or Italian sausage, sliced	1
2	cloves garlic, minced	2
2	medium onions, cut in eighths	2
1 cup	beef *or* vegetable broth*	250 mL
1 (5½ oz) can	tomato paste	156 mL
12	whole black peppercorns	12
2	whole cloves	2
1	large bay leaf, crushed	1
½ tsp	salt	2 mL
½ cup	fresh parsley, chopped	125 mL
½ cup	dry red wine (optional)	125 mL

* May use 1 bouillon cube dissolved in 1 cup/250 mL hot water.

Remove any fat and cut steak in 1-inch cubes. In large skillet, heat oil and brown meat. Transfer to large casserole or slow cooker. Sprinkle with flour. In same skillet, sauté sausage, onion, and garlic; add to beef. Add broth, tomato paste, peppercorns, cloves, bay leaf, and salt. Heat and stir to deglaze pan; add to meat. Cover and cook in 300⁰F (150⁰C) oven or slow cooker 4 to 5 hours (start on high, when simmering, reduce to low), until meat is tender. Taste and adjust seasonings; add parsley and wine. Serve with vegetables on hot plates. Small, whole potatoes, onions and beans, chopped carrots, parsnips, rutabaga, and broccoli stems complement the stew.

Yield: 8 servings

per serving (without vegetables)   **calorie breakdown**
calories 216   % protein 46
g fat 8.8   % fat 39
g fibre 1.5   % carbohydrate 15

MACARONI AND CHEESE

A Maritime cookbook would not be complete without a basic macaroni and cheese. Making the cheese sauce in the microwave is easy and quick. The fat may be reduced further by using a low-fat cheddar; be prepared for a sauce that is not as creamy as with regular cheddar cheese.

1½ cups	macaroni	375 mL
2 tbsp	butter	25 mL
2 tbsp	all-purpose flour	25 mL
½ tsp	salt	2 mL
¼ tsp	pepper	1 mL
1 tsp	Dijon mustard, optional	5 mL
1½ cups	1% milk	375 mL
1 cup	grated sharp cheddar cheese	250 mL
1 cup	bread crumbs	250 mL
2 tbsp	chopped fresh parsley	25 mL

In large saucepan, boil macaroni, uncovered, in 2 quarts (2 L) of boiling water 8 to 10 minutes, until al dente. Drain well, rinse with cold water. While macaroni is cooking, place butter in microwavable 1 quart (1 L) measure. Microwave on high 20 seconds, until melted. Whisk flour, salt, pepper, and mustard into melted butter to make smooth paste. Gradually whisk in milk. Microwave on high 3 to 4 minutes, until thickened, whisking after each minute. Stir cheese into white sauce and microwave on high 40 seconds, until cheese has melted. Place cooked macaroni in 2 quart (2 L) microwavable casserole. Pour cheese sauce over, stir gently. Combine bread crumbs and parsley. Sprinkle over top. Cover loosely with waxed paper and microwave on medium 6 to 8 minutes, until bubbly.

Yield: 4 servings

per serving	**calorie breakdown**
calories 484	% protein 17
g fat 17.8	% fat 33
g fibre 1.6	% carbohydrate 50

MARITIME BAKED BEANS

Regardless of which old cookbook we read, the recipe never varied. We replaced the diced salt pork with vegetable oil. While you may make baked beans in a slow cooker or in a pressure cooker, we have tried both and assure you that baking beans in a crock in the oven gives the best product.

2½ cups	(1 lb) dried Soldier or Jacob's Cattle beans	625 mL
¼ cup	brown sugar	50 mL
¼ cup	molasses	50 mL
1 tsp	dry mustard	5 mL
1 tsp	salt	5 mL
¼ tsp	pepper	1 mL
2 tbsp	oil	25 mL
1	medium onion, diced	1

Soak beans overnight in 7 cups (1.75 L) warm water.* Drain well, discarding water. Place in saucepan and cover with boiling water, return to boil, reduce heat, cover and simmer 1 hour. Drain and place in bean crock. Combine remaining ingredients and pour over beans. Add sufficient boiling water to barely cover. Bake, covered, in 300ºF (150ºC) oven 5 to 6 hours. Add hot water, as required, to keep beans moist. Uncover during last hour of cooking to brown. Serve with Steamed (page 253) or Maritime Brown Bread (page 251).

* For quick soak method, see Ross's Cowboy Beans, page 95.

Yield: 6 to 8 servings

per serving	**calorie breakdown**
calories 387	% protein 18
g fat 5	% fat 11
g fibre 18.8	% carbohydrate 70

SALSA MEATLOAF

Meatloaf is a perennial favourite. Maritimers use rolled oats as the meat extender while elsewhere bread crumbs are added. We have replaced the tomato sauce or soup with salsa, giving it a fresh, spicy taste. To both of us, the best part of meatloaf is the sandwich the next day.

1 lb	lean ground beef	450 g
1	medium onion, chopped	1
1 cup	quick cooking oats	250 mL
1 cup	tomato salsa*	250 mL
1	egg	1
½ tsp	salt	2 mL

* Choose hotness to suit personal taste.

In medium bowl, combine ground beef, onion, oats, ½ cup (125 mL) salsa, egg, and salt. Pack in 8 x 4 x 2½ inch (1.5 L) loaf pan. Bake in 350ºF (180ºC) oven 30 minutes. Spread remaining salsa over top. Return to oven and bake 15 minutes. Allow to stand 15 minutes before slicing and serving.

Yield: 6 servings

per serving	calorie breakdown
calories 264	% protein 29
g fat 13.4	% fat 45
g fibre 3.2	% carbohydrate 26

RUTABAGA AND APPLE SCALLOP

A common vegetable, the rutabaga or "swede" came from Scotland and grows readily in every province. Maritimers call it "turnip" or "yellow turnip," but what they are eating is rutabaga.

½	small rutabaga	½
2	apples	2
1 tbsp	brown sugar	15 mL
¼ tsp	salt	1 mL
pinch	pepper	
1 tsp	butter	5 mL
½ cup	whole wheat bread crumbs	125 mL

Peel and slice rutabaga in 1-inch (2 cm) strips, ¼ inch (0.5 cm) thick. Peel, core, and slice apples. Layer half turnip and apple in 6-cup (1.5 L) casserole. Sprinkle with half the sugar, salt, and pepper. Repeat layers. Dot with butter. Cover and bake in 350°F (180°C) oven 30 minutes. Uncover, sprinkle with bread crumbs and continue baking until rutabaga is tender, about 20 minutes.

Yield: 4 servings

Variations:
May cook in microwave, on high, with vented cover and without crumb topping, for about 20 minutes.
In place of apples, use 1 large onion, thinly sliced. Add 2 tablespoons (25 mL) vegetable dripping or water. Serve with roast beef or turkey.

per serving	**calorie breakdown**
calories 128	% protein 7
g fat 2.0	% fat 13
g fibre 2.7	% carbohydrate 80

Vegetarian Chili

Chili started in Texas with beef in tomato sauce. It evolved to beef plus dried beans in the sauce. Today, spicy tomato sauce is the only guaranteed ingredient.

½ cup	water	125 mL
1 (28 oz) can	tomatoes	796 mL
½ cup	bulgur	125 mL
2 tbsp	oil	25 mL
4	cloves garlic, minced	4
1 cup each of	diced onion, sliced celery, chopped green pepper, sliced mushrooms, sliced carrots	250 mL
1 (19 oz) can	kidney beans, including liquid	540 mL
1 (10 oz) can	pinto beans, including liquid	398 mL
1 (5½ oz) can	tomato paste	156 mL
1 tbsp	lemon juice	15 mL
1 tsp	ground cumin	5 mL
1½ tsp	chili powder	7 mL
½ tsp	salt	2 mL
¼ tsp	cayenne	1 mL
	grated cheddar cheese for garnish	

In liquid measure, combine water, liquid from tomatoes, and bulgur. Microwave on high 2 minutes, until hot. Set aside. In a large heavy saucepan, heat oil; sauté garlic, onion, celery, green pepper, and mushrooms 2 to 3 minutes. Add remaining ingredients, including drained tomatoes; bring to boil, reduce heat and simmer uncovered 20 minutes, stirring often. Add bulgur mixture and cook 15 minutes longer, stirring often. Taste and adjust seasonings; more chili powder may be desired. Serve hot, garnished with grated cheddar cheese.

Yield: 8 servings

per serving	**calorie breakdown**
calories 244	% protein 17
g fat 4	% fat 14
g fibre 11.8	% carbohydrate 69

ACADIAN CHICKEN FRICOT

A typical Acadian dish made with mackerel, clams, stewing hen or rabbit.
We use broiler chicken because stewing hens are hard to buy and slow to cook.

6	broiler chicken pieces, breasts and thighs	6
6 cups	hot water	1.5 L
1 tbsp	dried summer savoury	15 mL
1	bay leaf	1
1½ tsp	salt	7 mL
½ tsp	pepper	2 mL
1	large onion, diced	1
3 cups	peeled chopped potato	750 mL
2 cups	sliced carrots	500 mL
¼ cup	chopped fresh parsley (optional)	50 mL

Dumplings:

1 cup	flour	250 mL
2 tsp	baking powder	10 mL
½ tsp	salt	2 mL
1 tbsp	butter	15 mL
¾ cup	1% milk	175 mL

Remove skin and visible fat from chicken. In large saucepan, bring chicken, water, savoury, bay leaf, salt, and pepper to boil. Reduce heat, cover and simmer 20 minutes. Strain broth through colander and return it to saucepan. Remove meat from bones, cut into bite-size pieces and add to broth with onion, potatoes, and carrots. Discard bay leaf. Bring to boil, reduce heat and simmer 5 minutes.

To make dumplings, in small bowl, combine flour, baking powder, and salt. Cut in butter. Stir in milk with fork and mix only to moisten. Let rest 2 minutes. Drop dumplings by teaspoonful into fricot. Cover pot tightly, simmer 10 minutes. Serve in soup plates garnished with parsley.

Yield: 6 servings

per serving	calorie breakdown
calories 302	% protein 32
g fat 5	% fat 15
g fibre 3.3	% carbohydrate 53

Baked Ham with Sweet Mustard Sauce

Ham makes an attractive focal point for a buffet.

1 (5 lb)	half ham, butt end	2.3 kg
	whole cloves	
1 cup	brown sugar	250 mL
2 tsp	dry mustard	10 mL
⅓ cup	fine dry bread crumbs	75 mL
3 tbsp	cider vinegar	45 mL

Sweet Mustard Sauce:

¼ cup	brown sugar	50 mL
2 tbsp	dry mustard	25 mL
2 tsp	all-purpose flour	10 mL
¼ cup	vinegar	50 mL
¼ cup	water	50 mL
1	egg	1

Calculate cooking time for ham at 25 minutes per pound. Bake ham uncovered on shallow pan, in 325°F (160°C) oven. One hour before ham is to be done, remove from oven and trim off rind and fat. Score outside in diamond pattern and stud with cloves. Blend brown sugar, mustard, bread crumbs, and vinegar. Spread over top. Increase oven temp to 425°F (220°C) and continue baking until meat thermometer reads 160°F (75°C). Remove and let rest 15 minutes before carving.

To prepare sauce, in small saucepan, blend sugar, mustard, and flour. In liquid measure, whisk vinegar, water, and egg. Whisk liquid ingredients into dry ones, place over medium heat and cook, stirring constantly, until sauce is smooth and thick. Serve hot with baked ham. Makes about 3/4 cup (175 mL).

Yield: 12 servings

per serving	calorie breakdown
calories 266	% protein 38
g fat 6.4	% fat 22
g fibre 0.3	% carbohydrate 40

SQUASH RISOTTO

Risotto is an Italian creamy, seasoned rice dish. True risotto is made by repeatedly adding small amounts of stock to simmering rice. We have adapted the idea for a buffet or potluck casserole.

1 pkg	frozen squash, thawed*	400 g
¾ cup	brown rice	175 mL
1 tsp	oil	5 mL
1	small onion, diced	1
2	cloves garlic, minced	2
2 cups	apple juice or vegetable drippings	500 mL
1 tsp	salt	5 mL
¼ tsp	pepper	1 mL
1 tsp	celery seed	5mL
½ tsp	ground coriander	2 mL

*Substitute 1½ cups (375 mL) cooked, mashed squash.

In 2-quart (2 L) casserole, combine all ingredients. Cover and bake in 350⁰F (180⁰C) oven 1 hour, until rice is tender and liquid is absorbed. Add more liquid if casserole becomes dry. Risotto should be creamy.

Yield: 6 servings

per serving	calorie breakdown
calories 177	% protein 7
g fat 1.6	% fat 8
g fibre 1.1	% carbohydrate 85

Spiced Eye of Round

There are dozens of cuts of beef that can be roasted. The tenderloin is most tender; the standing or rolled rib is desirable for its marbled fat; the round is the leanest cut on the animal. For obvious reasons, we have chosen to feature eye of round. Because of its density, the number of servings per pound is greater than from any other roast of beef.

1 (3 lb)	eye of round roast	1350 g
2	cloves garlic	2
24	whole cloves	24
1 cup	red wine	250 mL
½ tsp	salt	2 mL
¼ tsp	pepper	1 mL
½ tsp	ground allspice	2 mL
½ tsp	ground cinnamon	2 mL
1	small bay leaf	1

Peel and cut garlic clove in long slivers. With boning knife, make narrow slits in top of roast and insert garlic sliver or whole clove in each one. In liquid measure, combine wine, salt, pepper, allspice, cinnamon, and bay leaf. Place roast in non-metal container of similar size or shape. Cover with wine mixture. If required, add more wine to cover meat. Cover and marinate in refrigerator for at least 12 hours.

At cooking time, bring marinade to a boil. Place roast in heavy, deep roasting pan or casserole; add hot marinade. Insert meat thermometer through a slit in sheet of aluminum foil and into centre of roast. Seal foil around edge of pan. Bake in 300°F (150°C) oven for about 1 hour or until meat thermometer reads 150°F (65°C) (medium rare). Remove from oven, allow to sit in marinade for 15 minutes before carving into thin slices. Alternatively, cool in marinade and refrigerate; slice and serve cold.

Yield: 10 servings

per serving	**calorie breakdown**
calories 138	% protein 78
g fat 3.1	% fat 21
g fibre 0	% carbohydrate 1

CREAMED ONIONS

An excellent vegetable dish to accompany any roast, creamed onions are economical and nutritious.

12	small yellow globe onions *or* 6 large onions, cut in half crosswise	12
1 cup	water	250 mL
½ tsp	salt	2 mL
4	black peppercorns	4
1	bay leaf	1
1 tbsp	butter	15 mL
2 tbsp	all-purpose flour	25 mL
1 tbsp	chopped fresh tarragon (optional)	15 mL

In medium saucepan, bring water to boil, add onions, salt, peppercorns, and bay leaf. Cover and simmer until tender. Using slotted spoon, transfer onions to hot serving dish. Strain cooking liquid, discarding peppercorns and bay leaf. Melt butter in same saucepan; work in flour with a fork; gradually whisk in cooking water and cook, stirring constantly until sauce thickens. Add tarragon. Pour over onions. Serve immediately or refrigerate and microwave at serving time.

Yield: 6 servings

per serving
calories 68
g fat 2.2
g fibre 1.9

calorie breakdown
% protein 9
% fat 27
% carbohydrate 64

Oriental Vegetable Stir-Fry

Bok choy is on the vegetable counter regularly, but we usually pass it by. If you like spinach and chard, give it a try.

1 tbsp	oil	15 mL
1	clove garlic, minced	1
6 cups	sliced bok choy (1 small bunch)	1.5 L
1 cup	diagonally sliced celery	250 mL
1 (15 oz) can	baby sweet corn	398 mL
2 tbsp	oyster sauce	25 mL

Heat oil in wok or heavy skillet. Add garlic, bok choy, and celery; stir-fry over medium heat until leafy part of bok choy wilts, 2 minutes. Add corn and oyster sauce; stir-fry to heat through. Serve immediately.

Yield: 4 servings

per serving
calories 127
g fat 4
g fibre 2.8

calorie breakdown
% protein 9
% fat 25
% carbohydrate 65

POTATO PANCAKES

Some form of pancake plays an important roll in the diet of most cultures; latkes (Yiddish word for "pancakes") have always been served with sour cream and applesauce in Jewish homes at the festival of Hanukkah. We serve them with sliced, cold, roasted meat. Small potato pancakes topped with decorative slices of smoked salmon are a great starter for a meal otherwise without potato.

1	large baking potato	1
1	egg, beaten	1
2 tbsp	finely chopped onion	25 mL
2 tbsp	all-purpose flour	25 mL
¼ tsp	salt	1 mL
pinch	pepper	
1 tbsp	oil	15 mL

Peel potato, grate by hand or in food processor. Place in towel and squeeze dry. Work quickly because potato will darken when exposed to air. Mix potato with egg; stir in onion, flour, salt and pepper. Heat half of oil in large skillet, add ¼ cup (50 mL) potato mixture per pancake. Flatten slightly with spatula. Fry over medium heat until browned on underside and crisp around edges, about 3 minutes. Turn, fry until crisp and golden brown, 2 to 3 minutes. Transfer to hot plate, place in warm oven. Repeat with remaining mixture adding more oil as necessary. Serve hot.

Yield: 2 servings

per serving	**calorie breakdown**
calories 172	% protein 10
g fat 7.1	% fat 37
g fibre 1.8	% carbohydrate 53

Stuffed Roasted Chicken

Our method of roasting chicken isn't looked on with favour by some poultry gurus, but it is an old method, and it works. We have used it for a total of 75 years without fail or unhappy incident. So, we want to share it. It results in evenly cooked, well-browned poultry. The paper bag offers protection, permits more even cooking than does a tent of foil and unlike a covered roasting pan produces crisp, brown skin.

1 (6-7 lb)	roasting chicken	3 kg
1	brown paper grocery bag free of lettering	1

Dressing:

8	slices whole wheat bread	8
2 tsp	oil	10 mL
1	medium onion, diced	1
1	large stalk celery, diced	1
2 tbsp	summer savoury	25 mL
½ tsp	salt	2 mL
¼ tsp	black pepper	1 mL

Wash chicken, remove any pinfeathers and entrails left in cavity, especially kidneys along back bone. Drain well on rack in sink. If bread is fresh, place on tray under broiler to dry on both sides.

To prepare dressing, in large saucepan, heat oil; sauté onion and celery until translucent. Remove from heat, add savoury, salt, and pepper. Break bread into small pieces, mix with onion mixture in saucepan. If making in advance, refrigerate until ready to cook chicken.

Just before cooking, stuff dressing lightly into neck area and cavity of chicken. Fold neck skin over to back of bird and secure with short skewer. Close cavity by threading skin on long skewer or inserting 4 skewers horizontally and lacing together with string. Tie legs and tail together with heavy cotton cord. Tie cord around body, securing wings. Insert meat thermometer into thickest part of thigh muscle, without touching the bone. Rub inside bottom of brown paper bag with a little oil. Place chicken in bag, cutting a slit for meat thermometer to go through. Fold top of bag over and crease well. Place package on rack in shallow roasting pan.

Roast in 325°F (160°C) oven 25 minutes per pound or until thermometer reads 185°F (90°C). The temperature at centre of dressing should be

165°F (75°C). Another test for doneness: leg moves easily when lifted and twisted. For optimum browning, during the last half hour of roasting, tear open top of paper bag and baste bird.

Let rest 15 minutes before carving.

After dinner, remove dressing and store separately in refrigerator.

Yield: 10 servings

per serving (no skin)
calories 424
g fat 11.1
g fibre 0.4

calorie breakdown
% protein 65
% fat 24
% carbohydrate 11

per serving (with skin)
calories 715
g fat 49.4
g fibre 0.4

calorie breakdown
% protein 30
% fat 63
% carbohydrate 7

SELECTING AND THAWING POULTRY

Carefully select a frozen bird that has pink skin colour. The package should be intact, without punctures. If the bird looks white and there are ice crystals inside the wrapper, leave it in the bin.

There are two recommended methods of thawing a bird. For a large turkey, the cold water method is preferred because refrigerator thawing takes too long. Place the sealed bird, breast side down, in sink of cold water. Allow 1 hour per 1 pound (2 hours per 1 kg) and turn the bird several times. When the surface responds to thumb pressure and legs move freely, remove bag and giblet package and wash bird. Store in refrigerator until roasting time.

Smaller turkeys and roasting chickens may be thawed in the same manner. The preferred method for birds of less than 10 pounds (4 kg) is in the refrigerator. Slit the bag along the back of bird and place bird on tray. Allow 5 hours per 1 pound (11 hours per 1 kg).

After the bird has been put in the oven to roast, scrub tools, surfaces, and sink with 2 quarts (2 L) of hot water to which 2 tablespoons (25 mL) of bleach have been added.

DUCHESS POTATOES

Similar to Potato Puff, this version offers party presentation.

6	medium potatoes	6
⅓ cup	milk	75 mL
1	egg	1
½ tsp	salt	2 mL
¼ tsp	pepper	1 mL
2 tsp	melted butter	10 mL
	paprika	

Peel potatoes and cut in half. In medium saucepan, bring 1 cup (250 mL) water to boil; add potatoes, cover, reduce heat and simmer 15 minutes, until soft. Drain, return to warm burner to dry off. Add milk and mash; whip in egg, salt, and pepper. Pipe mixture through pastry tube forming rosettes *or* shape into cones. Lightly brush with melted butter and sprinkle with paprika. Bake in 375⁰F (190⁰C) oven 15 minutes until golden brown. May be frozen.

Yield: 6 servings

per serving
calories 145
g fat 2.4
g fibre 1.9

calorie breakdown
% protein 10
% fat 15
% carbohydrate 75

MUSSEL CATAPLANA

There is a personal story behind this dish. We had lunched and networked on two topics for several months: whether to write a cookbook and where to go on a winter trip. The trip decision was easier to make, so we went to Portugal, had a grand time, including a feast of Cataplana at the O Telheiro do Infante restaurant at Sagres. That was the night we agreed to do the cookbook—just a stone's throw from where Henry the Navigator launched his newly trained sailors towards the New World.

1 lb	cultivated mussels	450 g
1	small chorizo sausage	1
2 tsp	olive oil	10 mL
2	cloves garlic, minced	2
1	medium onion, sliced	1
1	bay leaf	1
½ cup	dry white wine	125 mL
2	fresh tomatoes, peeled, seeded, and chopped parsley	2
1	lemon, cut into wedges	1

Scrub mussels and remove beards. Discard any that do not close when touched. Pierce chorizo sausage with fork and microwave on high, with vented cover, 3 minutes; drain and slice. Heat oil in a wok or large, heavy saucepan. Add garlic, onion, and sausage; sauté 2 minutes. Add bay leaf, white wine, tomatoes, and simmer gently 5 minutes. Add mussels, bring to boil, cover pan, reduce heat and simmer 5 minutes. Remove cover, if most mussel shells are not open, cook 1 minute longer. Discard any that have not opened. Remove bay leaf. Add chopped parsley. Serve in soup plates with lemon wedge to squeeze over cataplana.

Yield: 2 servings

per serving	**calorie breakdown**
calories 583	% protein 47
g fat 18.8	% fat 32
g fibre 1.7	% carbohydrate 22

LEMON MERINGUE PIE

You can take all kinds of shortcuts to get a passable lemon pie. However, there is only one way to achieve a remarkable lemon pie: use a large, fresh lemon.

1	baked (9-inch/23 cm) pastry crust*	1
1½ cups	granulated sugar	375 mL
6 tbsp	cornstarch	90 mL
1½ cups	water	375 mL
2	eggs, separated	2
1 tbsp	butter	15 mL
1	large lemon, grated rind and juice	1
1	egg white	1
⅓ cup	granulated sugar	75 mL

*see page 42

In medium saucepan, blend sugar and cornstarch. Whisk in water. Cook over medium heat, stirring constantly until mixture thickens. Reduce heat and continue stirring and cooking 1 minute longer. Remove from heat, set aside 2 tablespoons (25 mL) of sauce for meringue. Beat egg yolks slightly, whisk some of hot sauce into yolks. Gradually whisk yolk mixture into hot sauce, return to heat and continue cooking and stirring, 1 minute. Remove from heat, stir in butter, lemon juice, and rind. Pour into baked pastry crust.

For meringue, beat 3 egg whites until soft peaks form. Add ⅓ cup (75 mL) sugar, a spoonful at a time, beating continually, until peaks are stiff but not dry. Reduce speed and gradually add reserved sauce. Spread meringue on lemon filling. Bake in 325°F (160°C) oven for 20 minutes, until meringue sets and is lightly browned. Cool pie completely before serving. This meringue will not harden or weep.

Yield: 8 servings

per serving	**calorie breakdown**
calories 332	% protein 6
g fat 9.2	% fat 25
g fibre 0.7	% carbohydrate 70

TO BAKE AN UNFILLED PASTRY CRUST:

This method, called "baking blind," prevents the crust from shrinking during baking. Prick pastry all over with fork. Line with foil, shiny side toward crust. Fill with dried beans, dried peas or purchased ceramic pie beans. Bake in 400°F (200°C) oven, 8 minutes. Remove beans and foil, return to oven and continue baking until crust is golden brown. Cool on rack before adding cooked filling. Store dried beans or peas to use again.

SCIENTIFIC ADVICE ON MERINGUE

- Room temperature egg whites whip to greater volume.
- Meringue topping should be spread over warm filling.
- Reduce sugar to a maximum of 2 tablespoons (25 mL) per large egg white.
- Whip egg whites to soft peaks. With continued beating, slowly sprinkle in sugar and beat well after all sugar is added.
- Adding 2 tablespoons (25 mL) cooked cornstarch mixture to beaten meringue makes it easier to cut pie.
- Cooking temperature needs to be low, 325°F (160°C), and cooking time, 20 minutes.
- Cool pie quickly and store in refrigerator.

Fudge Sauced Pudding

Although a pudding mix can be purchased to make this dish, this old-fashioned recipe is much better.

2 tbsp	cocoa	25 mL
¾ cup	all-purpose flour	175 mL
¾ cup	granulated sugar	175 mL
2 tsp	baking powder	10 mL
½ cup	1% milk	125 mL
2 tbsp	oil	25 mL
1	egg	1
½ tsp	vanilla	2 mL
½ cup	lightly packed brown sugar	125 mL
¼ cup	cocoa	50 mL
1¾ cups	hot 1% milk	425 mL

Sift cocoa, flour, sugar, and baking powder into 2 quart (2 L) casserole. In liquid measure, whisk ½ cup (125 mL) milk, oil, egg, and vanilla. Pour over dry ingredients and stir to combine. Spread evenly in casserole, scraping down sides. Combine brown sugar and ¼ cup (50 mL) cocoa, breaking up lumps. Sprinkle evenly over pudding. Pour hot milk over top. Bake in 350°F (180°C) oven 40 minutes, until cake springs back when touched in centre. Serve warm.

Yield: 6 servings

per serving	**calorie breakdown**
calories 321	% protein 8
g fat 6.5	% fat 17
g fibre 1.9	% carbohydrate 75

QUICK RHUBARB PUDDING

You must have the cake mix and the package of gelatin. Beyond that, this dessert is fast and fantastic.

3 cups	chopped frozen rhubarb	750 mL
½ cup	granulated sugar	125 mL
1 (3 oz) pkg	strawberry flavoured gelatin	85 g
1 (8 oz) pkg	one-layer white cake mix	250 g
1 cup	boiling water	250 mL
1 tbsp	butter	15 mL

Spread rhubarb in 9-inch (2.5 L) square pan. Sprinkle with sugar and gelatin. Cover with dry cake mix. Pour boiling water evenly over top. Dot with butter. Bake in 350°F (180°C) oven 40 to 50 minutes, until toothpick inserted in centre comes out clean.

Yield: 6 to 8 servings

Variations:
This pudding can be made with other summer fruits and appropriate gelatin. The sweeter fruits will require less sugar.

per serving	calorie breakdown
calories 332	% protein 4
g fat 7	% fat 19
g fibre 1.5	% carbohydrate 77

Bananas Foster

We usually eat bananas raw or mashed as an ingredient in baked goods but this Caribbean recipe encourages warm, sunny thoughts in the middle of winter.

3	large firm ripe bananas	3
1 tbsp	lemon juice	15 mL
1 tbsp	butter, melted	15 mL
2 tbsp	brown sugar	25 mL
½ tsp	cinnamon	2 mL
2 tbsp	rum *or* orange juice	25 mL

Peel and cut bananas in half crosswise, then in half lengthwise. Brush with lemon juice and place in a lightly buttered baking dish. Combine remaining butter, brown sugar, cinnamon, and rum or orange juice; drizzle over bananas. Bake, uncovered in 350°F (180°C) oven 15 minutes, until bananas are soft and sauce bubbles. Baste once. Serve hot.

In the Microwave:
Cook on high, lightly covered, 4 to 5 minutes, basting once.

Yield: 4 servings

per serving	**calorie breakdown**
calories 148	% protein 3
g fat 3.4	% fat 21
g fibre 1.6	% carbohydrate 77

WILD BLUEBERRY GRUNT

This steamed cobbler, originally cooked in a pot over the open fire, is one of our most famous desserts known by various names, among them, "grunt" and "slump."

3 cups	wild blueberries, fresh or frozen	750 mL
½ cup	granulated sugar	125 mL
¼ tsp	nutmeg	1 mL
½ tsp	cinnamon	2 mL
⅓ cup	orange juice	75 mL

Dumplings:

1 cup	all-purpose flour	250 mL
2 tsp	baking powder	10 mL
¼ tsp	salt	1 mL
1 tsp	sugar	5 mL
1 tbsp	butter	15 mL
½ cup	1% milk (more or less)	125 mL

In deep skillet or wide saucepan, combine blueberries, sugar, nutmeg, cinnamon, and orange juice. Bring to boil, reduce heat and simmer, uncovered, stirring often, for 5 minutes.

To prepare dumplings, in medium bowl, combine flour, baking powder, salt, and sugar. Cut in butter and with fork stir in enough milk to make soft biscuit dough. Drop by spoonfuls on hot berry sauce. Cover tightly and simmer 15 minutes. No peeking! The dumplings should be puffed and cooked through. Transfer dumplings to serving dish, ladle sauce over top. Serve warm.

Yield: 6 servings

per serving
calories 228
g fat 2.7
g fibre 2.8

calorie breakdown
% protein 6
% fat 10
% carbohydrate 83

DATE PUDDING CAKE

Part of the Maritimes' heritage, this country recipe almost disappeared. Donna's Aunt Margaret brought it to us.

¾ cup	granulated sugar	175 mL
¼ cup	soft margarine	50 mL
1	egg	1
¼ cup	corn syrup	50 mL
1 cup	all-purpose flour	250 mL
1 cup	whole wheat flour	250 mL
1 tsp	baking soda	5 mL
1	orange, grated rind of	1
1 cup	sour milk*	250 mL
1 cup	chopped dates	250 mL

Topping:

¼ cup	orange juice	50 mL
2 tbsp	granulated sugar	25 mL

*see page 176

In medium bowl, cream sugar and margarine; beat in egg and corn syrup until light. In separate bowl, combine flours, baking soda, and orange rind. Add dry ingredients to creamed mixture alternately with sour milk. Fold in dates and spread batter in oiled 9-inch (2.5 L) square cake pan. Bake in 350⁰F (180⁰C) oven 35 minutes, until centre springs back when touched. To prepare topping, mix orange juice with 2 tablespoons (25 mL) sugar and pour over cake while hot. Serve warm or cold. If keeping more than 2 days, store covered in refrigerator.

Yield: 12 servings

per serving	**calorie breakdown**
calories 213	% protein 7
g fat 4.1	% fat 17
g fibre 2.7	% carbohydrate 76

APPLE BREAD PUDDING

Recipes for bread pudding were brought to Canada by the English. A nutritious dessert, most contain milk and egg, which are absorbed by the bread to form a custard when steamed or baked.

¼ cup	granulated sugar	50 mL
½ cup	low-fat cottage cheese*	125 mL
1	egg	1
1 cup	1% milk	250 mL
1 tsp	butter	5 mL
3	slices whole wheat bread	3
2	apples, peeled, cored, and sliced	2
¼ cup	raisins	50 mL
1 tsp	nutmeg	5 mL

*May substitute quark or yogurt cheese.

Beat or process sugar, cottage cheese, and egg. Blend in milk. Butter a 1 quart (1 L) casserole. Place slice of bread on bottom and cover with half the apple slices and raisins and one-third of the nutmeg. Cover with one-third milk mixture. Repeat layer and top with last slice of bread and remaining milk mixture. Sprinkle with nutmeg. Bake in 350°F (180°C) oven 50 minutes, until custard is set. Serve warm or cold.

Yield: 4 servings

per serving	**calorie breakdown**
calories 233	% protein 16
g fat 4.2	% fat 16
g fibre 3.1	% carbohydrate 68

Blueberry Cheesecake

Quark cheese is creamy, low in fat, and has a subtle taste. It is an old, soft, unripened cheese that originated in Germany. It is being revived as a replacement for cream cheese. The fat content varies from less than 1 per cent to a high of about 14 per cent. It depends on the amount of fat in the milk and the density of the cheese.

Crust:

20	Digestive biscuits (1½ cups/375 mL crumbs)	20
2 tbsp	granulated sugar	25 mL
¼ cup	butter, melted	50 mL

Filling:

1½ lb	quark or yogurt cheese	675 g
2	egg yolks	2
2 tbsp	all-purpose flour	25 mL
½ cup	granulated sugar	125 mL
1 cup	plain skimmed milk yogurt	250 mL
1	lemon, grated rind and juice	1
1 tsp	pure vanilla	5 mL
4	egg whites	4

Topping:

2 cups	wild blueberries, fresh or frozen	500 mL
¼ cup	granulated sugar	50 mL
½ cup	water	125 mL
3 tbsp	cornstarch	45 mL

In food processor or blender, process Digestive biscuits to fine crumbs. In 9-inch (2.5 L) springform pan, mix crumbs and sugar. Stir in melted butter and press firmly over bottom and 1 inch (2.5 cm) up sides of pan to form crust. Bake in 350°F (180°C) oven 8 minutes, until lightly browned. Cool.

In food processor or with stand mixer, beat quark cheese and egg yolks until smooth. Combine flour and sugar; add to cheese with yogurt, lemon juice and rind, and vanilla. Beat until smooth. Beat egg whites until stiff;

fold into cheese mixture. Pour over cooled crust. Bake in 350°F (180°C) oven 50 to 55 minutes, or until centre of cake is firm to touch. If filling darkens too soon, reduce temperature to 325°F (160°C). Turn oven off and leave cheesecake 1 hour. Remove from oven and cool completely.

In saucepan, heat blueberries, sugar, and ¼ cup (50 mL) water to boiling. Mix remaining ¼ cup (50 mL) water with cornstarch; stir into blueberries. Cook over medium heat, stirring constantly, until mixture thickens and clears. Cool slightly and spread over cooled cheesecake. Refrigerate until ready to serve.

Yield: 16 servings

per serving	calorie breakdown
calories 191	% protein 18
g fat 7	% fat 32
g fibre 0.9	% carbohydrate 50

Acadian Fruit Tart

The cookbook, A Taste of Acadie *contains a number of desserts from Acadian kitchens. Most of them are high in fat and sugar: Pork and Molasses Pie, Sugar Pie, Little Boats in Sauce, etc. One recipe, Petites Tarts au Lard, caught our eye and is a dessert that is pleasing to the eye. It was made in New Brunswick with a quarter pound of pork fat cubes but without the pork fat in Nova Scotia and Prince Edward Island.*

1	(8-inch/20 cm) unbaked pastry crust *	1
½ cup	seedless raisins, preferably golden	125 mL
2	medium apples, peeled, cored, and diced	2
1½ cups	whole cranberries, fresh or frozen	375 mL
1	egg	1
½ cup	granulated sugar	125 mL
1 tbsp	all-purpose flour	15 mL
¼ tsp	cinnamon	1 mL
2 tbsp	orange juice *or* water	25 mL

*see page 42

Place half the raisins in pastry crust. Top with half the apples and cranberries. Repeat with remaining fruit. In small bowl, whisk egg until frothy. Combine sugar, flour, and cinnamon; add to egg along with orange juice or water. Whisk until well mixed. Pour evenly over fruit. Bake in 400°F (200°C) oven 15 minutes. Reduce heat to 325°F (160°C) and bake 35 minutes longer, until fruit is bubbly and crust is brown and crisp. If crust and/or filling starts to brown too quickly, place foil tent over pie during last half of baking time. Serve warm or cold.

Yield: 6 servings

per serving
calories 360
g fat 13.6
g fibre 3.8

calorie breakdown
% protein 5
% fat 33
% carbohydrate 62

PUMPKIN ROLL

Sponge cake rolls are free of oil or butter and make good desserts as long as you don't fill them with whipped cream. Pumpkin, ginger, cinnamon, and nutmeg are good partners in this spicy dessert.

¾ cup	all-purpose flour	175 mL
1 tsp	baking powder	5 mL
1 tsp	cinnamon	5 mL
½ tsp	nutmeg	2 mL
½ tsp	ginger	2 mL
3	eggs	3
½ cup	granulated sugar	125 mL
½ cup	canned pumpkin	125 mL

Filling:

1 cup	quark cheese	250 mL
¼ cup	icing sugar	50 mL
½ cup	crushed ginger cookie crumbs	125 mL
	icing sugar to decorate	

Line a 15 x 10 x 2 inch (2 L) jelly roll pan with waxed paper. Sift flour, baking powder, and spices. In medium bowl, beat eggs until thick and lemon coloured. Continue beating, while gradually adding sugar, then pumpkin. Fold sifted dry ingredients into egg mixture. Spread batter into prepared pan. Bake in 375⁰F (190⁰C) oven 12 to 15 minutes, until top springs back when touched. Immediately loosen edges and invert cake on tea towel dusted with icing sugar; peel off paper. Starting at short end, roll up cake and towel together. Place on wire rack, seam side down to cool.

Beat together ingredients for filling. Unroll cooled cake and spread with filling. Roll up cake, without towel, refrigerate, covered. Dust with icing sugar before slicing and serving.

Yield: 12 servings

per serving	calorie breakdown
calories 185	% protein 15
g fat 2.1	% fat 10
g fibre 0.9	% carbohydrate 75

DARK FRUIT CAKE

This large, steamed, fruitcake is a full day's work. However, when done, you have enough cake for gifts and for the year.

2 lbs	seeded raisins	900 g
1 lb	seedless raisins	450 g
½ lb	currants	225 g
½ lb	candied red cherries	225g
½ lb	dates, cut in half	225g
½ lb	figs, cut in half	225g
2	slices candied pineapple, chopped	2
¼ lb	candied mixed peel	110 g
1¼ cups	all-purpose flour	300 mL
½ cup	butter	125 mL
½ cup	lightly packed brown sugar	125 mL
4	eggs	4
½ tsp	cinnamon	2 mL
½ tsp	nutmeg	2 mL
¼ tsp	cloves	1 mL
½ cup	strawberry jam	125 mL
2 tbsp	brandy *or* strong cold coffee	25 mL
1 tsp	lemon extract	5 mL
2 tsp	vanilla	10 mL

Line bottom and sides of 8 x 8½ inch (20 x 20 x 8 cm) fruitcake pan* with 2 layers heavy, brown paper. Oil inside layer.

In extra large bowl, combine all dried and candied fruits. Sprinkle ¼ cup (50 mL) flour over and stir to coat. Set aside. In medium bowl, cream butter and brown sugar; add eggs one at a time, beating after each addition. Combine remaining flour with cinnamon, nutmeg, and cloves; add to egg mixture alternately with jam. Stir in brandy or coffee, lemon extract, and vanilla. Pour evenly over fruit and stir only to combine. Pour into prepared pan. Cover with foil, secure with string, and place in steamer or on rack in large pot of boiling water so that water is not touching cake pan.

Steam 5 hours or until centre springs back when touched. Cake will look gummy. Remove foil and transfer to 250°F (120°C) oven; bake 1 hour. Let sit on rack 15 minutes, remove from pan, peel off paper, and cool thoroughly. Wrap in brandy soaked cheesecloth. Store in cool place in sealed tin for at least 1 month; resoak cheesecloth with brandy several times. May spread with almond paste and/or butter icing or serve plain; cut in fingers.

* May be made in large (9-inch/3 L) tube pan or several small loaf pans. Steaming and baking times will be reduced accordingly.

Yield: 128 slices

per slice
calories 76
g fat 1.0
g fibre 1.1

calorie breakdown
% protein 4
% fat 11
% carbohydrate 85

Good-For-You Pudding

This Christmas pudding is better than the old-fashioned plum pudding because we've replaced candied fruits with fresh fruits and vegetables.

1 cup	granulated sugar	250 mL
⅓ cup	oil	75 mL
1 cup	all-purpose flour	250 mL
1 tsp	baking soda	5 mL
1 tsp	nutmeg	5 mL
½ tsp	allspice	2 mL
½ cup	chopped cranberries	125 mL
1 cup	seeded raisins	250 mL
1	medium potato, peeled and grated (1 cup/250 mL)	1
1	large carrot, peeled and chopped (1 cup/250 mL)	1
1	large apple, peeled and chopped (1 cup/250 mL)	1
½ cup	walnuts, chopped	125 mL

In large bowl, beat sugar and oil. Add flour, baking soda, nutmeg, and allspice, mixing well. Stir in remaining ingredients. Pack into lightly oiled pudding mold or heat resistant bowl. Cut a circle of waxed paper to fit on top of pudding in the mold. Set mold in shallow pan of boiling water and bake 350°F (180°C) oven for 2 hours, or until centre springs back when touched. Let cool 10 minutes, unmold and serve warm with brandy sauce or hard or caramel sauce.

To reheat, place in saucepan of boiling water on top of stove, cover and steam for 30 minutes or microwave on high, covered, 3 to 5 minutes.

Variation:
Steam pudding on top of stove. Tie a piece of foil over top of mold. Place mold on rack in saucepan of simmering water, halfway up sides of mold. Cover, steam for 2 to 3 hours, depending on shape of mold. Add more boiling water as required.

Brandy Sauce:

2 tbsp	butter	25 mL
2 tbsp	all-purpose flour	25 mL
½ cup	lightly packed brown sugar	125 mL
1 cup	1% milk	250 mL
¼ cup	brandy	50 mL

In saucepan, melt butter; combine flour and brown sugar and blend into butter. Stir in milk. Cook over medium heat, stirring constantly, until sauce thickens. Remove and add brandy. Serve hot over steamed pudding. Makes 1½ cups (375 mL).

Yield: 12 servings

per serving
calories 269
g fat 9.2
g fibre 2.8

calorie breakdown
% protein 5
% fat 29
% carbohydrate 66

TRIFLE

The only thing trifling about this very special English dessert is its name. The wonderful combination of ingredients results in a dessert that tempts indulgence. The red raspberries and green kiwi fruit convey "Merry Christmas, Happy New Year."

¼ cup	granulated sugar	50 mL
3 tbsp	all-purpose flour	45 mL
2 cups	1% milk	500 mL
2	eggs	2
1 tsp	vanilla	5 mL
½	sponge cake (recipe follows)	½
½ cup	raspberry jam*	125 mL
½ cup	sherry	125 mL
3	kiwi fruit	3
2 cups	frozen raspberries, thawed*	500 mL
¾ cup	whipping cream	175 mL
1 tbsp	icing sugar	15 mL
½ tsp	vanilla	2 mL

*May substitute strawberry jam and frozen strawberries.

To Cook Custard in Microwave:
In 4-cup (1 L) microwavable bowl, mix sugar and flour well. Stir in milk. Microwave on high 5 minutes or until hot and slightly thickened, stirring twice. Beat eggs; whisk about ½ cup (125 mL) of the hot sauce into eggs and then whisk egg mixture into thickened sauce. Microwave on medium for 1½ minutes, stirring twice. Stir in vanilla. Cover with plastic wrap to prevent skin formation; refrigerate.

To Cook Custard Sauce on Stovetop:
In medium saucepan, mix sugar and flour; stir in milk and cook over medium heat, stirring constantly until thickened; remove from heat. Beat eggs, whisk some of the sauce into eggs, then stir into saucepan. Return to heat and cook, stirring constantly until custard bubbles. Remove from heat, stir in vanilla and cool as above.

To Assemble Trifle:

Cut sponge cake into ½-inch (1 cm) slices. Spread one side of each slice with jam and arrange plain side out in 2-quart (2 L) clear glass bowl, cutting pieces where necessary to cover bottom and sides of bowl. Sprinkle sherry evenly over cake pieces. Peel and slice 3 kiwi fruit, reserving slices of one for garnish. Reserving ¼ cup (50 mL) whole raspberries for garnish, layer kiwi and raspberries over cake. Pour cooled custard over fruit. Refrigerate until ready to serve. Just before serving, beat whipping cream, adding icing sugar and vanilla near end. Spread whipped cream over top. Garnish with reserved raspberries and remaining kiwi slices.

Yield: 8 to 10 servings

per serving trifle	calorie breakdown
calories 281	% protein 8
g fat 5.8	% fat 19
g fibre 4.3	% carbohydrate 73

Sponge Cake

A traditional sponge cake is made with 6 eggs, but this recipe produces an excellent cake using just 3 eggs, thus reducing the amount of fat by 50 per cent. A sponge cake differs from a standard cake because it contains no butter, shortening, or oil—the only fat comes from the egg yolks.

3	eggs, room temperature	3
1 cup	granulated sugar	250 mL
½ tsp	vanilla	2 mL
1 cup	sifted cake and pastry flour *or* ⅞ cup (225 mL) all-purpose flour	250 mL
½ tsp	baking powder	2 mL
6 tbsp	warm water	90 mL

Beat eggs until thick and lemon coloured, continue beating while adding sugar a spoonful at a time; add vanilla. Mix flours and baking powder; add to egg mixture alternately with warm water, starting and ending with flour. Spoon batter into oiled and floured 9-inch (3 L) tube pan. Bake in 325°F (160°C) oven 40 to 50 minutes, until centre springs back when touched. Invert pan over funnel. Remove cake from pan when cool.

Yield: 16 slices

per serving sponge cake
calories 91
g fat 1
g fibre 0

calorie breakdown
% protein 8
% fat 10
% carbohydrate 82

BANANA POPPY SEED MUFFINS

Bananas give them flavour and poppy seeds give them crunch—a winning combination in a muffin.

1¾ cups	whole wheat flour	425 mL
¾ cup	granulated sugar	175 mL
1 tsp	baking powder	5 mL
2 tbsp	poppy seeds	25 mL
½ tsp	nutmeg	2 mL
¼ cup	oil	50 mL
1 cup	overripe mashed banana (2 medium)	250 mL
1	egg	1
1 tsp	baking soda	5 mL
⅓ cup	hot water	75 mL

In medium mixing bowl, combine flour, sugar, baking powder, poppy seeds, and nutmeg. In liquid measure, beat oil, mashed banana, and egg with a fork. Add to flour mixture, stirring only to moisten. Stir baking soda into hot water and quickly pour into batter; blend only to mix. Spoon into lightly oiled or lined muffin cups. Bake in 400⁰F (200⁰C) oven 15 minutes. Let stand 10 minutes, remove from pan, cool on wire rack. Freeze well.

Yield: 12 muffins

per muffin
calories 173
g fat 5.3
g fibre 2.6

calorie breakdown
% protein 7
% fat 26
% carbohydrate 66

CHRISTMAS BREAD

Christmas bread has always been served Christmas morning before gifts are opened in the Routledge home. It can be made ahead of time and frozen. If you have a bread maker with a dough option, this recipe will work; add the dough ingredients as listed to bread pan and pick up the directions after the first rising.

2½ cups	all-purpose flour	625 mL
2 tbsp	granulated sugar	25 mL
1 tsp	salt	5 mL
1½ tsp	instant yeast	7 mL
¾ cup	hot water (130°F/55°C)	175 mL
1 tbsp	oil	15 mL
1	egg	1
2 tsp	soft butter	10 mL
½ cup	brown sugar	125 mL
1 tsp	cinnamon	5 mL
½ cup	raisins *or* currants	125 mL

Icing:

1 tbsp	soft butter	15 mL
1 tbsp	milk	15 mL
1 cup (approx)	icing sugar	250 mL

In large bowl, mix 1 cup (250 mL) of the flour, sugar, salt, and yeast. Stir in hot water and oil. Add egg and beat until mixture is smooth and elastic. Mix in enough of remaining flour to make a soft dough. Turn on floured surface and knead 5 minutes. Return to bowl, cover and let rise in warm place until double in bulk, 1 hour. Punch down, let rest 5 minutes. Roll a rectangle 24 x 12 inch (60 x 30 cm). Spread with soft butter and sprinkle with brown sugar, cinnamon, and raisins or currants. Roll up jelly roll fashion, starting at long edge. Pinch edges to seal.

For Tea Ring:
Bring ends together and pinch to form circle. Carefully lift ring into oiled 9-inch (3 L) tube pan placing seam down. Use scissors to cut slits in top of dough at 1-inch (2 cm) intervals.

For Wreath:
Bring ends together and pinch to form circle. Carefully lift ring onto oiled cookie sheet, forming even circle with seam down. Use scissors to cut halfway through the dough at 1-inch (2 cm) intervals. Twist each piece so that cinnamon rings are exposed and the dough resembles a wreath.

For Christmas tree:
Cut the roll into 16 pieces. Place pieces, with cinnamon rings exposed, in shape of tree on oiled cookie sheet, the last roll forms tree trunk. Leave space between rolls for them to rise and give tree shape.

Cover with tea towel and let rise in a warm place until double in size. Bake in 350°F (160°C) oven until golden brown. Time will depend on the shape of the bread; Christmas tree and wreath will take 15 to 20 minutes; tea ring will take 20 to 25 minutes.

Make butter icing by beating together butter, milk, and enough icing sugar to make a soft icing.

Cool bread on wire rack. When slightly warm, drizzle icing over top; decorate with red and green cherries and toasted almonds.

Yield: 16 servings

per serving	calorie breakdown
calories 163	% protein 7
g fat 2.6	% fat 14
g fibre 1	% carbohydrate 79

Mom's Oatmeal Cookies

Donna's mom made these cookies for lunch boxes and to accompany her evening cup of tea. She wrapped the cylinders in foil and kept them in the refrigerator, unbaked, for several weeks. We prefer to bake them all at once and freeze them.

1 cup	soft margarine	250 mL
½ cup	packed brown sugar	125 mL
1 cup	granulated sugar	250 mL
2	eggs	2
1 tsp	vanilla	5 mL
1 tsp	nutmeg	5 mL
½ tsp	cinnamon	2 mL
1½ cups	whole wheat flour	375 mL
1½ tsp	baking powder	7 mL
½ tsp	baking soda	2 mL
½ tsp	salt	2 mL
3½ cups	quick cooking oats	875 mL
½ cup	chopped walnuts (optional)	125 mL

In large bowl, beat margarine, sugars, eggs, vanilla, nutmeg, and cinnamon until smooth and creamy. Combine flour, baking powder, baking soda, and salt; beat into creamed mixture. Stir in oats and nuts, if using. Turn on floured surface and knead 5 times. Form into two logs, 1½ inches (4 cm) in diameter. Wrap in waxed paper and chill. When ready to bake, slice ¼ inch (0.5 cm) thick with sharp knife; place on ungreased cookie sheet 1 inch (2 cm) apart. Bake in 350°F (180°C) oven 12 minutes. Immediately remove from pan, cool on wire rack. Freeze well.

Yield: 6 dozen

per cookie (without nuts)
calories 68
g fat 3
g fibre 0.5

calorie breakdown
% protein 7
% fat 39
% carbohydrate 55

MARITIME BROWN BREAD

This is a basic bread of the area, eaten with beans and potato scallop. We argued about how sweet our recipe should be, compared to the old-time recipes. Remember, children probably eat this bread drizzled with more molasses.

½ cup	lukewarm water	125 mL
1 tsp	sugar	5 mL
1 tbsp	active dry yeast	15 mL
2 cups	quick cooking oats	500 mL
2½ cups	*boiling* water	625 mL
2 tbsp	oil	25 mL
⅔ cup	molasses	150 mL
2 tsp	salt	10 mL
3 cups	all-purpose flour	750 mL
3 cups	whole wheat flour	750 mL
1 cup	raisins (optional)	250 mL

Dissolve sugar in ½ cup (125 mL) warm water. Add yeast and set aside for 10 minutes, until foamy. In large bowl, pour boiling water over oats. Stir in oil, molasses, and salt. Add 2 cups (500 mL) all-purpose flour and beat vigorously to develop elasticity. Stir in yeast mixture and whole wheat flour. Add raisins, if using. Turn on floured surface and knead 6 minutes, working in remaining cup (250 mL) all-purpose flour as required to form soft dough. Return to mixing bowl, cover and let rise in warm place, until double in bulk, about 1½ hours. Punch down, let rest 5 minutes. Shape into loaves and place in lightly oiled loaf pans. Cover with tea towel and let rise in warm place until double in size, 1 hour. Bake in 350°F (180°C) oven 45 to 50 minutes, until bread sounds hollow when rapped with knuckles. If bread browns too quickly, reduce temperature. Remove from pans immediately; cool on wire rack. Freezes well.

Yield: 3 large or 2 double loaves

per slice	**calorie breakdown**
calories 140	% protein 12
g fat 1.5	% fat 9
g fibre 2.6	% carbohydrate 79

Date Bread

An old standard, date bread belongs on the winter tea table.

1 cup	all-purpose flour	250 mL
1 cup	whole wheat flour	250 mL
¾ cup	granulated sugar	175 mL
1 tsp	baking powder	5 mL
½ tsp	baking soda	2 mL
¾ cup	water	175 mL
1	medium orange, cut up and seeded	1
2 tbsp	oil	25 mL
1	egg	1
1 cup	chopped dates	250 mL

In medium bowl, combine flours, sugar, baking powder, and soda. In blender or food processor, process water, orange, oil, and egg until quite smooth. Add to flour mixture; stir until combined. Fold in dates. Turn into oiled 8 x 4 x 2½ inch (1.5 L) loaf pan. Let rest 15 minutes. Invert another loaf pan over top and bake in 325°F (160°C) oven 30 minutes. Remove inverted pan and bake 25 to 30 minutes, until toothpick inserted in centre comes out clean. Cool in pan 10 minutes; remove and cool completely on wire rack. Wrap and store 24 hours before slicing. Freezes well.

Yield: 16 slices

per slice	**calorie breakdown**
calories 141	% protein 7
g fat 2.0	% fat 12
g fibre 2.4	% carbohydrate 80

STEAMED BROWN BREAD

Some Maritimers prefer yeast brown bread with baked beans for Saturday night supper. Others must have steamed brown bread.

1 cup	whole wheat flour	250 mL
1 cup	all-purpose flour	250 mL
1 cup	cornmeal	250 mL
1½ tsp	baking soda	7 mL
½ tsp	salt	2 mL
⅓ cup	granulated sugar	75 mL
1 cup	raisins	250 mL
½ cup	molasses	125 mL
1¼ cups	buttermilk	300 mL
3 tbsp	oil	45 mL
1	egg	1

In medium bowl, combine flours, cornmeal, baking soda, salt, sugar, and raisins. In liquid measure, whisk molasses, buttermilk, oil, and egg. Add to dry ingredients, mixing only to moisten. Turn into oiled 1-quart (1 L) mold, cover with waxed paper, and secure with string. Place on rack in steamer or large saucepan with boiling water halfway up mold. Steam 2 to 3 hours, depending on mold size and shape. A tube mold will cook in 2 hours; a solid mold will take 3 hours. When done, centre will spring back when touched. Invert on wire rack, remove mold after 10 minutes.
Serve hot.

Yield: 16 slices

per slice	**calorie breakdown**
calories 134	% protein 8
g fat 2.4	% fat 15
g fibre 2.1	% carbohydrate 77

CRANBERRY ORANGE BREAD

One of the prettiest fruit breads, this one is ideal from Thanksgiving until Christmas.

1 cup	all-purpose flour	250 mL
1 cup	whole wheat flour	250 mL
¾ cup	granulated sugar	175 mL
½ tsp	baking soda	2 mL
1 tsp	baking powder	5 mL
1	orange, grated rind and juice	1
	hot water	
2 tbsp	oil	25 mL
1	egg	1
½ cup	currants	125 mL
1 cup	cranberries, fresh or frozen, cut in half	250 mL
2 tbsp	slivered almonds *or* hazelnuts for topping	25 mL

In medium mixing bowl, combine flours, sugar, baking soda, and baking powder. In liquid measure, combine orange rind, juice, and enough hot water to make ¾ cup (175 mL); whisk in oil and egg. Pour into flour mixture and stir until combined. Fold in currants and cranberries. Spoon batter in greased 8 x 4 x 2½ inch (1.5 L) loaf pan. Lightly press nuts on top. Let rest on counter 15 minutes. Invert another loaf pan over top and bake in 325°F (160°C) oven, 30 minutes. Remove inverted pan and continue to bake 25 to 35 minutes, until toothpick inserted in centre comes out clean. Cool in pan 10 minutes; remove and cool completely on wire rack. Wrap and store 24 hours before slicing.

Yield: 16 slices

per slice
calories 127
g fat 1.8
g fibre 2

calorie breakdown
% protein 8
% fat 12
% carbohydrate 79

BAKED RHUBARB

It is quicker to stew rhubarb on top of the stove in a saucepan. However, if you want perfect chunks of fruit floating in pink nectar, it is better to bake it.

3 cups	chopped rhubarb, fresh or frozen	750 mL
¾ cup	granulated sugar	175 mL
2-inch	stick cinnamon	5 cm
¼ cup	water	50 mL

Combine all ingredients in baking dish. Cover and bake in 350⁰F (180⁰C) oven 30 minutes, until tender. Chill. Remove cinnamon before serving.

Yield: 4 servings

per serving
calories 162
g fat 0.2
g fibre 1.8

calorie breakdown
% protein 2
% fat 1
% carbohydrate 97

MICROWAVED PORRIDGE

*No breakfast was more common in the Maritimes than porridge. Some
started it at night and hung it over the waning fire. Later on they put it on
the back of the warm wood stove. Others cooked a large pot in the morning.
In the modern kitchen, each person creates his own. Believe me, making
porridge is an art. You start by selecting from four kinds of rolled oats displayed on the grocery shelf. You then choose from among the various dried
and fresh fruits that may be placed under or over the rolled oats. Next you
choose between hot and cold water and/or milk and/or juice. Finally, there's
all the flavourings, sweeteners, and dairy products that may go on top.
Donna is a regular porridge eater and here's her recipe.*

6	Thompson raisins	6
⅓ cup	quick cooking oats	75 mL
⅔ cup	cold tap water	150 mL
1	shake of salt	1
1 tsp	brown sugar	5 mL
½ cup	homogenized milk	125 ml

Drop the raisins into a cereal bowl and cover with oats. Add cold water
and salt. Microwave on medium 2 to 2½ minutes, until mixture heaves in
bowl. Remove and stir. Sprinkle with sugar and add milk. (I like lots of
milk.)

Yield: 1 serving

per serving
calories 241
g fat 6
g fibre 3.1

calorie breakdown
% protein 14
% fat 22
% carbohydrate 64

CRANBERRY RELISH

Blending cranberries with apples and oranges for a relish probably started with native rock or bog cranberries. Today we make it for the holiday season with cultivated bog cranberries and less sugar.

1 (12 oz) pkg	cranberries, washed and drained	340 g
1	large red apple, washed, quartered, and cored	1
1	medium orange, washed, quartered, and seeded	1
½ cup	granulated sugar	125 mL

Grind fruit coarsely using a meat grinder or pulse action on food processor. Stir in sugar and let stand for 2 hours. Stir and store in refrigerator. Keeps 1 month.

Yield: 1½ cups

per 2 tablespoons
calories 60
g fat 0.4
g fibre 2.2

calorie breakdown
% protein 2
% fat 2
% carbohydrate 96

Divinity Fudge

A divine finale to dinner for two, and there's absolutely no fat in it.

2½ cups	granulated sugar	625 mL
¼ tsp	salt	1 mL
½ cup	corn syrup	125 mL
½ cup	hot water	125 mL
2	egg whites, room temperature	2
1 tsp	pure vanilla	5 mL

In medium saucepan, combine sugar, salt, corn syrup, and hot water; stir while bringing to boil. Boil without stirring until candy thermometer reads 260°F (135°C), hard ball stage. Toward end of cooking, with stand mixer, beat egg whites until soft peaks form. When syrup is ready, pour in thin, steady stream over egg whites, beating at high speed. Do not scrape bowl. Add vanilla and continue beating until stiff peaks form. When too thick for mixer, beat by hand until candy loses its sheen. Quickly turn into buttered 9-inch (2.5 L) square pan and spread evenly. When cool, cut into 25 squares. Alternatively, drop quickly, by spoonfuls on waxed paper.

May add nuts, if desired.

Yield: 25 pieces

per piece	**calorie breakdown**
calories 103	% protein 1
g fat 0	% fat 0
g fibre 0	% carbohydrate 99

MULLED CRAN-APPLE CIDER

A modern mulled cider, this is the hand and tummy warmer for gathering family and friends that makes you forget about alcoholic beverages.

1 cup	water	250 mL
6-inch	stick cinnamon	15 cm
12	whole cloves	12
1 qt	cranberry juice	1 L
1 qt	apple cider	1 L

In small saucepan, combine water, cinnamon, and cloves. Bring to boil, reduce heat and simmer 15 minutes. Strain, discarding spices. Pour cranberry juice, apple cider and spiced water into 3 quart (3 L) saucepan; bring to boil. To serve, pour into heat resistant punch bowl on hot tray. Garnish with orange pinwheels and whole cranberries.

Refrigerate leftover cider; serve cold or reheat.

Yield: 2 quarts (2 L) or 14 (6 oz/175 mL) servings

per serving
calories 82
g fat 0
g fibre 0

calorie breakdown
% protein 0
% fat 0
% carbohydrate 99

SPANISH COFFEE

Following a Portuguese dinner of cataplana, we suggest a neighbourly Spanish dessert.

½	fresh lemon	½
1 tsp	sugar	5 mL
2 oz	brandy	60 mL
2 oz	Tia Maria	60 mL
2 cups	strong, hot coffee	500 mL
¼ cup	whipped cream	50 mL
2 tbsp	Tia Maria	30 mL

Coat rim of glass mug with half lemon; dip in sugar to coat. Pour brandy and 2 oz (60 mL) Tia Maria into mugs. Fill with coffee; top with cream. In glass measure, microwave 2 tablespoons (30 mL) Tia Maria on high for 20 seconds. Flame and quickly pour over cream. Serve.

Yield: 2 servings

per serving
calories 263
g fat 1.8
g fibre 0.0

calorie breakdown
% protein 1
% fat 13
% carbohydrate 85

Too Good to Leave Out

As we sorted through our files, we came across the odd recipe that was woven into family history, sometimes through both our families. We also had two recipes that were excellent snacks for energetic children, yet wouldn't fit the low-fat guidelines. As we worked along, we decided to create this chapter for those few special dishes we wanted to share. After all, every eating regime deserves an occasional liberty.

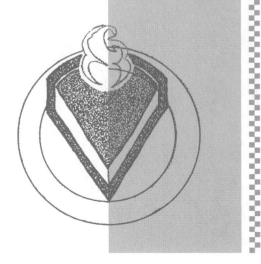

GUACAMOLE

This avocado dip is a staple in Latin American cooking. Because the innocent appearing avocado fruit is so high in fat and calories, we could not include it in our Mexican menu, but it is "too good to leave out."

1	ripe avocado	1
2 tbsp	low-fat salad dressing	25 mL
2 tbsp	lime or lemon juice	25 mL
½ tsp	salt	2 mL
few drops	hot pepper sauce	
2	green onions, thinly sliced	2
1	tomato, peeled, seeded, and diced	1
1	jalapeño pepper, seeded and diced (optional)	1

Cut avocado in half and remove pit; spoon flesh into small bowl and mash until fairly smooth. Beat in salad dressing, lime or lemon juice, salt, and hot pepper sauce. Stir in onions, tomato, and jalapeño, if using. Spoon into serving dish, cover tightly with plastic wrap, and refrigerate until ready to serve. Serve with tortilla or pita crisps.

Note:
Guacamole will discolour if left uncovered. It is best served within a few hours.

Yield: about ¾ cup (175 mL)

per serving: (2 tbsp/25 mL) **calorie breakdown**
calories 73   % protein 5
g fat 6.5   % fat 73
g fibre 1.9   % carbohydrate 22

Honey Garlic Spareribs

A finger-licking food we do occasionally crave. We have chosen the leanest spare ribs, back ribs. In fat content, they are certainly a better choice than chicken wings. Ask your butcher to saw the ribs in half for finger-size nibblers.

2 lb	pork, back spareribs	900 g
1	small onion, chopped	1
1	bay leaf	1
3	cloves garlic, minced	3
½ cup	honey *or* corn syrup	125 mL
¼ cup	soya sauce	50 mL
¼ cup	rice vinegar	50 mL
2 tsp	grated fresh ginger (optional)	10 mL

Cut ribs into individual pieces and place in shallow casserole with onion and bay leaf. Bake, uncovered, in 350°F (180°C) oven for 30 minutes. Remove from oven, drain off juices. In small bowl, combine garlic, honey or corn syrup, soya sauce, vinegar, and ginger (if using). Pour over ribs and stir. Bake, covered, in 350°F (180°C) oven for 15 minutes. Remove cover, stir and bake uncovered, 15 minutes longer. May be made ahead and reheated. Serve hot with rice.

Yield: 4 servings as main course; 12 as starter

per serving
calories 418
g fat 20
g fibre 0.5

calorie breakdown
% protein 20
% fat 42
% carbohydrate 38

Mariner's Lasagna

We combined seafood with the lasagna technique, and voilà, a sumptuous dish.

9	whole wheat or spinch lasagna noodles	9
¼ cup	butter *or* margarine	50 mL
2	cloves garlic, minced	2
1	medium onion, diced	1
2 cups	sliced mushrooms	500 mL
⅓ cup	all-purpose flour	75 mL
1½ cups	chicken broth, salted	375 mL
2 cups	1% milk	500 mL
2 lbs	cooked seafood (scallops, shrimp, etc)	900 g
¼ tsp	white pepper	1 mL
1 tbsp	chopped fresh parsley	15 mL
1 tbsp	chopped fresh basil *or* ½ tsp (2 mL) dried	15 mL
4 cups	grated low-fat Mozarella cheese	1 L
¼ cup	grated Parmesan cheese	50 mL

Cook lasagna noodles according to package directions. Drain, cover with cold water. In large saucepan, melt butter; sauté garlic and onion 2 minutes. Add mushrooms and sauté 1 minute. Sprinkle with flour, stir well to blend with butter. Stir in chicken broth. Add milk, cook over medium heat until mixture thickens, stirring constantly. Remove from heat; add seafood, pepper, parsley, and basil to sauce. Spread a thin layer of seafood sauce in 9 x 13 inch (3.5 L) baking dish. Cover with 3 lasagna noodles. Spread one-third remaining seafood sauce over noodles. Cover with one-third of the Mozarella cheese. Repeat layers twice, ending with cheese. Sprinkle with Parmesan cheese. Bake, uncovered, in 350⁰F (180⁰C) oven 30 to 40 minutes, until hot and bubbly. Let stand 10 minutes before cutting.

Yield: 8 servings

per serving	**calorie breakdown**
calories 828	% protein 41
g fat 35.3	% fat 40
g fibre 1.4	% carbohydrate 19

SCALLOPS BUBBLY BAKE

This recipe, acquired from the Boston Cooking School Cookbook, *first published in 1896, has existed for many years in Atlantic Canada under various names.*

1 lb	scallops	450 g
½ cup	dry white wine	125 g
⅓ cup	butter	75 mL
½ cup	minced onion	125 mL
½ cup	diced celery	125 mL
1 cup	sliced mushrooms	250 mL
1	bay leaf	1
¼ cup	all-purpose flour	50 mL
1 cup	1% milk	250 mL
salt and white pepper to taste		

Topping:

1 tbsp	butter	15 mL
1 cup	coarse bread crumbs	250 mL
¼ cup	grated cheddar cheese	50 mL

In stovetop-safe 1 qt (1 L), glass casserole, combine scallops and wine; refrigerate 1 hour. Bring scallops and wine to a boil, reduce heat and simmer gently for 1 minute. Drain scallops, reduce heat and simmer gently for 1 minute. Drain scallops, reserving liquid (about 1 cup/250 mL). In medium saucepan, melt butter, add onion, celery, mushrooms and bay leaf; sauté 2 minutes. Sprinkle flour over vegetables and stir over medium heat to mix well. Add milk and reserved liquid; cook, stirring constantly, until mixture thickens and comes to the boiling point. Remove bay leaf. Season sparingly with salt and pepper. Pour over scallops in casserole, and carefully stir to combine.

For topping, melt butter; pour over bread crumbs and cheese. Toss to combine. Spread over top of scallop mixture. Bake in 350°F (180°C) oven for 20 minutes, until top is golden brown and mixture bubbles around edges. Serve with mashed potatoes or rice.

Yield: 4 servings

per serving
calories 509
g fat 22.6
g fibre 1.52

calorie breakdown
% protein 24
% fat 43
% carbohydrate 33

Peking Duck

The Chinese national dish; an unusual meal ideal for a conversational dinner.

Mandarin Pancakes:

2½ cups	all-purpose flour	625 mL
¾ cup	boiling water	175 mL
¼ cup	cold water	50 mL
1 tbsp	sesame oil	15 mL

Roasted Duckling:

1 (5 lb)	duckling	2.2 kg
3 tbsp	honey	45 mL
¼ cup	warm water	50 mL
4	green onions, cut in 3-inch julienne strips	4
	Hoisin sauce	

To make pancakes, in medium bowl, beat flour and boiling water until smooth. Stir in enough of the cold water to make a stiff dough. Turn dough on oiled surface and knead 5 minutes, until smooth and elastic. Form into long roll, cut in 15 pieces, and cover with plastic wrap to prevent drying. Roll each piece between waxed paper into a 4-inch (10 cm) thin pancake. In small, heavy skillet, fry on both sides in 1 teaspoon (5 mL) sesame oil, adding more as required. Overlap on plate and keep warm.

To prepare duckling, clean and wash bird. Place on rack, breast down, over roasting pan. In liquid measure, combine honey and water; brush over duckling. Roast in 400°F (200°C) oven 30 minutes, brushing twice with honey mixture. Remove from oven and turn duckling on back. Drain off fat. Reduce temperature to 325°F (160°C) and roast for 1 to 1½ hours, brushing several times with honey mixture. Duckling is done when drumstick lifts and twists easily. Remove and transfer to hot platter. Remove skin and slice meat into 1-inch (2 cm) by 3-inch (7 cm) strips. Cover and keep hot.

Serve pancakes on hot plates. Pass meat and green onions to wrap in pancakes, which are dipped into Hoisin sauce and eaten with fingers.

Yield: 5 servings

per serving	calorie breakdown
calories 443	% protein 29
g fat 11.1	% fat 23
g fibre 2.1	% carbohydrate 4

Lemon Birthday Cake

This was the first birthday cake Marg made for her children. Now the batter is put into cartoon character pans for her grandchildren.

2½ cups	sifted cake and pastry flour	625 mL
1 tbsp	baking powder	15 mL
½ tsp	salt	2 mL
1½ cups	granulated sugar	375 mL
½ cup	soft margarine	125 mL
1 cup	1% milk	250 mL
2	eggs	2
1 tsp	lemon extract	5 mL

Cut waxed paper circles to cover bottoms of two 8-inch (1.3 L) round cake pans. Sift flour, baking powder, and salt; stir in sugar. In large bowl, cream margarine. Add dry ingredients plus ¾ cup (175 mL) of the milk and beat on low speed for 2 minutes. Add remaining milk, eggs and lemon extract and beat on low speed, 1 minute. Divide batter between prepared pans; smooth tops and bake in 375°F (190°C) oven 20 to 30 minutes, until centre springs back when touched. Let stand 10 minutes. Run knife around edge of pan to loosen cake and invert on wire racks. Peel off waxed paper and cool.

Lemon Filling:

¾ cup	granulated sugar	175 mL
3 tbsp	cornstarch	45 mL
1 cup	boiling water	250 mL
1	egg	1
1	lemon, juice and rind	1
1 tbsp	butter	15 mL

In medium saucepan, combine sugar and cornstarch. Whisk in water and cook over medium heat, stirring constantly, until clear and thick. Remove from heat. Beat egg slightly, whisk some of hot sauce into egg and gradually whisk egg mixture into hot sauce. Return to heat and continue cooking and stirring, 1 minute. Remove from heat, stir in lemon rind and juice, and butter. Cool before spreading between cake layers.

Butter Cream Frosting:

4½ cups (1 lb)	icing sugar (more or less)	1250 mL
¼ cup	soft butter	50 mL
¼ cup	homogenized milk	50 mL
1 tsp	pure vanilla	5 mL

In large bowl, beat 2 cups icing sugar, butter, and milk, until smooth. Beat in remaining icing sugar until frosting is smooth and of spreading consistency. Beat in vanilla. Spread on top and sides of cake.

Add extra icing sugar to small amount of frosting to make stiffer; colour with food colouring and use to write "Happy Birthday" on cake.

Yield: 12 to 16 servings

per serving	calorie breakdown
calories 583	% protein 3
g fat 13.7	% fat 21
g fibre 0.1	% carbohydrate 76

Donna's Chocolate Devil's Food Cake, Filling, Icing, and Glaze

The all-time favourite cake at Donna's house. There was enough batter for a large loaf pan plus cupcakes that provided lunchbox desserts. Later, with the filling and glaze, it became a requested birthday and wedding cake.

4 cups	all-purpose flour	1 L
2 tsp	baking soda	10 mL
1 tsp	baking powder	5 mL
1 cup	soft margarine	250 mL
4 cups	lightly packed brown sugar	1 L
4	large eggs	4
2 tsp	pure vanilla	10 mL
⅔ cup	dark cocoa	150 mL
1 cup	sour milk*	250 mL
1 cup	hot water	250 mL

*see page 176

Prepare cake pans: Place 12 baking cups in muffin pan and line two 9-inch (1.5 L) round cake pans with waxed paper.*
   Sift together flour, baking soda, and baking powder. Set aside. Using stand mixer and large bowl, cream margarine until light. Beating continuously, add 2 cups sugar, then eggs, one at a time, then remaining sugar. Beat until light and fluffy. Reduce mixer speed; add vanilla and cocoa, taking care to mash lumps. Blend in one-third flour mixture, then half of milk. Repeat ending with flour. Add hot water, all at once and stir quickly to blend. Pour into prepared pans. Bake in 350°F (180°C) oven, until center springs back when touched. Layer cakes require 40 minutes; cupcakes 20 minutes. Let stand 10 minutes. Remove cupcakes from pan and cool on wire rack. Run knife around edge of round pans to loosen cake; invert on wire racks. Peel off waxed paper and cool. Cake is better second day; freezes well before or after icing.

*Alternatively, make 12 cupcakes and a 9 x 13 inch (3.5 L) cake.

Filling for Layered Cake:

2 tbsp	dark cocoa	25 mL
½ cup	lightly packed brown sugar	125 mL
2 tbsp	cornstarch	25 mL
1 cup	homogenized milk	250 mL
1 tsp	butter	5 mL
½ tsp	pure vanilla	2 mL
2 tbsp	liqueur (optional)	25 mL

In 2 cup (500 mL) liquid measure, combine cocoa, brown sugar, and cornstarch; stir in milk. Microwave on high 3 to 4 minutes, stirring twice, until thick and bubbly. Remove, add butter and vanilla; cover and chill. Split cake layers with serrated knife. If desired, drizzle each layer with 1 tablespoon (15 mL) liqueur. Spread with filling.

Icing for Loaf or Layered Cake:

4 squares	unsweetened chocolate, chopped	4
¼ cup	soft butter	50 mL
6 tbsp	hot water	75 mL
3 cups	icing sugar	750 mL

In saucepan, over low heat, melt chocolate, stirring constantly. Remove from heat, beat in butter, hot water and icing sugar, until thick and creamy. Spread icing over top and sides of layer cake and tops of cupcakes.

Glaze:

8 squares	semi-sweet chocolate, chopped	8
½ cup	whipping cream	125 mL

In saucepan over low heat, melt chocolate, stirring constantly. Remove and gradually beat in whipping cream, until shiny. Pour on top of cake and drizzle down sides. When firm, slice cake using hot, dry knife.

Yield: 22 servings

per serving	**calorie breakdown**
calories 581	% protein 4
g fat 20.5	% fat 31
g fibre 2.8	% carbohydrate 65

CHOCOLATE CHEESECAKE

Designed for chocoholics, enjoyed by most people, and allowed for dieters, this is the ultimate cheesecake. Make it only when more than ten people are being served.

1¼ cups	chocolate wafer crumbs	300 mL
2 tbsp	granulated sugar	25 mL
¼ cup	melted butter	50 mL

Filling:

1 cup	(8 oz/225 g) quark cheese	250 mL
½ cup	(4 oz/115 g) softened cream cheese	125 mL
¾ cup	granulated sugar	175 mL
3	eggs	3
8 squares	semi-sweet chocolate, melted	8
1 tsp	almond extract	5 mL
1 tsp	pure vanilla	5 mL

Topping:

4 squares	semi-sweet chocolate, melted	4
¼ cup	sour cream	50 mL
¼ cup	liqueur of choice	50 mL

In 9-inch (2.5 L) springform pan, combine crumbs and sugar. Stir in butter and press firmly. Using stand mixer and large bowl, whip quark and cream cheese until smooth; continue beating while gradually adding sugar, then eggs, one at a time. Drizzle in chocolate (at room temperature) while continuing to beat. Add flavourings, scrape side of bowl and distribute evenly over crust. Bake in 300°F (150°C) oven 1 hour, until centre is firm to touch. Turn off oven and leave 1 hour. Remove and cool on wire rack, then in refrigerator 4 to 24 hours.

To prepare topping, blend 4 squares chocolate with sour cream and liqueur. Transfer cake to serving plate and spread with topping.

Yield: 16 servings

per serving
calories 310
g fat 17.1
g fibre 1.7

calorie breakdown
% protein 6
% fat 48
% carbohydrate 46

Estella's Pound Cake

Donna's elder daughter liked to baby-sit for a neighbour, Estella, a mother who put out home-baked treats for sitters. Imagine going baby-sitting and finding this smashing cake topped with fudge icing as your evening snack.

3 cups	all-purpose flour	750 mL
2 tsp	baking powder	10 mL
1 cup	butter	250 mL
2 cups	granulated sugar	500 mL
3	eggs	3
1 tsp	lemon extract	5 mL
2 tsp	pure vanilla	10 mL
2 tbsp	cherry liqueur *or* fruit juice	25 mL
1 cup	1% milk	250 mL

Sift together flour and baking powder. Set aside. With stand mixer, beat butter until lemon coloured. Continuing to beat, gradually add sugar; then eggs, one at a time. Reduce speed and add flavourings; half flour mixture, then milk and remaining flour mixture. Divide between two oiled or nonstick 8 x 4 x 2½ inch (1.5 L) loaf pans. Smooth top and fill corners higher than centre. Let rest 15 minutes. Invert another loaf pan on top and bake in 350⁰F (180⁰C) oven 20 minutes. Remove inverted pan and bake 30 to 35 minutes longer, until centre springs back when touched. Cool on wire rack 20 minutes before removing from pan. Cool and store in sealed container. Freezes well.

Yield: 32 slices

per serving	**calorie breakdown**
calories 163	% protein 5
g fat 6.8	% fat 37
g fibre 0.4	% carbohydrate 57

Peanut Butter Cookies

A child's cookie because of the excellent balance of nutrients, it is one in which the fat calories in the peanut butter keep good company. We were surprised to find it wasn't in traditional Maritime cookbooks because it was a standard in our families' cookie jars.

¾ cup	soft margarine	175 mL
½ cup	granulated sugar	125 mL
1 cup	brown sugar	250 mL
2	eggs	2
1 cup	peanut butter	250 mL
1 cup	all-purpose flour	250 mL
1½ cups	whole wheat flour	375 mL
2 tsp	baking soda	10 mL

In large bowl, beat margarine, sugars, eggs, and peanut butter until smooth and fluffy. Combine flours and baking soda; stir into creamed mixture, mix well. Drop by teaspoonful on ungreased cookie sheets. Press flat with floured fork. Bake 375°F (190°C) 10 to 12 minutes, until golden brown. Remove from cookie sheets and cool on wire rack. Store in covered container or freeze.

Yield: 5 dozen

per cookie
calories 89
g fat 4.6
g fibre 0.7

calorie breakdown
% protein 9
% fat 46
% carbohydrate 46

Chocolate Peanut Breakaways

Donna's kitchen has made hundreds of batches of these for children who like everything about them, beginning with the name. Over the years she adjusted ingredients to make them more healthful.

1½ cups	soft margarine	375 mL
1¼ cups	lightly packed brown sugar	300 mL
¼ cup	molasses	50 mL
1	egg	1
½ tsp	baking soda	2 mL
⅔ cup	natural wheat bran	150 mL
2 cups	whole wheat flour	500 mL
1 6-oz	package chocolate chips	170 g
1½ cups	salted, red-skinned peanuts	375 mL

In medium bowl, beat margarine, brown sugar, molasses, and egg until smooth. Reduce speed and beat in baking soda, bran and half of flour. Stir in remaining flour, chips, and nuts. Spread in 9 x 13 inch (3.5 L) ungreased baking pan and bake in 375°F (190°C) oven 20 minutes, until brown and firm to touch. Cool 10 minutes on wire rack; cut into squares. When cool, remove from pan and store in sealed container. These freeze well.

Yield: 35 squares

per serving	**calorie breakdown**
calories 200	% protein 6
g fat 13.1	% fat 57
g fibre 1.7	% carbohydrate 37

APRICOT SLICE

Marg was never a "squares" fan until she tried this recipe from her Aunt Muriel.

⅔ cup	chopped dried apricots	150 mL
⅓ cup	soft butter	75 mL
¼ cup	granulated sugar	50 mL
1⅓ cup	all-purpose flour	325 mL
1 cup	brown sugar	250 mL
½ tsp	baking powder	2 mL
¼ tsp	salt	1 mL
2	eggs	2
½ cup	chopped pecans	125 mL

Whipped creamy icing:

¼ cup	soft butter	50 mL
6 tbsp	icing sugar	90 mL
2 tbsp	cold 1% milk	25 mL
2 tbsp	boiling water	25 mL

In small saucepan, cook apricots in barely enough water to cover for 5 minutes, until soft. Set aside to cool. In 9-inch (2.5 L) square cake pan, using fingers, combine butter, granulated sugar, and 1 cup (250 mL) flour. Spread to cover pan and press firmly. Bake in 325⁰F (160⁰C) oven 10 minutes, until lightly browned. Set aside.

In medium bowl, combine brown sugar, remaining ⅓ cup (75 mL) flour, baking powder, and salt. Add eggs; beat until smooth and light. Stir in apricots, including liquid, and pecans. Spread over base and bake in 350⁰F (180⁰C) oven 30 minutes, until set. Cool in pan on wire rack.

To prepare icing, in small bowl, beat butter and icing sugar until creamed. Add milk and beat until smooth. Continue to beat while adding boiling water, 1 teaspoon at a time. Icing thickens as beating continues, 5 to 7 minutes. Spread over cooled apricot cake. To serve, cut into squares.

Yield: 36 squares

per square	calorie breakdown
calories 96	% protein 5
g fat 4.1	% fat 37
g fibre 0.2	% carbohydrate 58

Scotch Squares

Scotch cakes are made as a Christmas treat. This recipe has the same ingredients. The difference is in the method. It's fast and rewarding, mainly because there is less handling of the dough.

1 lb	soft butter	454 g
¾ cup	granulated sugar	175 mL
4 cups	sifted all-purpose flour	1 L
¼ cup	granulated sugar (for rolling)	50 mL

Using stand mixer and large bowl, beat butter until fluffy and light in colour; beat in ¾ cup (175 mL) sugar. Reduce mixer speed and add flour to blend. Spread in ungreased 9 x 13 inch (3.5 L) baking pan and smooth top with spatula. Bake in 325°F (160°C) oven 40 minutes, until lightly browned. Remove to wire rack, cool 10 minutes, and cut into 1½-inch (4 cm) squares. Immediately roll each one in sugar. Store in sealed container in cool place or in freezer.

Yield: 48 squares

per serving	calorie breakdown
calories 123	% protein 4
g fat 7.8	% fat 56
g fibre 0.3	% carbohydrate 40

Almond Toffee

Donna can trace this recipe to a 1939 edition of the Minneapolis Star *newspaper. It was always been associated with Christmas. Some believe it came to the Maritimes with the Loyalists. A true toffee, it has been made by generations of the Young family.*

½ cup	toasted slivered almonds	125 mL
½ lb	butter	225 g
1⅓ cups	lightly packed brown sugar	325 mL
2 oz	semi-sweet baking chocolate	56 g

In small, heavy skillet over medium heat, toast almonds until golden, stirring often. Butter 9-inch (2.5 L) square baking pan and spread with half of almonds. In large, heavy skillet combine butter and sugar. Over medium heat, stir until butter melts and ingredients blend together. Set timer for 12 minutes and cook with constant figure-eight stirring. (Ignore the phone.) If heat is too low, candy will remain sugary; if too high, it will burn. When time is up, candy will pour readily into prepared pan. Continue to stir while pouring. Chop chocolate and sprinkle on top. Allow to melt; spread evenly. Distribute remaining nuts and press into chocolate. Cool at room temperature, invert on cutting surface and break into bite-size pieces. Store quickly in sealed container in cool place, before it's all eaten.

Yield: 25 pieces

per piece	**calorie breakdown**
calories 240	% protein 2
g fat 16.8	% fat 59
g fibre 1.9	% carbohydrate 39

Salted Nut Brittle

The Maritime Farmer *weekly newspaper published interesting recipes. Years ago, Donna copied this one. She makes it every Halloween for the neighborhood and in between for special friends.*

2 cups	granulated sugar	500 mL
1 cup	corn syrup	250 mL
½ cup	water	125 mL
2 cups	salted mixed nuts	500 mL
2 tbsp	butter	25 mL
2 tsp	pure vanilla	10 mL
2 tsp	baking soda	10 mL

Butter large cookie sheet and place on bread board. In large and deep heavy saucepan, combine sugar, corn syrup and water. Over medium heat, stir until sugar dissolves. Insert candy thermometer and boil to 230°F (110°C), thread stage. Add nuts and stir to combine. Reduce heat to medium-low and continue boiling, stirring frequently until thermometer reads 304°F (152°C), hard crack. Remove from heat; stir in butter, vanilla, and baking soda. Beat to cool slightly; mixture will foam. Pour on large, buttered cookie sheet and spread with spoon. As soon as possible, butter hands and stretch in all directions. Turn over and stretch again. Brittle should be very thin. Cool and break. Store in sealed container.

Yield: 20 large pieces

per piece	**calorie breakdown**
calories 234	% protein 4
g fat 9.5	% fat 35
g fibre 0.8	% carbohydrate 61

Food Guide Pyramid

A Guide to Daily Food Choices

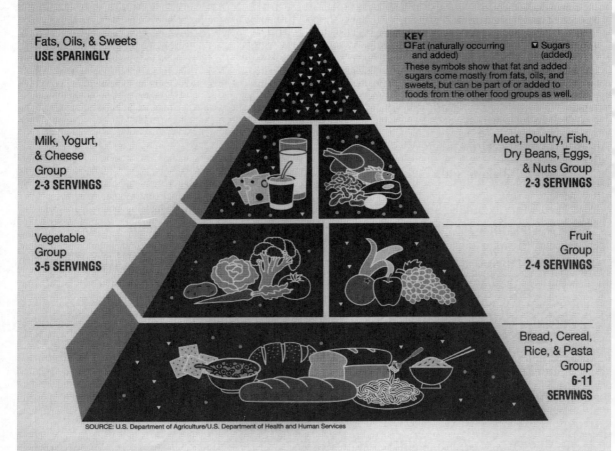

Fats, Oils, & Sweets
USE SPARINGLY

KEY
☐ Fat (naturally occurring and added)   ☑ Sugars (added)
These symbols show that fat and added sugars come mostly from fats, oils, and sweets, but can be part of or added to foods from the other food groups as well.

Milk, Yogurt, & Cheese Group
2-3 SERVINGS

Meat, Poultry, Fish, Dry Beans, Eggs, & Nuts Group
2-3 SERVINGS

Vegetable Group
3-5 SERVINGS

Fruit Group
2-4 SERVINGS

Bread, Cereal, Rice, & Pasta Group
6-11 SERVINGS

SOURCE: U.S. Department of Agriculture/U.S. Department of Health and Human Services

Use the Food Guide Pyramid to help you eat better every day. . .the Dietary Guidelines way. Start with plenty of Breads, Cereals, Rice, and Pasta; Vegetables; and Fruits. Add two to three servings from the Milk group and two to three servings from the Meat group.

Each of these food groups provides some, but not all, of the nutrients you need. No one food group is more important than another — for good health you need them all. Go easy on fats, oils, and sweets, the foods in the small tip of the Pyramid.

To order a copy of "The Food Guide Pyramid" booklet, send a $1.00 check or money order made out to the Superintendent of Documents to: Consumer Information Center, Department 159-Y, Pueblo, Colorado 81009.

U.S. Department of Agriculture, Human Nutrition Information Service, August 1992, Leaflet No. 572

Health Santé
Canada Canada

CANADA'S
Food Guide
TO HEALTHY EATING

Enjoy a variety
of foods from each
group every day.

Choose lower-
fat foods
more often.

Grain Products
Choose whole grain
and enriched
products more
often.

Vegetables & Fruit
Choose dark green and
orange vegetables and
orange fruit more often.

Milk Products
Choose lower-fat
milk products more
often.

Meat & Alternatives
Choose leaner meats,
poultry and fish, as well
as dried peas, beans and
lentils more often.

Canada

Comparison of Dietary Fats

Fatty acid content normalized to 100 per cent

DIETARY FAT	Saturated Fat	Monounsaturated Fat	Alpha-Linolenic Acid (Omega-3)	Linoleic Acid
Canola oil	7%	21%	11%	61%
Safflower oil	10%	76%	Trace	14%
Sunflower oil	12%	71%	1%	16%
Corn oil	13%	57%	1%	29%
Olive oil	15%	9%	1%	75%
Soybean oil	15%	54%	8%	23%
Peanut oil	19%	33%	Trace	48%
Cottonseed oil	27%	54%	Trace	19%
Lard*	43%	9%	1%	47%
Beef tallow*	48%	2%	1%	49%
Palm oil	51%	10%	Trace	39%
Butterfat*	68%	3%	1%	28%
Coconut oil	91%	2%	2%	7%

*Cholesterol Content (mg/Tbsp): Lard 12; Beef tallow 14; Butterfat 33. No cholesterol in any vegetable-based oil.

Source: POS Pilot Plant Corporation, Saskatoon, Saskatchewan, Canada June 1994

Legend:

☐ SATURATED FAT

■ MONOUNSATURATED FAT

POLYUNSATURATED FAT
- Linoleic Acid
- Alpha-Linolenic Acid (An Omega-3 Fatty Acid)

CANOLA COUNCIL OF CANADA   400-167 LOMBARD AVENUE   WINNIPEG   MANITOBA   CANADA   R3B 0T6

BIBLIOGRAPHY

Benoit, Madame Jehane. *Encyclopedia of Canadian Cuisine.* Toronto, ON: Canadian Homes Magazine, 1963.

Boudreau, Marielle Cormier and Melvin Gallant. *A Taste of Acadie.* Fredericton, NB: Goose Lane Editions, 1991.

Canadian Home Economics Association. *The Laura Secord Canadian Cookbook.* Toronto: McClelland & Stewart Ltd., 1966.

Healthy Home Cooking, Series, Alexandria, Va.: Time-Life Books Inc., 1988.

Herbst, Sharon Tyler. *Food Lover's Companion,* Hauppauge, N.Y.: Barron's Educational Series, Inc., 1990.

Hullah, Evelyn. *Cardinal's Handbook of Recipe Development,* Don Mills, ON: Cardinal Biologicals Ltd., 1984.

New Brunswick Home Economics Association. *New Brunswick Recipes.* Sackville, New Brunswick: The Tribune Press Ltd., 1958.

Nightingale, Marie. *Out of Old Nova Scotia Kitchens.* Toronto, ON: Pagurian Press Ltd., 1971.

Routledge, Margaret E. and Eleanor E. Wein. *Food Study, A Canadian Manual.* Fredericton, NB: University of New Brunswick, 1978.

INDEX